Child Psychotherapy

Child Psychotherapy:
The Initial Screening
and the Intensive
Diagnostic Evaluation

RICHARD A. GARDNER, M.D.

Clinical Professor of Child Psychiatry
Columbia University, College of Physicians and Surgeons

JASON ARONSON INC.
Northvale, New Jersey
London

First softcover edition 1993

Copyright © 1993 by Richard A. Gardner

10 9 8 7 6 5 4 3 2 1

Library of Congress Cataloging-in-Publication Data

Gardner, Richard A.
    Child psychotherapy : the initial screening and the intensive
diagnostic evaluation / by Richard A. Gardner.
        p.   cm.
    Includes bibliographical references and index.
    ISBN 1-56821-031-0 (pbk.)
    1. Mental illness—Diagnosis.   2. Behavioral assessment of
children.   3. Interviewing in child psychiatry.   I. Title.
    [DNLM: 1. Psychotherapy—in infancy & childhood.   2. Mental
Disorders—diagnosis.   3. Mental Disorders—in infancy & childhood.
WS 350.2   G228c   1993]
RJ503.5.G37   1993
618.92′89075—dc20
DNLM/DLC
for Library of Congress   93-16824

Manufactured in the United States of America. Jason Aronson Inc. offers books and cassettes. For information and catalog write to Jason Aronson Inc., 230 Livingston Street, Northvale, New Jersey 07647.

To Patricia Ann

You and this book
both represent
a culmination and
a commencement

Other Books by Richard A. Gardner

The Boys and Girls Book About Divorce
Therapeutic Communication with Children:
   The Mutual Storytelling Technique
Dr. Gardner's Stories About the Real World, Volume I
Dr. Gardner's Stories About the Real World, Volume II
Dr. Gardner's Fairy Tales for Today's Children
Understanding Children: A Parents Guide to Child Rearing
MBD: The Family Book About Minimal Brain Dysfunction
Psychotherapeutic Approaches to the Resistant Child
Psychotherapy with Children of Divorce
Dr. Gardner's Modern Fairy Tales
The Parents Book About Divorce
The Boys and Girls Book About One-Parent Families
The Objective Diagnosis of Minimal Brain Dysfunction
Dorothy and the Lizard of Oz
Dr. Gardner's Fables for Our Times
The Boys and Girls Book About Stepfamilies
Family Evaluation in Child Custody Litigation
Separation Anxiety Disorder: Psychodynamics and Psychotherapy
Child Custody Litigation: A Guide for Parents
   and Mental Health Professionals
The Psychotherapeutic Techniques of Richard A. Gardner
Hyperactivity, The So-Called Attention-Deficit Disorder,
   and The Group of MBD Syndromes
The Parental Alienation Syndrome and the Differentiation
   Between Fabricated and Genuine Child Sex Abuse
Psychotherapy with Adolescents
Family Evaluation in Child Custody Mediation, Arbitration,
   and Litigation
The Girls and Boys Book About Good and Bad Behavior
Sex Abuse Hysteria: Salem Witch Trials Revisited
The Parents Book About Divorce - Second Edition
The Psychotherapeutic Techniques of Richard A. Garnder - Revised
The Parental Alienation Syndrome: A Guide
   for Mental Health and Legal Professionals
Self-Esteem Problems of Children: Psychodynamics
   and Psychotherapy
Conduct Disorders of Children: Psychodynamics and Psychotherapy
True and False Accusations of Child Sex Abuse

Contents

Acknowledgments

I deeply appreciate the dedication of my secretaries Linda Gould, Carol Gibbon, Donna La Tourette, and Susan Monti to the typing of this manuscript in its various forms. I am grateful to Barbara Christenberry for her diligence in editing the manuscript. She provided useful suggestions and, at the same time, exhibited respect for my wishes regarding style and format. I am grateful to Colette Conboy for her valuable input into the production of the first edition of this book, from edited manuscript to final volume. I appreciate the efforts of Robert Tebbenhoff of Lind Graphics for his important contributions to the revised edition.

My greatest debt, however, is to those children and families who have taught me so much over the years about the development and alleviation of psychopathology. What I have learned from their sorrows and grief will, I hope, contribute to the prevention and alleviation of such unfortunate experiences by others.

Introduction

It has been my experience that many therapists rush too quickly into the psychotherapeutic process without spending proper time on the diagnostic evaluation. No patient would want a doctor to embark upon a treatment program without first making certain that a proper diagnosis has been arrived at. The word *diagnosis* is derived from the Greek, meaning *to know through* or *to know in depth*. A diagnosis, then, is not simply a label; rather, it is a body of knowledge about the patient that serves as the foundation for the treatment. It is the purpose of this book to provide the reader with the details for conducting what I consider to be a proper and thorough diagnostic evaluation in the true sense of the term.

The first section describes my initial diagnostic evaluation. Generally, this is a two-hour interview in which I see the child, mother, and father, in varying combinations as warranted. But I do not walk "cold" into this interview. Rather, at the time of the initial telephone call (which deserves discussion in its own right), the parent is advised that a 13-page questionnaire will be sent and that this is to be brought to the first interview. This questionnaire provides me with a significant amount of information that I have found to be most useful at the time of this initial consultation. I outline herein in detail the various areas that should be explored during this initial meeting.

When therapy is indicated, I then embark upon what I refer to as the intensive evaluation. This involves a few interviews with the child, one to two individual interviews with each of the parents, a joint interview with the parents, and a family interview. In addition, it may involve evaluations by other parties when warranted. The data collection process also includes the assessment of information from previous examiners, the school, and any other sources that may be useful. All this information is then pulled together and presented to the parents. This intensive evaluation not only serves to provide me with an in-depth understanding of the child's and family's problems (the two go together) but serves as a foundation for the treatment that is to follow.

Therapists who are willing to involve themselves in the kind of evaluation described in this book will contribute significantly to their understanding of their patients' problems and will enhance their therapy efficacy.

Part One

The Initial
Screening Evaluation

Let's start at the very beginning—a very good place to start.

Maria Trapp, *The Sound of Music*

My initial screening interview is two hours. This generally gives me the opportunity to get enough of a "feel" for the situation to provide me with guidelines regarding how I should proceed further. At that point, I not only make a decision on the basis of information acquired during the interview but on information obtained from an extensive questionnaire (to be discussed in detail below) that the parent brings to the first interview. If, however, by the end of the two hours I still do not have enough information to come to a definite decision, I have no hesitation scheduling a third. I feel no inner compulsion to pressure myself into coming to a conclusion under any kind of time restraints. If therapy is warranted,

I will generally recommend the more extensive evaluation, which I will discuss in Chapter Two .

1 WHO SHALL BE SEEN IN THE INITIAL CONSULTATION?

There are many ways to conduct the initial screening interview. Various combinations of child and/or parent(s) in different sequences, with one or more interviewers, may be utilized. For example, the child may be seen alone, the parent(s) alone, the child and parent(s) together, or a total family interview may be held. There may be one interviewer for all or separate interviewers seeing one or more individuals at a time. Of all the possible approaches, I personally prefer the first interview to be conducted with the child and parents together, individually and in varying combinations— as warranted. All things considered, I believe this arrangement to have the greatest number of advantages and the fewest drawbacks as compared to the other commonly used methods. Moreover, I believe that the clinical interviews are best conducted by one person.

Those who first see the parents alone claim that it provides an atmosphere in which information can be obtained without the child's distractions, and the parents need not be inhibited for fear that they may needlessly embarrass or otherwise harm the child by their open disclosures of his or her problems.

I consider the child's "distractions" to be a potentially rich source of information that is lost when the child is not there. Also, I have found that the direct confrontation has been more therapeutic than not. It helps crystallize in the child's mind (and also in the parents') the nature of the problems and this may be the first step toward their alleviation. If what is said is too painful the child's defenses can be relied upon to protect him or her. One can be quite sure that the child has been confronted many times before with the manifestations of the difficulties, but to do so again in the accepting and sympathetic environment of the therapist's office may be salutary. Such discussion fosters healthy communication between parents and child, and this kind of open conversation is often lacking in families in which children suffer psychological problems.

The three person interview also provides the therapist with the opportunity to observe directly interactions between the parents and the child. Seeing the parents alone in the initial interview deprives the therapist of first-hand observation of the patient. No matter how astute the parents may be in describing their child, they cannot provide the interviewer with as accurate a picture as his or her actual presence can.

In such an interview, I usually encourage hesitant parents to speak up. I tell them that my experience has been that it is in their child's best interests to discuss openly what directly pertains to the child in his or her presence and that we will have the opportunity later to talk about their own (the parents') personal matters which are less directly concerned with the child. Knowing that they will have subsequent time alone with me often makes it easier for them to discuss the child's problems in his or her presence.

There are some who take great pains to keep the child-therapist dyad completely separate from all therapeutic work and/or contact with the parents. From the outset, they will arrange for the parents to be counseled by a colleague, with whom there are occasional conferences. Proponents of this approach claim that the child's relationship with the therapist will be diluted and contaminated by any contact the therapist may have with the parents; that the patient will not have the feeling of having the therapist all to him- or herself and the treatment will thereby suffer. There are some therapists who take this so far that they will have absolutely no contact at all with the parents at any time.

I have formidable criticisms of this approach. It deprives the therapist of the opportunity of seeing the parents first-hand. No matter how accurate the child's description, he or she most often has distortions, which may be clarified via direct contact with the parents. And the colleague working with the parents is likely to have distortions about the child because information about him or her has been filtered through the parents. The child's problems are inextricably involved with the family's, and the therapist, by isolating the dyad, removes it from the field within which the problems have arisen and taken place and within which they must be worked through. Furthermore, the arrangement precludes joint interviews with the parents that can be a valuable source of information about family dynamics and interpersonal relations.

I have not found that my relationships with my child patients have suffered because of contact with parents (and these have varied from occasional interviews to actual stimultaneous therapy with one of the parents, usually the mother). In fact, such contacts and involvements have most often deepened my relationship with the child. The child will follow the parents. If the latter have respect for and faith enough in the therapist to consult him or her themselves, this enhances the child's involvement; whereas when the opposite is true, when there is no contact, the child's loyalty becomes divided between the therapist and the parents. In such a situation therapy can be deeply undermined, if not made entirely impossible.

There are some who feel quite strongly that the child should be seen alone in the first interview, but they will work subsequently with the parents in varying degrees. They reason that such an approach communicates to the child, from the very beginning, that *he* or *she* is the patient; they hold that this is vital if subsequent work is to be successful. I do not consider this to be such an important consideration because, more often than not, I see the parents as equally worthy of my clinical attention. I prefer to communicate to all that they are each to be clinically evaluated and that the greatest concentration is yet to be determined—therefore, the three person interview.

In addition, proponents of this method claim that taking the child away from the parents in the waiting room provides a direct opportunity to observe the child's reaction to separation—with special regard to the degree of separation anxiety. The assumption here is that there are children who do not have such anxiety. It is hard for me to imagine any child who would not be fearful going off alone in a room with an adult stranger in a setting which is probably unlike anything he or she has ever seen before. Not only is nothing learned when such separation is demanded but worse, the resulting fears interfere with the therapist's obtaining information about the child—all for the purpose of observing how he or she reacts under extreme tension. I would go further and say that such enforced separation often interferes with or delays the formation of the warm, friendly, trusting relationship which is a *sine qua non* of treatment. Another disadvantage of this approach is that it may place the therapist in the position of having to force or drag the child into his or her office. This is probably the only *never* I mention in this book, but I use it here without hesitation. This should *never* be. Such a struggle is totally antithetical to the process and goals of therapy, and adherence to the dictum of seeing the child alone in the beginning of the first session merely invites such a deplorable situation.

It is for these reasons and others that my initial two-hour interview is one in which all three parties are invited, that is, the child and both the parents. During that time they are seen in any combination that one can imagine, either individually or jointly. Generally, younger children (below the age of 11 or so) are invited to come into my consultation room together with their parents. Adolescents (13 and above) are first brought in alone, and the parents join us subsequently. In this way, I provide the adolescent with a separate experience from the parents, which is important for youngsters of this age to have. However, the parents are still brought in, which gets across the message that I am going to involve them in the treatment as well. (Some adolescents object to parental involvement, usually as a manifestation of specious independence or as a way of preventing parental disclosures. There is rarely a good reason.) Regarding children between ages 11 to 13, I utilize a number of criteria to decide how I will structure the initial invitation. If the youngster appears to be a mature individual, I may treat him or her like an adolescent and invite the child in first. In contrast, if the youngster appears to be younger and immature, I will invite the parents to join us. And, if I have any doubts about which way to go, I will ask the child how he or she would like to structure the interview, that is, whether the child wishes to accompany me alone or to be joined by the parents. Sometimes the discussion that takes place in the waiting room over this issue can, in itself, provide useful information about the family.

2 THE INITIAL TELEPHONE CALL

Although one of my secretaries almost invariably answers my telephone, they make no appointments—whether it be the first appointment or any other appointment in the total course of the treatment. When a person calls to make an appointment, he or she is informed that I will be available to speak during certain call times, during which period I can generally speak in a more leisurely manner regarding the appointment. If the day is particularly tight (often the case), I will converse with the parent during the evening. I generally find a ten-minute conversation necessary before setting up the initial appointment. My purpose here is to get some information about the nature of the child's problems in order that I may be in a better position to deal with unexpected events that may occur during the initial consultation. Because of the unpredictability of children, therapists who work with them must be prepared to deal with many more "surprises" than those who treat adults.

But there are other reasons for my acquiring more information before making the initial appointments. Sometimes, an appointment might not be necessary. A parent might call requesting a consultation regarding how to tell the children about an impending separation. In such cases I may refer the caller to my *The Parents Book About Divorce* (1977, 1979a) to read the section on telling children about an impending separation. I am careful, however, to reassure such callers that I am not turning them away; rather, I am trying to save them money in that the cost of the pocket edition of my book is far less than a consultation. I inform them also that if this does not prove sufficient, then I will be happy to set up an appointment for a consultation. On a number of occasions I have received calls from distraught parents at the time of a sudden death of a spouse, and there is a family argument regarding whether or not children should attend the funeral services and burial. Often I can provide meaningful advice in a short time, and no consultation is necessary.

Sometimes the symptoms described are short-lived and the parent is not aware of the fact that all children exhibit at times transient symptomatology such as tics, gastrointestinal complaints, or a wide variety of fears. On occasion symptomatic reactions to parental divorce may be the reason for the parent's call. In many such situations I will advise the parents to wait awhile because such symptoms are predictable and are usually transient. The authors of DSM-III are most appreciative of this phenomenon, and this is reflected in the stipulation that time considerations must be taken into account before many childhood diagnoses are warranted.

Some parents who anticipate custody litigation may call requesting therapy in the hope that they can then use the therapist as an advocate in the litigation. It behooves the therapist to "smell these out" over the telephone in order to avoid sticky and compromising situations. (I consider myself to have an excellent sense of smell in these situations.) If there is any doubt about such a caller's true motives, I will inform the individual that a decision must be made *before the first interview* as to whether my services are requested for the purpose of *litigation* or for *therapy*. I inform such callers that I am receptive to following either path; however, once one course is chosen I will not switch to the other and I will be asking that the appropriate document be signed—*again before the first interview*—which strictly confines me to a particular path. The reasons for my rigidity on this point relate to important legal issues (Gardner, 1982, 1986).

On one occasion a mother called to make the initial appointment and, after telling me the presenting problems, told me that I would have to promise her something before she would make the first appointment. I immediately smelled something foul, but I didn't know what it would be. She then told me that her child was adopted and that I must promise her that under no circumstances would I ever reveal this to him. I told her that I would make no such promise and that I cannot imagine the child's therapy proceeding without this topic being discussed at some point in the treatment. I reassured her that I would not scream the fact in the child's face as soon as he entered the room, but I would not agree to such a restriction throughout the whole course of the treatment. She advised me that other doctors had agreed to this restriction. I advised her then to consult these other doctors and that I was giving her my opinion on the subject.

Another mother, again after telling me her daughter's problems, also asked me to make a promise. (Again, smelly odors emanated through the telephone wires.) This time the mother informed me that the child was diagnosed as having a learning disability at the age of three and the parents were advised to start the child in school a year later than they had originally planned. In order to protect the child from the psychological trauma of such late commencement into the educational process, they told the girl that she was one year younger than she really was. Again, I informed the mother that I would not confront the child with this fact during the first minute of my first session, but I would not agree to be part of this conspiracy throughout the whole course of the treatment. The mother informed me that the school principal, all the teachers, and all the extended family members on both sides had agreed to withhold this information from the child. I informed the mother that I considered her not to have learned the lesson that Richard Nixon sadly learned, namely, that it is unreasonable to expect a few hundred people to keep a secret. And so we too parted ways.

A common problem that can easily be obviated in the initial telephone call is the one in which a divorced mother sets up an appointment and informs the therapist that her former husband will be paying her bills and that the therapist should be billing him directly. In response to such callers I generally respond that I will be happy to do so if her former husband will call me and tell me directly that he will be paying for my services. Often I will get the response that he is required to pay all medical bills as a stipulation of the divorce decree and that if I have trouble getting the money from him she is sure that the court will order him to pay. Any therapist who is naive or gullible enough to accept a patient under these circumstances does not get my pity.

A divorced mother will call asking for a consultation. I inform her that my usual procedure is to see both parents and the child, in varying combinations, during a two-hour consultation. The mother informs me that she is divorced, with the implication that that fact in itself is justification for my not involving her former husband in the therapy. I will generally then ask if the child's father still maintains some involvement with him or her. If the answer is in the affirmative, I then recommend that the mother consult with the father and invite him to join us during the first interview. I generally do this before a specific appointment is made. This insures that the mother will at least invite the father (who, of course, may or may not accept). My experience is that they most often do. The mother may argue that it would not be a good idea to have her former husband join us because "all we'll do is fight." My response to such a mother goes along these lines: "It is certainly not my goal to get you to fight. However, this I can tell you: I already know that as long as you and your husband cannot be in the same room together without fighting, your child will continue to have problems. I cannot imagine helping your son(daughter) with his(her) problems, as long as there is such severe animosity between you and your ex-husband. I can tell you now that one of my goals in therapy will be to help the two of you to reduce the hostilities. If that wasn't one of my goals, I wouldn't be qualified to help your child. Also, although the fighting is certainly unpleasant, I will probably learn some important things from it that will be useful in your child's treatment." Here again I have most often been successful in getting both parties to attend the initial interview.

On occasion, the calling mother may respond to my request for the father's involvement with "My husband doesn't believe in psychiatry. He told me that if I want to take Sally to a psychiatrist, it's okay with him but he doesn't want to get involved. To which I will replay, "Please tell your husband that my experience has been that the more involvement I have on the part of both parents, the greater the likelihood the treatment will be successful. If your husband refuses to involve himself entirely, I will do the best I can, but please inform him that I'll be working under compromised circumstances." I call this the "ball-is-in-your-court-baby principle." I basically say to the husband that the choice is his; if he wants me to conduct therapy under optimum circumstances, he will involve himself. If he doesn't do so, there will be less of a likelihood that the treatment will be successful, and he will have thereby contributed to its failure. Again, most often husbands appear when this message is transmitted to them. I might say here parenthetically, for those readers in private practice, that those husbands who do not *believe in* psychiatry are not famous for their *paying for* psychiatry. Doing everything reasonable to bring both parents into the initial interview establishes also a certain precedent, namely, that their involvement in the child's treatment is important and my urging them both to be present at the outset is a clear statement of this.

During this initial telephone conversation some parents ask my fee. Without hesitation I give my response. At the time of this writing my answer is this: "My standard fee is $90 for 45-minute sessions and $120 for full-hour sessions. The fee for the initial two-hour consultation, therefore, will be $240. Following that, there is a possibility of some lowering, but not below $75 for 45-minute sessions and $100 for full-hour sessions. This can be determined at the time of the consultation on the basis of your financial situation and insurance coverage." I know of many therapists who refuse to discuss fees over the telephone. This is not only injudicious but alienating. It cannot but engender distrust on the patient's part. It is reasonable for a patient to conclude from such an answer that "I guess he's going to try and get as much as he can." And such a conclusion is warranted. The argument that the discussion may have psychoanalytic significance is not justified. The caller is not an analytic patient; he or she is just a parent who is entitled to know what the therapist charges. Later in this chapter, I will discuss further the issue of fees.

Before closing, I inform the caller that I will be sending a questionnaire that I would like both parents to fill out. As will be discussed below, this questionnaire is quite comprehensive and provides me with a significant amount of "upfront" information at the time of the initial consultation. Attached to the questionnaire is a face letter (Figure 3.1) which I consider to be quite important. For parents who have not asked about the fees, they are provided this information with the questionnaire so that there is no disappointment, incredulity, amazement, or other reactions that may result in nonpayment of the fees. It also informs the parents that they will have the obligation themselves to pay me and that I will not pursue third parties for payment. (Many patients feel no guilt over doctors' doing this.)

3 THE QUESTIONNAIRE

I have found my questionnaire extremely valuable for the large majority of consultations. It provides the therapist with an immense amount of information in a few minutes, information that might take hours to obtain via direct questioning. The questionnaire provides information useful in ascertaining for the presence of psychogenic disturbances as well as diagnosing children who suffer with what I refer to as the Group of Minimal Brain Dysfunction Syndromes (GMBDS). I prefer to use this term over MBD because MBD implies a single disease entity. Rather, we are dealing here with a group of syndromes. It is unreasonable to attempt to assess for both psychogenic problems and the presence of GMBDS in a single two-hour interview. The questionnaire helps the examiner determine which are the areas that should most appropriately be focused on in the initial consultation. It tells the examiner where the "smoke" is so that he or she can know where to look for the "fires."

Furthermore, it has certain fringe benefits. It is detailed and thorough, thereby creating a good impression with many parents. This "good impression" helps establish a good relationship with the parents, which can ultimately contribute to the child's having a better relationship with the therapist. Furthermore, it provides examiners with a well-organized format on which to base their re-

Figure 3.1

Dear

Attached please find the questionnaire I would like you to fill
out about your child. Please bring it with you at the time of
your first appointment. In addition, I would appreciate your
bringing copies of any other material that you suspect might be
useful to me, e.g. reports from psychologists, psychiatrists,
child study teams, learning disability consultants, teachers,
etc. Please make copies of these reports so that I can have
them for my files.

My fee for consultations is $120/60-minute session. Unlike
reports from other medical specialists, child psychiatric
reports are generally quite lengthy and time consuming to
prepare. Accordingly, if a written report is desired, there is
an additional charge for its preparation, dictation, and review,
which is prorated at the aforementioned rate. My fee for
treatment ranges from $90/45-minute session down to $75/45-
minute session, the exact fee to be determined at the time
treatment is instituted. Payment is due at the time services
are rendered.   hours have been set aside for the initial
consultation with your child. I would appreciate your paying
my secretary the $ fee at the time of the consultation.
My secretary will be happy to provide receipts and assist in
the preparation of forms for subsequent reimbursement to you
by insurance companies and other third party payers.

Please know that I will do everything possible to be helpful
to your child. If you have any questions regarding the above,
please do not hesitate to call my office.

Sincerely,

Richard A. Gardner, M.D.
Clinical Professor of
    Child Psychiatry
Columbia University, College
    of Physicians and Surgeons

RAG/lg
encl.

ports. When dictating a report the examiner merely peruses the questionnaire and dictates information directly from it. The organization is already there and the examiner is saved the trouble of thumbing through notes, shifting back and forth, etc.

Basic Data

Most questionnaires request name, address, telephone number, etc. for the child and then for each of the parents. With the burgeoning divorce rate in recent years, fewer children are living in homes with both natural parents. Many other combinations are being seen and it is important that the examiner have a clear idea of the child's family structure and the exact nature of his or her relationships with the various adults who are involved in the child's care. Therefore, immediately after I get basic information about where the child is living (address, telephone number, school), the parent is asked to place checks in the appropriate places in the present placement table (Figure 3.2) to indicate the child's relationships with the adults with whom he or she is living (column A), as well as those who are involved in his or her care but living elsewhere (column B). For example, a boy might be living with his natural mother and stepfather. Checks for these individuals would be placed in column A. His natural father might be living with his new wife, the child's stepmother. Checks for these individuals would be placed in column B. The parent would then place numbers 1 and 2 next to the checks in column A for the natural mother and stepfather and the number 3 next to the check for the natural father in column B. More data on the nonresidential stepmother would generally not be obtained here (unless the situation specifically warranted its inclusion). Because the home address for the natural mother and stepfather has already been obtained, only their business addresses are requested. Then information about the natural father's home and business is requested. Although this type of inquiry may appear cumbersome at first, it is ultimately easier than the explanations that parents are required to provide when the questionnaire asks simply for data about the mother and father. In addition, columns A and B provide at-a-glance information about present placement.

Information about the referral source is then requested (Figure 3.3) as well as the reasons for the consultation. Just a few lines are available for this because I only wish the parent to make a brief

Figure 3.2

PLEASE BRING THIS COMPLETED FORM WITH YOU AT THE TIME OF YOUR FIRST APPOINT-

MENT ON_____AT_____

IT IS PREFERABLE THAT BOTH PARENTS ACCOMPANY THE CHILD TO THE CONSULTATION.

Child's name_____Birth date_____Age___Sex_____
            last   first   middle

Home address_____
            street   city   state   zip

Home telephone number_____
                 area code   number

Child's school_____
           name   address   **grade**

Present placement of child (place check in appropriate bracket):

	Column A Adults with whom child is living	Column B Non-residential adults involved with child
Natural mother	( )___	( )___
Natural father	( )___	( )___
Stepmother	( )___	( )___
Stepfather	( )___	( )___
Adoptive mother	( )___	( )___
Adoptive father	( )___	( )___
Foster mother	( )___	( )___
Foster father	( )___	( )___
Other (specify)	_____ ___	_____ ___

Place the number 1 or 2 next to each check in Column A and provide the
following information about each person:

1. Name_____Occupation_____
      last   first

    Business name_____Business address_____

    _____Business tel. No. (   )_____

2. Name_____Occupation_____
      last   first

    Business name_____Business address_____

    _____Business tel. No. (   )_____

Place the number 3 next to the person checked in Column B who is most involved
with the child and provide the following information:

3. Name_____Home address_____
                                           street

    _____Home tel. No. (   )_____
    city   state   zip

    Occupation_____Business name_____

Figure 3.3

Business address_____Bus. Tel. No. ( )_____

Source of referral: Name_____Address_____

_____Tel. No. ( )_____

Purpose of consultation (brief summary of the main problems):_____

_____

_____

_____

_____

PREGNANCY
  Complications:
    Excessive vomiting_____hospitalization required_____

    Excessive staining or blood loss_____

    Threatened miscarriage_____

    Infection(s) (specify)_____

    Toxemia_____

    Operation(s) (specify)_____

    Other illness(es) (specify)_____

  Smoking during pregnancy_____average number of cigarettes per day_____

  Alcoholic consumption during pregnancy_____describe, if beyond an occa-

    sional drink_____

  Medications taken during pregnancy_____

  X-ray studies during pregnancy_____

  Duration_____weeks

DELIVERY
  Type of labor: Spontaneous_____Induced_____
  Forceps: high_____mid_____low_____
  Duration of labor_____hours

  Type of delivery: Vertex (normal)_____breech_____Caesarean_____

  Complications:
    cord around neck_____

    cord presented first_____

    hemorrhage_____

14

statement here. To provide more space would probably result in a repetition of material to be obtained subsequently.

Pregnancy

It is probable that many, if not most, of the causes of the GMBDS exert their effects during pregnancy. Although genetic factors and those related to delivery and afterwards are certainly seen, it is probable that most of the cases of MBD are the result of interferences that occurred during the gestational period.

One should get further information about any of the complications of pregnancy that may have been checked off on the questionnaire. Most women stain during pregnancy. If, however, prolonged periods of bed rest were required, or hospitalization was necessary, then one could assume that this complication was in the pathological range. It is probable that many children's MBD is the result of maternal infections that get transmitted to the embryo and fetus. Sometimes such infections are subclinical and so we have no information about them. When they produce clinical symptoms, especially if severe, then the likelihood of their being of etiological significance is greater. The maternal infections that have most conclusively been demonstrated to produce fetal brain dysfunction are cytomegalic inclusion disease, toxoplasmosis, rubella, herpes simplex, and syphilis. Toxemia has been associated with the GMBDS. One should, therefore, inquire about high blood pressure, seizures, and proteinuria. Most women vomit during pregnancy. Vomiting can cause dehydration that might result in fluid and nutriment deprivation for the fetus. The crucial question is how much vomiting is necessary to cause fetal deprivation? If hospitalization was required, especially for intravenous fluid replacement, then it is possible that vomiting was the cause of the child's MBD. However, it would only be under suspicion as an etiological factor.

A standard warning on many drug labels is that safe administration during pregnancy has not been established. Accordingly, any medication that was taken over time during the pregnancy should be noted by the examiner. Thalidomide has probably been one of the more widely publicized causes of congenital anomalies and intellectual impairment. Other drugs that have been known to cause brain dysfunction include aminopterin, diphenylhydantoin, methotrexate, and high doses of vitamin D. And there are probably many other drugs, as yet unimplicated, that will ultimately be shown to have such effects.

Exposure to X-radiation has also been implicated. The most common story is of a woman who presents with nausea, vomiting, and other gastrointestinal symptoms. Pregnancy may not have been suspected, especially if the woman is single or over 40. The patient may undergo a number of radiological examinations (GI series, gall bladder studies, barium enema, et cetera) in the attempt to ascertain the cause of the vomiting. By the time the correct diagnosis is made, the woman may have been exposed to significant amounts of X-radiation. Most radiologists now inquire into the recent menstrual history to be sure that they are not exposing a pregnant woman to X-rays.

Smoking during pregnancy has been associated with low birth weight, increased fetal and neonatal death rate, and impairments in the child's physical, neurological, and intellectual growth. And there appears to be a correlation between the amount of smoking and the incidence of these effects. Excessive alcoholic ingestion can cause what has been referred to as the *fetal alcohol syndrome*. These babies exhibit alterations in growth, facial dysmorphism and other disturbances of body morphogenesis, as well as low birth weight. The GMBDS and mental retardation have been described in these children.

One also wants to learn about the duration of the pregnancy. Traditionally the mother's report on this has not been too reliable because many mothers do not know exactly when they became pregnant. One definition of prematurity (a term falling into disuse) used to be that a child whose gestation was less than 37 weeks was considered premature. Because of the unreliability of this figure, the child's birth weight was subsequently used and children under 2500 grams (5.5 pounds) were considered premature. But, this criterion has also been found wanting because there were some babies below this weight who showed none of the traditional manifestations of prematurity. Accordingly, new criteria (the *gestational age*) are being used to determine if the infant's birth weight is indeed a problem, and these will be presented below when I discuss the significance of the birth weight. The duration of pregnancy figure, however, can still serve as a clue (admittedly a poor one) as to whether there were problems regarding the pregnancy's duration. It is more significant if the gestational age (see below) has been determined by the physician, using recently developed physiological and neurological criteria. Only babies born after the early 1970s were so examined. In time, all knowledgeable mothers may refer to the child's gestational age at birth rather than the duration of the pregnancy.

Delivery

The delivery is another period when the child may be exposed to factors that can produce MBD. Inducing labor runs certain risks for the child, more so in the past than in the present. The physician may miscalculate the pregnancy's duration (especially if he or she relies too heavily on the mother's estimate) and deliver the baby before it can thrive optimally in the extrauterine environment. In the past oxytocin, the drug most commonly used to initiate and maintain uterine contractions, was administered by buccal tablet. One had no control over the duration of its action. Accordingly, uterine contractions might persist after it was determined that cephalopelvic disproportion was present and the fetus was being traumatized. In addition, drugs such as oxytocin can produce tetanic contractions of the uterus. These can cut off blood circulation from the placenta to the fetus and thereby cause anoxia in the child. In recent years such drugs can be given by intravenous drip, which can be carefully controlled. Once trouble is suspected, the oxytocin is immediately discontinued. Because there is no reserve of the drug present in the body (as is the case with buccal tablets) uterine contractions due to the drug can be quickly interrupted. The mother who was spontaneously delivered does not run the risk of these complications.

High forceps delivery is practically unknown today. Just about all obstetricians recognize the danger of its producing trauma to the infant. It is generally agreed among obstetricians that low forceps delivery is without danger, but mid-forceps delivery may cause some trauma. Most obstetricians will choose to do a Caesarean section rather than expose the child to the traumatic risks of mid-forceps delivery.

Mothers may not be completely reliable regarding the accuracy of their reports on the duration of labor. Considering all the things they have to think about during this time, they cannot be seriously faulted for such impairment in their recollection. Strictly speaking, labor is considered to begin when the cervix starts to dilate, and is considered to be continuing as long as there is progressive cervical dilation. Most women enter the hospital already partially dilated, so cervical observation and the more objective reporting of the onset is no longer possible. The clinical definition of the onset is the time when contractions begin to occur at a frequency greater than one every five minutes. Labor is considered to be going on as long as such contractions are *regular and continuous*. Normally, the duration of labor for the first pregnancy is 12–14 hours. Labors more than 16 hours should be considered prolonged, with an increased risk for fetal damage. The normal duration of second and subsequent labors is 8–10 hours, with more than 12 hours being considered prolonged. Of course, there is no exact cut-off point for defining prolonged labors. The longer beyond these figures the labor goes, the greater likelihood there will be fetal distress and damage.

Head trauma incurred during labor is a common cause of brain damage. The most common manifestations of birth trauma that may be associated with brain injury are cephalhematoma, facial nerve paralysis, brachial palsy, phrenic nerve paralysis, fracture of the clavicle, and hematoma of the sternocleidomastoid muscle.

Breech deliveries are generally more traumatic than vertex. Caesarean sections, especially those that are resorted to because of complications that have interfered with delivery via the birth canal, have also been associated with the GMBDS. It is probable that it was not the Caesarean section *per se* that caused the MBD, but the complications that caused the obstetrician to utilize this method of delivery. When a child is born with the umbilical cord around the neck, there may have been some compromise of blood circulation from the placenta to the fetal brain. When the cord presents first, there may be compression of the blood circulation to the child, with resultant impairment of circulation to the infant's brain. Excessive blood loss during labor may also reduce the amount of blood reaching the infant.

As mentioned, birth weight is no longer considered to be the criterion of prematurity. In fact, most neonatologists discourage the use of the term prematurity. Low-birth-weight babies, that is, those weighing less than 2500 grams, are divided into two categories: (1) those whose birth weights are appropriate for their gestational age (AGA) and (2) those whose weights are low, that is, they are small for gestational age (SGA). As mentioned above, we now have objective physiological and neurological criteria for determining gestational age and do not have to rely on a mother's recollection of when she thinks she became pregnant. The babies in these two groups are quite different. Consider, for example, two babies whose birth weight is 1500 grams. One baby is found to have a gestational age of 31 weeks and the other 37 weeks. Because 1500 grams is about normal for 31 week fetuses, the first baby would be considered AGA. The second would be considered SGA. The assumption is made that the second baby has only grown to the 31 week size in a 37 week pregnancy. Something has happened to retard the child's growth. The second child is more likely to exhibit difficulties that would include GMBDS. The first is more likely to develop normally in that nothing serious is considered to have happened to it, although its low birth weight is still an abnormality that may cause difficulty. The questionnaire asks the parent for the birth weight as well as whether it was an AGA or SGA baby. Many parents are not familiar with these terms, but in time knowledge of them should become more widespread.

Babies of large size (over 9 pounds) are also at greater risk for the development of MBD, in that their deliveries are more likely to be traumatic. Babies of long gestation (over 42 weeks) are also likely to have complications such as MBD because the aging placenta becomes more inefficient in its functioning and meconium aspiration is also more likely in such infants.

Post-Delivery Period
[While in the Hospital]

The healthy child breathes spontaneously at birth. At most, the child requires some clearing of the nasal passages. The traditional slap on the buttocks to get the child breathing is considered by most obstetricians to be unnecessary. The usual nasopharyngeal aspiration provides enough stimulation to induce breathing. The longer the delay in breathing the greater the likelihood the child will suffer with cerebral anoxemia. The normal infant spontaneously cries at birth. A delayed cry is also an index of infant depression, especially of respiration and bodily response to stimulation. A fairly objective statement about the newborn's overall physical condition at the time of birth is the Apgar score (Figure 3.4). At one, two, and five minutes after birth, the child is given a score of 0, 1, or 2 on five items. The five physiological functions evaluated are heart rate, respiratory effort, muscle tone, reflex irritability, and general color. With a maximum score of 2 in each category, the maximum score

Figure 3.4

   infant injured during delivery_____

   other (specify)_____

Birth Weight_____
  Appropriate for gestational age (AGA)_____
  Small for gestational age (SGA)_____

POST-DELIVERY PERIOD (while in the hospital)
  Respiration: immediate_____delayed (if so, how long)_____

  Cry: immediate_____delayed (if so, how long)_____

  Mucus accumulation_____

  Apgar score (if known)_____

  Jaundice_____

  Rh factor_____transfusion_____

  Cyanosis (turned blue)_____

  Incubator care_____number of days_____

  Suck: strong_____weak_____

  Infection (specify)_____

  Vomiting_____diarrhea_____

  Birth defects (specify)_____

  Total number of days baby was in the hospital after the delivery _____

INFANCY-TODDLER PERIOD
  Were any of the following present--to a significant degree--during the
  first few years of life? If so, describe.

  Did not enjoy cuddling _____

  Was not calmed by being held and/or stroked _____

  Colic_____

  Excessive restlessness_____

  Diminished sleep because of restlessness and easy arousal _____

  Frequent headbanging_____

  Constantly into everything_____

  Excessive number of accidents compared to other children_____ is 10. A score of 1, 2, or 3 is considered severe depression; 4, 5, 6, or 7 is moderate depression; and 8, 9, or 10 is no depression. Most mothers are not aware of the existence of this figure, and many who are do not know what recording was made on their child. When the figure can be obtained, it is a valuable bit of information.

About 40% of newborns exhibit a transient physiologic jaundice (icterus neonatorum). There are two causes of this type of jaundice: 1) Increased destruction of red blood cells in order to reduce the high fetal red cell concentration (necessary for intrauterine existence) to the lower levels necessary after birth. 2) The immature liver is inefficient in its capacity to metabolize bilirubin and other products of red blood cell destruction. Generally, the jaundice appears on the second to fourth day and ends betweeen the seventh and fourteenth. Jaundice due to Rh incompatibility (erythroblastosis fetalis) or ABO incompatability (icterus praecox) usually begins during the first 24 hours and is severer. Whereas transfusions are not necessary for physiological jaundice, they are for the treatment of Rh incompatability and severe forms of ABO incompatability. Recently developed immunological treatment with RhoGAM (an anti-Rh + antibody globulin) can prevent Rh incompatibility disorder in mothers who have not yet been sensitized. Less common causes of jaundice in the newborn are congenital obliteration or obstruction of the bile ducts, septicemia, hepatitis, and a variety of blood dyscrasias. The most common examples of brain damage caused by high bilirubin levels is the kernicterus resulting from icteric degeneration of the basal ganglia as well as other cerebral centers.

Cyanosis is a concomitant of anoxia, which may cause cerebral ischemia and nerve cell dysfunction and degeneration. Anoxia may be seen in prematurity in association with the respiratory distress syndrome (hyaline membrane disease), maternal toxemia, and any other condition in which the neonate is under stress. Intracranial hemorrhage (most often caused by birth trauma and hemorrhagic disease of the newborn), congenital atalectasis, hyaline membrane disease, and various congenital heart diseases can also cause cyanosis. The need for incubator care may be a clue to the presence of apnea, cyanosis, and a variety of diseases affecting respiration and circulation.

The normal baby has a strong suck. A weak suck at birth is generally suggestive of some pathological process. Often it is one manifestation of general neurological depression. Meningitis may be the result of infections in the newborn. Generally it is caused by organisms found in the mother's vagina infecting the fetus and producing septicemia in the newborn infant. Infected circumcisions, umbilical stumps, and otitis media, once common causes of meningitis, are less common today.

A variety of congenital anomolies may be associated with neurophysiological impairment. This is especially true of those disorders that directly involve the central nervous system and/or the tissues and bones in which it is encased. The most common disorders in this category are meningocele, meningomyelocele, meningoencephalocele, hydrocephalus, and spina bifida. Congenital cardiac anomalies may also be associated with cerebral nerve cell degeneration. This is especially true of the cyanotic forms that are associated with hypoxic spells such as the tetralogy of Fallot. If the child was in the hospital for more than five days, one should inquire about the reasons. Usually, a stay beyond that time was necessitated by some physical disorder that may be associated with the GMBDS.

The Infancy-Toddler Period

The normal human infant enjoys being hugged and caressed. This desire is present from birth and the child who is deprived of such gratification may become listless, lose his or her appetite, withdraw interest from the environment, become marantic, and even die. If a child, from the day of birth, does not respond to stroking and cuddling, then some interfering factor is usually present. Sometimes the mother herself is impaired in her desire and/or capacity to fondle her baby. Or she does so with such tension that the child does not find it a gratifying experience. Such mothers may consider breast feeding "disgusting" and may show other signs of inhibition in maternal capacity. Such a mother will generally react similarly to her other children. The child's hyporeactivity in such situations should be considered psychogenic.

If, however, the child is described as not having reacted to cuddling and stroking from birth and the siblings are described as having done so, then it is more likely that the child's impairment is due to some physical disease such as mental retardation, autism, and brain dysfunction. At times the GMBDS child may be differentiated from the retarded and autistic by its hyperreactivity to such stimulation. The autistic and retarded child may be described as lying in the mother's arms limp and unresponsive "like a sack of potatoes." The GMBDS child, however, may respond to stroking by becoming irritable, crying, and fighting off such stimulation. These reactions may be a manifestation of the same mechanisms that produce hyperactivity and impulsivity.

A history of colic is often described by parents of MBD children. They may look back upon the first year or two of the child's life as a nightmare in which they hardly slept. The cry of such children is often shrill and piercing, described by parents as "a sound like a siren," "an animal in acute distress," and "the high thin note of static on the radio."

These children are often described as the "last to go to sleep at night and the first to get up in the morning." Their restlessness in bed may interfere with the sleep of others in the household. They may frequently knock themselves against the sides of their cribs or bang their heads. After they begin to walk, they are constantly into everything and their curiosity is even greater than that of the normal toddler (whose curiosity is usually insatiable). Some parents say of MBD children that "their terrible twos started at nine months." They are heedless to danger and are accident prone. This does not appear to be on a psychogenic basis. They are not compelled by some deep psychopathological self-destructive need to harm themselves. Rather their accident proneness is the result of their neurophysiological impairments: their inability to learn well from experience, their intellectual deficits, their problems in adequately processing incoming stimuli, etc. They may be well known to the doctors at the nearby emergency room, and they may have a number of scars which serve to remind observers of their accidents but not themselves.

Developmental Milestones

Parents are not renowned for the accuracy of their recollections regarding the times at which their children reached the various developmental milestones (Figure 3.5). Many parents, rather than saying that they do not recall, provide a figure that is no more than a guess. Obviously, such information is of little value to the examiner. Yet it is important for the examiner to get such data because developmental lags are commonly seen in children with the GMBDS. Furthermore, the data provide vital information regarding the presence of the developmental type of soft neurological sign. The ques-

Figure 3.5

DEVELOPMENTAL MILESTONES

If you can recall, record the age at which your child reached the following developmental milestones. If you cannot recall, check item at right.

	age	I cannot recall exactly, but to the best of my recollection it occurred		
		early	at the normal time	late
Smiled				
Sat without support				
Crawled				
Stood without support				
Walked without assistance				
Spoke first words besides "ma-ma" and "da-da"				
Said phrases				
Said sentences				
Bowel trained, day				
Bowel trained, night				
Bladder trained, day				
Bladder trained, night				
Rode tricycle				
Rode bicycle (without training wheels)				
Buttoned clothing				
Tied shoelaces				
Named colors				
Named coins				
Said alphabet in order				
Began to read				

COORDINATION

Rate your child on the following skills:

	Good	Average	Poor
Walking			
Running			
Throwing			
Catching			
Shoelace tying			
Buttoning			
Writing			
Athletic abilities			

tionnaire allows the parent the face-saving "out" of being able to say that the information has been forgotten. In addition, three categories of response can be provided under the "I cannot recall exactly" heading: it occurred 1) early, 2) at the normal time, and 3) late. When developmental questions are so posed, the information the examiner does get is more likely to be useful.

The normal times at which the milestones occur is subject to significant variation, but the later beyond the normal range the capacity is reached the greater the likelihood that pathology is present. Smiling usually occurs by two months, sitting with support at six–seven months, crawling at seven months, standing without support at 10–11 months, and walking without support at 12–14 months. There is greater variability regarding the normal range for the onset of speech.

The words *ma-ma* and *da-da* are poor criteria for determining the age of speech onset because parents are likely to hear such articulations in the normal babbling sounds of the infant. (This is especially true for first babies.) Accordingly, the question for determining the age of onset of first words asks for words other than these. Nine to 14 months is generally the time for the appearance of single words. The appearance of first phrases and first sentences is very variable. First phrases appear at about 18 months and short sentences at about 24 months, but the normal range is so variable that the age of onset of these functions is of limited diagnostic value. However, it is important for the examiner to appreciate that there are children who do not speak at all until three and even four years of age who do not have any neurological impairment. I believe that the failure to speak between two and four, when there is no demonstrable organic cause (such as MBD, severe hearing loss, retardation, autism or schizophrenia) is a manifestation of psychogenic problems. The period between four and five appears to be a crucial one for the onset of speech. My experience has been that if a child does not start to speak by four it may or may not be a sign of organic pathology. However, if a child does not utilize *intelligible* speech by five years of age it is almost invariably a sign of severe pathology. In such cases I generally consider mental retardation and autism or other forms of childhood schizophrenia. The GMBDS children, although sometimes lagging with regard to the time of speech onset, are not generally so late that they do not start until five or after. In addition, the child who has not started to utilize intelligible speech by five may never do so. Such children must be differentiated from those with elective mutism. The latter know how to speak, but generally confine themselves to communicating verbally with certain people (usually their parents).

The general assumption is made that children cannot voluntarily control their bowel movements until they are old enough to walk. Accordingly, the parent who states that a child was bowel trained at six months and started to walk at 12 months is not providing valid information. One possibility here is that the child had a fairly regular schedule and the parent caught him or her at the right moment for placement on the potty or toilet. Bowel training for day and night usually occurs between two and three years of age. Bladder training occurs later and is more variable. Many children are bladder trained during the day (commonly established by two-three years of age) before nocturnal control is achieved. So great is the normal variation for nighttime wetting that there is no good cutoff point in childhood which can be used to define the pathological. It is a disservice to a child to automatically assume that nighttime wetting after the age of five or six, for example, is automatically a manifestation of psychiatric problems. It may be the result of neurophysiological immaturity or physiological hyperirritability. When bowel and bladder training are late in the GMBDS child, a number of factors may be operative: neurophysiological lag, hyperirritability, impaired attention to internal stimuli, and intellectual deficit.

Children of two to three generally pedal a tricycle and by six or seven ride a bicycle without training wheels. The ability to button clothing generally occurs at three to four and tying shoelaces at five to six. At four most children can name the majority of colors and by five to six name a few coins. Most can repeat the letters of the alphabet at four to five years and start to read between five and six. It is in the area of reading that the GMBDS child may exhibit his or her problems most dramatically.

Coordination

The evaluation of coordination may be quite subjective. This is true not only for the parent, but for the examiner as well. The parents' views, however, often do have merit, especially if they are only asked to state whether the child is "good," "average," or "poor" compared to others with regard to the ability to perform certain functions that depend upon coordination capacity. The questionnaire (Figure 3.5) focuses on such functions that involve fine and/ or gross motor coordination.

Comprehension and Understanding

The questions in this section of the questionnaire (Figure 3.6) attempt to provide the examiner with information about the child's general level of intelligence. This may be a very highly charged area for the parents of the GMBDS child. They generally will view the child to be brighter than he or she may be. They may use rationalizations such as, "His intelligence is really normal but he's *slower* to understand than other children." Others may even describe the child as "basically very bright" even though there is little if any evidence that this is the case. The parents may hold to the statement made by some professionals that "MBD children's intelligence is in the normal range." I do not believe that the average child who is correctly diagnosed as having MBD is of normal intelligence. Although there are many GMBDS children with above average and even superior IQs, there are many more in the low average and borderline range. The average GMBDS child in my experience has an IQ of about 90, that is, at the bottom of the normal range. The professional who says that the average MBD child has a normal IQ is ignoring all we know about the ways in which such children's deficits impair them on most, if not all, of the WISC-R subtests, the very test used to assess these children's intelligence.

The first question in this section of the questionnaire (Figure 3.6) is essentially directed to parents who are defensive about or denying their child's possible intellectual impairment. The second asks more directly about intelligence.

School

It is in school, more than anywhere else, that the GMBDS child's deficits may reveal themselves. Many GMBDS children are not recognized as being different from others until they attend school. There the teacher has the opportunity to compare the child to others his or her age, and is generally knowledgeable enough about what is age appropriate to be able to recognize atypical behavior quite readily. In addition, it is in school that the learning impairments, so commonly seen in GMBDS, may first become apparent.

Figure 3.6

COMPREHENSION AND UNDERSTANDING

Do you consider your child to understand directions and situations as well as other children his or her age?_____If not, why not?_____

_____

How would you rate your child's overall level of intelligence compared to other children? Below average_____Average_____Above average_____

SCHOOL

Rate your child's school experiences related to <u>academic learning</u>:

	<u>Good</u>	<u>Average</u>	<u>Poor</u>
Nursery school			
Kindergarten			
Current grade			

To the best of your knowledge, at what grade level is your child functioning: reading_____spelling_____arithmetic_____

Has your child ever had to repeat a grade? If so, when_____

Present class placement: regular class_____special class (if so, specify)

_____

Kinds of special therapy or remedial work your child is currently receiving

_____

Describe briefly any academic school problems_____

_____

_____

Rate your child's school experience related to <u>behavior</u>:

	<u>Good</u>	<u>Average</u>	<u>Poor</u>
Nursery school			
Kindergarten			
Current grade			

Does your child's teacher describe any of the following as significant classroom problems?

Doesn't sit still in his or her seat_____

Frequently gets up and walks around the classroom_____

Shouts out. Doesn't wait to be called upon _____

Won't wait his or her turn_____

Lastly, it is in the school, more than anywhere else, that the child's capacity for self-inhibition is tested, and it is in school, therefore, that the GMBDS child's impulsivity is likely to cause him or her the most difficulty.

The questionnaire sections that refer to school (Figures 3.6 and 3.7) are divided into two categories: academic learning and behavior. In the academic section the questions attempt to provide the examiner with specific information regarding the child's level of academic performance. The questions have been designed to focus on information that will provide the examiner with as accurate a picture as possible of the child's academic functioning: specific grade levels in reading, spelling, and arithmetic; history of grade repeat; type of class (regular or special); and special therapy or remedial work.

The second section is devoted to school behavior. Again, the aim is to get information that is as specific as possible. The checklist in the middle of this section focuses on many of the most common complaints made by teachers about GMBDS children. These problems are manifestations of their hyperactivity (Doesn't sit still in his or her seat); impulsivity (Shouts out. Won't wait his or her turn); impaired concentration (Typically does better in a one-to-one relationship); and impaired ability to project oneself into another's situation (Doesn't respect the rights of others). Finally, both sections provide the parent with the opportunity to describe other school problems that may not have been referred to in the questions previously posed.

Peer Relationships

Information about peer relationships is less useful than school behavior, but more useful than home behavior in diagnosing GMBDS. The requirement for self-restraint is greatest in school, least at home, and somewhere in the middle of these with peers. Teachers will tolerate the least degree of antisocial behavior, parents the most, and peers an amount between these two. The questions posed about peer relationships (Figure 3.7) attempt to focus specifically on the most common problems with friends that GMBDS children have. The most sensitive indices of whether the GMBDS child is relating well to peers is his or her degree of reaching out to them and whether they are seeking the child. The age of playmates (younger, older, same age) also tells something about the child's de-

Figure 3.7

Does not cooperate well in group activities_____

Typically does better in a one-to-one relationship_____

Doesn't respect the rights of others_____

Doesn't pay attention during storytelling_____

Describe briefly any <u>other</u> classroom behavioral problems_____

_____

_____

PEER RELATIONSHIPS

Does your child seek friendships with peers?_____

Is your child sought by peers for friendship?_____

Does your child play primarily with children his or her own age?_____

   younger_____older_____

Describe briefly any problems your child may have with peers_____

_____

_____

HOME BEHAVIOR

All children exhibit, to some degree, the kinds of behavior listed below. Check those that you believe your child exhibits to an excessive or exaggerated degree when compared to other children his or her age.

Hyperactivity (high activity level)_____

Poor attention span_____

Impulsivity (poor self control)_____

Low frustration threshold_____

Temper outbursts_____

Sloppy table manners_____

Interrupts frequently_____

Doesn't listen when being spoken to_____

Sudden outbursts of physical abuse of other children_____

Acts like he or she is driven by a motor_____

Wears out shoes more frequently than siblings_____

Heedless to danger_____

Excessive number of accidents_____

Doesn't learn from experience_____

Poor memory_____

More active than siblings_____

gree of success with friends. Also, the quality of the friendships is important to learn about, whether the children are normal or atypical, whether they are sought after or in the fringe group.

Home Behavior

Home behavior is a poor criterion on which to determine whether a child's behavior is pathological. Practically all siblings fight. At what level does the normal degree of rather fierce sibling rivalry end and the pathological begin? All children exhibit poor table manners at times. Where does one draw the line between normal table sloppiness and the pathological? And, as mentioned, parents will tolerate greater degrees of atypical behavior than teachers and peers. Yet pathology can certainly manifest itself in the home. In order to ascertain whether the child's home behavior may be pathological, the parent is asked to check those items (Figure 3.7) in which the child's behavior is exaggerated or excessive when compared to other children the child's age. Included here again are those behavioral patterns that relate to some of the primary manifestations of GMBDS, viz., hyperactivity, poor attention span, impulsivity, and memory impairments.

Interests and Accomplishments

Most of the previous items have focused on the child's deficits. Such emphasis may be upsetting to the parent who is filling out the questionnaire. For the parents' well-being, as well as providing the examiner with a more balanced picture of the child, a section (Figure 3.8) is devoted to the child's assets. An inquiry into hobbies, interests, and accomplishments may provide useful diagnostic information. Reading is obviously not likely to be the favorite pastime of the GMBDS child. Watching TV or listening to music may be (I don't claim these to be pathognomonic for the disorder). A GMBDS child may have deep involvement in sports and do well in them. Success in this area, then, provides information about the child's coordination. Others may do well in school but are abysmally poor in sports. In short, the areas of interest and pleasure may provide information about the child's healthy areas of neurophysiological functioning.

Figure 3.8

INTERESTS AND ACCOMPLISHMENTS
  What are your child's main hobbies and interests?_____

_____

  What are your child's areas of greatest accomplishment?_____

_____

  What does your child enjoy doing most?_____

_____

  What does your child dislike doing most?_____

_____

MEDICAL HISTORY
  If your child's medical history includes any of the following, please note
  the age when the incident or illness occurred and any other pertinent information.
    Childhood diseases (describe any complications)_____

_____

    Operations_____

_____

    Hospitalizations for illness(es) other than operations_____

_____

    Head injuries_____

    _____with unconsciousness_____without unconsciousness_____

    Convulsions_____

    _____with fever_____without fever_____

    Coma_____

    Meningitis or encephalitis_____

    Immunization reactions_____

    Persistent high fevers_____highest temperature ever recorded_____

    eye problems_____

    ear problems_____

    poisoning_____

Medical History

In this section of the questionnaire (Figure 3.8), an attempt is made to learn about any illnesses that occurred after the newborn child left the hospital, illnesses that might have been of etiological importance in the child's MBD. The traditional childhood diseases, such as measles and mumps, were occasionally associated with central nervous system complications such as encephalitis. Fortunately, with the advent of new vaccines, we are seeing much less of these disorders. A history of coma and/or seizures associated with such an illness is suggestive of central nervous system involvement even though medical attention may not have been sought. Operations may provide a clue to the etiology. For example, the child with frequent bouts of otitis media requiring myringotomies is suspect for hearing impairment which may interfere with speech and learning. There is hardly a child who does not sustain occasional head trauma. But when it is associated with unconsciousness or coma, then brain dysfunction (not necessarily permanent) must be suspected.

There was a time when a child who only had seizures with fever was considered to be neurologically normal. Such children were considered to have "febrile seizures," which were not taken as seriously as those that occurred in the afebrile state. One reflection of this relaxed attitude toward febrile convulsions was the view that such seizures did not warrant anticonvulsant medication. The traditional treatment of such seizures was to warn the mother to give the child elixir phenobarbital (or other anticonvulsant medication) as soon as the child showed signs of illness—especially a febrile illness. Unfortunately, children have a way of spiking fevers so rapidly that mothers were often unaware that the child was getting sick and so did not often give the anticonvulsant in time to prevent the convulsion. Many pediatric neurologists today take such seizures more seriously. They hold also that in addition to the basic pathology that causes the seizures, a seizure per se can result in superimposed damage to the brain. A grand mal seizure includes an apneic phase and this can cause cerebral hypoxia. Accordingly, a child with febrile seizures may be placed on maintenance anticonvulsant medication if there is a family history of seizures, signs of organic cerebral dysfunction, or other factors indicative of a high risk of further brain dysfunction. I have seen a few children with MBD who had febrile seizures that went untreated because they were "only febrile." I believe that the extent of their brain dysfunction would have been far less had they been on medication to prevent their convulsions.

Meningitis and encephalitis, especially when associated with coma, is highly correlated with residual brain damage and is one of the more generally accepted causes of GMBDS. Encephalitides are also known to be a concomitant of untoward immunization reactions. There are some children who easily run persistently high fevers with practically any infection. Others may manifest such fevers without known cause. Children with fevers of unknown etiology may have some kind of neurophysiological dysfunction which is akin to and possibly a symptom of GMBDS. The same factors that have produced neurophysiological abnormalities in other parts of the brain may be causing impaired functioning of temperature regulatory mechanisms.

Reading difficulties can be the result of pathological processes anywhere along the pathway from the eye to the occipital cortex (as well as in neurological systems that are interconnected). Strabismus, squinting, tearing, holding the book at a distance, holding the book too close, inclining the head to the side while reading, and easy reading fatigability are all suspicious signs of ocular problems that can contribute to reading difficulties—problems that can usually respond to optometric and/or ophthalmological treatment. Such considerations are all too often neglected in the GMBDS workup and the parent's indicating a history of eye problems should alert the examiner to their presence.

Ear disorders, such as chronic infections, can involve the brain. The child who has trouble hearing or trouble understanding what he or she hears may not only have some disorder of the external ear but of the central auditory processing mechanisms as well. Auditory examination is all too often neglected in the GMBDS workup. The parents' recording a history of ear problems should warrant the examiner's further investigation.

Although lead has been implicated more than other substances as an etiological factor in GMBDS, the ingestion of other substances must be considered. The impulsivity, poor judgment, and intellectual impairment of children makes them more likely to ingest drugs, poisons, and other dangerous substances. Accordingly, poisons should not only be viewed as primary etiological agents, but as potentially causing superimposed brain damage as well.

Last, my experience has been that a specific etiological factor cannot be found in the vast majority of GMBDS children. These are the children, I believe, whose only etiological factor is the fact that they are at the 15th-25th percentile level on the normal bell-shaped curve and are considered, in our society, to have a disease.

Present Medical Status

Most of the examiners for whom this book is written do not have scales in their offices for the purpose of measuring height and weight. Accordingly, it is useful to get these figures (Figure 3.9). They are not as likely to be significantly distorted by the parents as some of the other information provided, and the examiner, by merely looking at the child, can generally determine whether the figures provided are roughly accurate.

It is also important for the examiner to know whether the child is presently suffering with any illnesses, because the symptoms of such disorders can affect one's findings. For example, acute allergic reactions can cause the kind of agitation that can sometimes be confused with hyperactivity. The allergic child, however, will manifest other signs of allergy (sniffling, rash, conjunctivitis, etc.) to help the examiner in the differential diagnosis. The medications a child is taking are also important to know about. We have a long way to go in learning about the various factors that can produce GMBDS. It is possible, and even probable, that long-term use of certain medications might cause nerve cell dysfunction. In addition, the drugs a child is taking may affect performance on the diagnostic tests that are given. A child taking phenobarbital as an anticonvulsant is not likely to be as alert when taking the WISC-R, for example, as the child who is not taking barbiturates.

Family History—Mother

One is interested in the mother's age at the time of the pregnancy with the patient because the older the mother the greater the likelihood she will give birth to a child with various kinds of anomalies and malformations. One is also interested in the past history of spontaneous abortion because it is reasonable to assume that if the mother tends to lose and reject embryos and fetuses, those that are retained may be subject to the same kinds of rejection processes. Accordingly, there may be a greater likelihood of impairment in such mothers' retained fetuses than in fetuses of mothers with no previous history of spontaneous abortion. This is especially the case when chromosomal malfunctions habitually cause the abortions. In

Figure 3.9

PRESENT MEDICAL STATUS

Present height_____Present weight_____

Present illness(es) for which child is being treated_____

_____

Medications child is taking on an ongoing basis_____

_____ _____

FAMILY HISTORY - MOTHER

Age_____ Age at time of pregnancy with patient_____

Number of previous pregnancies_____Number of spontaneous abortions

(miscarriages)_____Number of induced abortions_____

Sterility problems (specify)_____

School: Highest grade completed_____

   Learning problems (specify)_____grade repeat_____

   Behavior problems (specify)_____

Medical problems (specify)_____

Have any of your blood relatives (not including patient and siblings) ever

had problems similar to those your child has? If so, describe_____

_____

_____

FAMILY HISTORY - FATHER

Age_____Age at the time of the patient's conception _____

Sterility problems (specify)_____

School: Highest grade completed_____

   Learning problems (specify)_____grade repeat_____

   Behavior problems (specify)_____

Medical problems (specify)_____

Have any of your blood relatives (not including patient and siblings) ever

had problems similar to those your child has? If so, describe_____

_____

addition, one is also interested in the past history of induced abortions. A mother with a history of sterility problems may be rejecting fertilized eggs and providing an intrauterine environment that is not optimally conducive to the healthy growth and development of the fertilized ovum. It is reasonable to speculate that the embryo that does finally grow to maturity is being exposed to the same detrimental influences and has a greater likelihood of being malformed.

One does well to inquire into the presence of significant medical problems because many maternal illnesses (infectious, metabolic, toxic, etc.) can have a significant effect on the developing embryo and fetus. Lastly, one wants to learn if blood relatives of the mother had symptoms similar to the child's when they were younger. As mentioned, genetic factors are probably operative in some children with GMBDS and this aspect of the inquiry may elucidate this etiological factor. It is also important to get information about the mother's school history, especially regarding learning disabilities and hyperactivity. The questions on maternal history of school learning problems, grade repeat, and behavior problems are designed to provide information in these areas.

Family History—Father

Sterility problems on the father's part may contribute to less than optimum sperm conditions for conception and a higher risk of embryonic abnormalities. One should give serious attention to the father's school history with regard to learning problems, grade repeat, and behavior problems, because present evidence suggests that the genetic factors appear more along the paternal than the maternal line. Although one should inquire into the father's medical problems, they are far less liklely to be of etiological significance for the MBD child. Again, one should inquire into the presence of the child's symptoms in the father's blood relatives to evaluate the presence of genetic factors.

Psychological Symptoms

Figures 3.10–3.13 present a list of a wide variety of psychological symptoms that are generally considered to be primarily, if not exclusively, psychogenic. Whereas most of the material in the questionnaire that has thus far been presented and discussed relates to

Figure 3.10

Most children exhibit, at one time or another, one or more of the symptoms listed below. Place a P next to those that your child has exhibited in the PAST and an N next to those that your child exhibits NOW. Only mark those symptoms that have been or are present to a significant degree over a period of time. Only check as problems behavior that you suspect is unusual or atypical when compared to what you consider to be the normal for your child's age. Then, on page 12, list the symptoms checked off on pages 9-12 and write a brief description including age of onset, duration, and any other pertinent information.

Thumb-sucking ___

Baby talk ___

Overly dependent for age ___

Frequent temper tantrums ___

Excessive silliness and clowning ___

Excessive demands for attention ___

Cries easily and frequently ___

Generally immature ___

Eats non-edible substances ___

Overeating with overweight ___

Eating binges with overweight ___

Undereating with underweight ___

Long periods of dieting and food abstinence with underweight ___

Preoccupied with food--what to eat and what not to eat ___

Preoccupation with bowel movements ___

Constipation ___

Encopresis (soiling) ___

Insomnia (difficulty sleeping) ___

Enuresis (bed wetting) ___

Frequent nightmares ___

Night terrors (terrifying night-time outbursts) ___

Sleepwalking ___

Excessive sexual interest and pre-occupation ___

Frequent sex play with other children ___

Excessive masturbation ___

Frequently likes to wear clothing of the opposite sex ___

Exhibits gestures and intonations of the opposite sex ___

Frequent headaches ___

Frequent stomach cramps ___

Frequent nausea and vomiting ___

Often complains of bodily aches and pains ___

Worries over bodily illness ___

Poor motivation ___

Apathy ___

Takes path of least resistance ___

Ever trying to avoid responsibility ___

Figure 3.11

Poor follow-through ___

Low Curiosity ___

Open defiance of authority ___

Blatantly un-cooperative ___

Persistent lying ___

Frequent use of profanity to parents, teachers, and other author-ities ___

Truancy from school ___

Runs away from home ___

Violent outbursts of rage ___

Stealing ___

Cruelty to animals, children, and others ___

Destruction of property ___

Criminal and/or dangerous acts ___

Trouble with the police ___

Violent assault ___

Fire setting ___

Little, if any, guilt over behavior that causes others pain and dis-comfort ___

Little, if any, response to pun-ishment for anti-social behavior ___

Few, if any, friends ___

Doesn't seek friendships ___

Rarely sought by peers ___

Not accepted by peer group ___

Selfish ___

Doesn't respect the rights of others ___

Wants things own way with exag-gerated reaction if thwarted ___

Trouble putting self in other person's position ___

Egocentric (self-centered) ___

Frequently hits other children ___

Argumentative ___

Excessively cri-tical of others ___

Excessively taunts other children ___

Ever complaining ___

Is often picked on and easily bullied by other children ___

Suspicious, distrustful ___

Aloof ___

"Wise-guy" or smart aleck attitude ___

Brags or boasts ___

Bribes other children ___

Excessively competitive ___

Often cheats when playing games ___

"Sore loser" ___

"Doesn't know when to stop" ___

Poor common sense in social situations ___

Often feels cheated or gypped ___

Feels others are persecuting him when there is no evidence for such ___

Typically wants his or her own way ___

Very stubborn ___

Obstruction-istic ___

Negativistic (does just the opposite of what is requested) ___

Figure 3.12

Quietly, or often silently, defiant of authority ____

Feigns or verbalizes compliance or cooperation but doesn't comply with requests ____

Drug abuse ____

Alcohol abuse ____

Very tense ____

Nail biting ____

Chews on clothes, blankets, etc. ____

Head banging ____

Hair pulling ____

Picks on skin ____

Speaks rapidly and under pressure ____

Irritability, easily "flies off the handle" ____

Fears
dark
new situations ____
strangers ____
being alone ____
death ____
separation from
 parent ____
school ____
visiting other
 children's homes ____
going away to
 camp ____
animals ____
other fears
(name)

_____ ____

_____ ____

Anxiety attacks with palpatations (heart pounding), shortness of breath, sweating, etc. ____

Disorganized ____

Tics such as eye-blinking, grimacing, or other spasmodic repetitious movements ____

Involuntary grunts, vocalizations (understandable or not) ____

Stuttering ____

Depression ____

Frequent crying spells ____

Excessive worrying over minor things ____

Suicidal preoccupation, gestures, or attempts ____

Excessive desire to please authority ____

"Too good" ____

Often appears in-sincere and/or artificial ____

Too mature, frequently acts older than actual age ____

Excessive guilt over minor indiscretions ____

Asks to be punished ____

Low self-esteem ____

Excessive self-criticism ____

Very poor toleration of criticism ____

Feelings easily hurt ____

Dissatisfaction with appearance or body part(s) ____

Excessive modesty over bodily exposure ____

Perfectionistic, rarely satisfied with performance ____

Frequently blames others as a cover-up for own short-comings ____

Little concern for personal appearance or hygiene ____

Little concern for or pride in personal property ____

"Gets hooked" on certain ideas and remains preoccupied ____

Compulsive repetition of seemingly meaningless physical acts ____

Shy ____

Inhibited self-expression in dancing, singing, laughing, etc. ____

Recoils from affectionate physical contact ____

Figure 3.13

Withdrawn ___	Mute (refuses to speak) but can ___	Flat emotional tone ___
Fears asserting self ___	Gullible and/or naive ___	Speech non-communicative or poorly communicative ___
Inhibits open expression of anger ___	Passive and easily led ___	Hears voices ___
Allows self to be easily taken advantage of ___	Excessive fantasizing, "lives in his (her) own world" ___	Sees visions ___
Frequently pouts and/or sulks ___		

As requested above, please first list below symptoms marked with the letter P and next to each symptom give descriptive information such as age of onset, age of termination, and other important data. Then list symptoms marked with an N and provide similar information.

P or N   Symptom   Brief Description

_____   _____   _____

_____   _____   _____

_____   _____   _____

_____   _____   _____

_____   _____   _____

_____   _____   _____

_____   _____   _____

_____   _____   _____

_____   _____   _____

_____   _____   _____

_____   _____   _____

_____   _____   _____

_____   _____   _____

_____   _____   _____

_____   _____   _____

neurophysiological dysfunction, the symptoms presented here are more likely to provide information about psychogenic disturbances. Some of the psychological disorders manifested by the symptoms are purely psychogenic in etiology; others are secondary to primary neurophysiologic disturbances, especially GMBDS.

Because most if not all children are likely to exhibit many of these symptoms at some time in their development, the parent is asked to check *only* those items that have exhibited themselves over a period. Without this instruction many parents would check most of the items. Furthermore, one wants to differentiate between those symptoms that existed in the past and those that are presently causing difficulty. Finally, in order to obtain further information about symptoms that have been checked in Figures 3.10–3.13, the parent is asked to provide further details about each symptom, for example, age of onset, age of termination, and other important data.

Siblings

In the questionnaire, Figure 3.14 provides only limited space for information about siblings. This is purposeful. The questionnaire is lengthy enough as it stands, and detailed information about siblings may not be warranted. However, some of the "key words" provided about the siblings may serve as a clue to the examiner that a more detailed inquiry during the interviews is justified. If a sibling, however, warrants treatment, then the examiner should ask the parent to fill out a separate questionnaire for that child.

Names and Addresses of Other Professionals Consulted

Information from other professionals is most often useful. The questionnaire's face letter requests that parents bring copies of reports from previous examiners, and these can often provide valuable information. For the sake of completion, the questionnaire also asks for the names and addresses of previous examiners in order to insure that all reports will be received. Last, the parent is invited to record any additional comments. Although the questionnaire attempts to be thorough, there are often special issues relevant to the patient that may not have been focused upon.

Figure 3.14

SIBLINGS

	Name	Age	Medical, social, or academic problems
1.			
2.			
3.			
4.			
5.			

LIST NAMES AND ADDRESSES OF ANY OTHER PROFESSIONALS CONSULTED

1. _____

2. _____

3. _____

4. _____

ADDITIONAL REMARKS

Please use the remainder of this page to write any additional comments you wish to make regarding your child's difficulties.

4 INTERVIEWING THE CHILD AND PARENTS TOGETHER

Interviewing the parents and child together in the initial interview is not traditional. The traditional practice is for the therapist to invite the child alone into the consultation room while leaving the parent(s) in the waiting room. One of the main arguements given for utilizing this procedure is that separating the child from the parents at the outset communicates to the child that he or she is to have a special private relationship with the therapist—a relationship not shared with the parents. Proponents of this practice claim that this enhances the likelihood of a good therapist-patient relationship being established. I am dubious about this. In fact, I believe that the practice is more likely to work in just the opposite way, that is, having an exclusive relationship with the child—a relationship in which the parents are excluded—is more likely to interfere with the development of a good therapist-patient relationship in that it is likely to alienate the parents and thereby lessen their involvement with, respect for, and support of the therapist in his or her relationship with the child. Furthermore, pressuring the child to separate from the parents at that time may lessen the likelihood that a good relationship will be established. The tensions and anxieties that such separation engenders may produce untoward reactions to the therapist at the outset— reactions that will compromise the development of a good relationship.

Another reason often given for separating the child from the parents at the outset is that it allows the therapist to observe whether the child has "separation anxiety." It is difficult, however, to imagine any child not being anxious in circumstances where the therapy is an unknown, the therapist is a stranger, and the child has never before been in the clinic or office and has little appreciation of what is going on. It is likely that the youngster has been told something like, "You're going to see a nice lady," "We're taking you to see a nice man who'll be playing lots of games with you," or "We're taking you to see a teacher who will help you learn better." Because such explanations are cover-ups, they may not be believed and may therefore create tension. Or the child may be told that he or she is going to see someone who will help with the youngster's "problems." Although the child may not have the faintest idea what the parents mean by the word "problems," he or she is not likely to anticipate that the experience is going to be a pleasant one.

Thus, if a child exhibits anxiety when separating from the parents to go with the therapist, it is likely that this is a normal response. In fact, it is reasonable to say that not being anxious at that point would probably reflect significant psychopathology indicating that the child's capacity to form deep relationships is so impaired that it makes no difference whether he or she is with a parent or a stranger. Or it may reflect such a defect in the parent-child relationship that the child welcomes an opportunity to go off with a stranger. But these are unusual situations. Most often the child is anxious and does not want to be separated from the parents in strange surroundings. One of the worst experiences a child therapist can have is that of trying to force or cajole a screaming, panicky child into accompanying the examiner alone into a private office. As the child desperately implores the parents not to let the stranger take him or her off, the presence of others in the waiting room cannot but increase the child's humiliation. Once in the consultation room, the likelihood of gaining any meaningful information from the child is almost nil. The word *never* is not one that I like to use. However, I have no problem using it with regard to a therapist's forcibly carrying a panic-stricken child into his or her consultation room at the beginning of the initial interview. This should *never* be done. There is no situation in which it is warranted, and there is no question that it may compromise significantly the treatment—even to the point where it may not be possible, so great may be the initial psychological trauma caused by this injudicious (and even simple-minded) approach to the treatment of the child.

Many therapists argue that another reason for seeing the parents alone first is that the child's disruptions and interferences will inhibit the data-collection process. I disagree with this point. The disruptions and interferences can be an important source of information, especially with regard to the relationship that the child has with each of the parents. The ways in which the parents handle these disruptions can be a useful source of information. Another argument given for seeing the parents alone is that they may not be comfortable revealing certain information in front of the child and may even deprive the therapist of this vital data. My experience has been that many parents in this category are overprotective and their hesitation to provide information in the interview with the child is a clue to the presence of this symptom. (Their failure to provide this information does not deprive the therapist of the opportunity to obtain it, because time is still set aside for them to be seen alone during the course of the two-hour consultation.) Last, no matter how accurate the parents' description of the child is, it is very difficult, if not impossible, for the therapist to gain a reasonable appreciation of the kind of person the child is without actually seeing him or her. Although one could argue that asking to see pictures of the child might provide some information in this regard, it is clearly far less efficacious than the actual experience of interviewing the child him- or herself at the outset.

If the child absolutely refuses to come into the consultation room with the parents, the boy or girl should be allowed to sit outside. For example, if a boy obstinately refuses to leave the waiting room, the examiner might say something along these lines: "Your parents and I will be talking over there in my office. You're invited to come in and join us at any time. If you change your mind, we'll be happy to allow you to join us in the conversation, which, of course, will be about you anyway." If after ten or fifteen minutes he is still outside, the examiner might go out and try to draw the child into a general discussion in the hope of becoming a more familiar figure so that the child will become more receptive. For example, if the child is looking at baseball cards I might say, "You know, I'm not up with baseball these days. I used to be interested in it when I was a kid. I lived near the Yankee Stadium in the Bronx and the Yankees were my favorite team. Who are the big heroes now? Who's your favorite team?" In this way I try to establish some area of common interest with the child in the hope that it will catalyze and facilitate his involvement with me. Having similar interests can play a role in "breaking the ice." Or the therapist might send a parent out to the waiting room if that approach seems preferable. At the very worst, the child will never come into the examiner's office and will never become a patient. Under such circumstances, therapists should lose no sleep at night but should be satisfied with the knowledge that they have tried their best to engage the child and have therefore "done their duty."

Once the parents and child are in the room, I again depart from the traditional approach. In my own training in the 1950s, I was taught that the unstructured interview is best because it allows for free revelations from the universe of information that may come

before the evaluator, and that specific questions are likely to be con-
taminating and restricting. Subsequent experience has led me to
conclude that one need not lose the benefits of the open-ended inquiry if one asks specific questions. Both types of inquiry can provide useful information. Thus, during training, I was taught that
the best question to begin with was something along the lines of:
"Well, why have you come here?" or "So what's the problem?" The
rationale for this approach is that since the question is an open one
and does not draw the patient into specific areas, it therefore does
not have any contaminants. Although this position is certainly valid,
it does not give proper consideration to the fact that posing open-
ended questions to a person who is tense or fearful will not yield
helpful information. Accordingly, the initial interview is best begun
with general questions that any human being would ask another in
a new situation. One might ask whether the parents had trouble
finding the office or whether they had difficulty because of the
weather. These are innocuous enough questions and are not likely
to contaminate anything. They do, however, serve to lessen anxiety
and make the examiner (a total stranger) more familiar and "human."

The chairs have been previously arranged so that the four of
us form a circle. Even at this point one is already gathering information. Who sits where? Are common courtesies observed? Is there
jockeying or vying for a particular seat? Does the child sit in his
own chair or does he cling to a parent? If so, which one and how
is this responded to—with warm caresses, cold stiffness, rejection,
and so on?

The child, at this point, may not wish to sit. If the activity engaged in appears to have possibilities for providing information that
will be helpful, I may permit the "digression." For example, a child
might attempt to reduce anxiety by trying to find similarity between the therapist's office and some other place that is familiar
to him or her. Such a child might say: "I have a ball at home that's
just like that." To such a comment I might reply: "Yes, you'll find
that there are lots of things here that are just like those you've seen
in other places." One adolescent, who had previously been in treatment with another therapist, on entering his first session, commented sneeringly: "You shrinks are all the same." He then glanced
around the room and while pointing to different objects said: "The
same stupid couches and those pictures of your crazy kids on the
desk." Had I addressed myself to his hostility I would have missed

the point entirely. I merely commented that he was perfectly right that Dr. X and I did have a number of things in common. He needed to see us as similar in order to be more relaxed and my response served to help him to be so.

Some parents, at this point, will make a humorous comment which may help to alleviate their anxiety. If they get a smile from the therapist, he or she becomes less menacing. It behooves the therapist, in this phase, to hear their message and comply with the parents' request for a friendly response. A poker face or austere, humorless mien will only increase anxiety and lessen the chances of obtaining accurate information. For example, as one family was taking seats, the father chose the larger, deeper chair and laughingly stated: "I hope I don't fall asleep in there. It looks so comfortable." The remark clearly revealed his desire to desensitize himself to his anxiety and avoid the anticipated threats of the interview. I smiled and replied: "I hope you don't. I usually find that I have a little more difficulty getting information from someone who is sleeping." The father laughed and seemed more relaxed. I did not go into the sources of his anxiety nor did I psychoanalyze the remark. I responded at the exact level at which he was functioning and directed my attention to his true request. A humorous response does more to reduce anxiety at such a time than direct statements about how the interview is really not so bad. With my response he had the *living experience* that I was benevolent.

Actually many things can happen at this point and the therapist must be alert to appreciate their meaning and sufficiently flexible to alter the interview in order to derive the maximum benefit from what may occur. Therapists do well to appreciate, however, that the most likely reason for atypical comments and responses during this very early phase relate to the need to reduce the anxiety associated with this first screening interview.

It is important to appreciate that most children under the age of ten or eleven are extremely uncomfortable about revealing deficiencies to a mental health examiner, even to the point of lying. This is not only true during the first session, but throughout the course of therapy and even at the time of termination. So common is this reluctance that I consider it normal and am often suspicious about the motivations of the child who openly admits deficiencies. This is another reason why examiners do well not to "push the point" regarding getting a child to admit inappropriate or maladaptive behavior. This phenomenon is one of the primary reasons why I have developed a variety of techniques, the purpose of which is to obtain information and provide input to a child who does not willingly discuss his or her problems.

The child is then asked a series of simple questions that will probably be easy to answer, questions about what the youngster's name is and how it is spelled and about his or her address, telephone number, age, school grade, teacher's name, the names and ages of the parents and siblings, and so forth. As the child gets "the right answers," fears are alleviated and the child is then in a better position to answer the more open-ended questions about why he or she is there. The specific questions only take a few minutes, do not contaminate, and will provide the examiner with a patient who will generally be in a good position to give accurate answers to the questions that will follow. What is even more important is that the examiner is much more likely to develop a good relationship with the child by starting in this way—with sensitivity to the child's fears—rather than by using an approach likely to produce more alienation and tension. Some insecure or dependent children will request, either by words or gesture, that a parent respond for them even though they know the correct answer, or they will look for reassurance that they have given the appropriate response.

Early in the discussion of the patient's problems, the therapist should try to learn about the type of preparation the child was given prior to the interview. Parents who use duplicity to "protect" their children from what they consider to be the detrimental effects of their knowing that they will be seeing a psychiatrist or other mental health professional will often tell their children absolutely nothing about the nature of the interview or will inform them that they are going to talk to a "nice man(woman)" or use some other euphemism or ruse. The parents may have been vague about the kind of doctor I am or may have tried to give their children the impression that I am a general physician, pediatrician, or tutor. In such cases I simply tell such children that I am a psychiatrist and ask them if they know what that is. If they do not, I tell them that I am the kind of doctor who tries to help people who have "troubles, worries, or problems." I specifically say "tries" in order to emphasize the point that my job is to try to help people and that I cannot promise to do so. At that point, or subsequently, I will get across the idea that an important determinant as to whether or not I can be helpful is how much cooperation and involvement I have on the part of the child and both parents. Early in treatment I want to create an atmosphere of cooperative working together. If the mother and/or father appears upset by the disclosure that I am a psychiatrist, I usually tell the parent(s) that I appreciate that their withholding information was motivated by the desire to do what they thought was best for the child, but that it has been my experience that children are not so fragile as many adults think and that such concealment engenders distrust of the parents and unnecessary anxiety in the child. I tell them also that, all things considered, the arguments are overwhelmingly in favor of an open and honest discussion of just who I am and what my purpose is.

If the child becomes upset by the disclosure, I usually try to find out exactly what he or she considers to be the implications of going to a psychiatrist. Most often they involve fears that the child will be considered crazy or that people will laugh at him or her. If the child does not directly verbalize these fears, I will usually state: "Some kids think that only crazy people see psychiatrists. Do you think that?" If the answer is in the affirmative, I usually say, "Most of the people I see are not that sick that anyone would call them crazy. They just have some things wrong with *certain parts* of themselves which they want to change. I emphasize the words "certain parts" in order to get across the idea that I do not view the child to be suffering with all-pervasive psychopathology and is a total misfit, rather I consider the problems to be confined to certain specific areas. Such circumscribing of the deficits lessen the likelihood that the child will generalize from the isolated deficiencies and consider him- or herself totally loathsome. And for the nonpsychotic child, I will add, "Although I know you only a short time, I do have some information about you. I have spoken to your mother on the phone, and I have also had a chance to talk to you for a little while now. Although I don't know you very well, I can tell you already, from everything I do know about you, that there is nothing I have learned so far which would lead me to believe that you are crazy or insane." However, if the child appears to be psychotic, I will say, "That word *crazy* is a cruel word and sometimes people who have trouble like yours are laughed at and called crazy. I know that there are parts of you that you would like to change and that you would like to be more like other children. We psychiatrists think that it's sad to have such problems, and we do not laugh at people with them and call them names. People who do that often have something wrong with themselves."

Some children, in this early phase of the interview, may describe a few problems, but usually with some hesitation. A child might say, for example, "I don't get along with friends." To this response, I will ask, "In exactly what way?" Concrete examples serve well to clarify the exact nature of the problem. As mentioned in Chapter Three, generalizations are far less valuable in treatment than specific examples. If the child cannot describe the specifics, I will turn to the parents to provide them. In order to obtain such information, I usually look vaguely half-way between them so as not to focus on one, but rather to determine if either tends to be more active or to dominate. Throughout the interview my position is that of the *ignorant interrogator*. I use the word ignorant here in the true sense of the word, that is, as someone who is unknowing and that I am interrogating continually in order to lessen my ignorance.

I go back and forth, between child and parents, ever clarifying, ever adding to my knowledge. If there are contradictions between what the child says and what the parents say (a common occurrence), I might say to the child, "Now you say one thing and your parents say just the opposite. What about that? I don't understand. I'm confused." The question should be posed in the spirit of an honest, open desire to learn the truth and not with the implication that the therapist is trying to prove any particular person right or wrong. Such additional back-and-forth inquiry may result in agreement as to the presence or nature of a particular problem. If it does not, the particular line of inquiry should be abandoned for the time being, with a comment such as, "Well, it seems that you and your parents see it differently. Let's go on and talk about some of the other problems. Perhaps later I will be able to get a clearer picture about what's going on."

Although some children may suffer some embarrassment over their problems discussed so openly, there are compensatory therapeutic benefits to be derived from such confrontation. They clarify the reasons for the child's being in the therapist's office, and this serves to make them more ego-alien and more amenable to treatment. The therapist, a significant figure of authority, agrees that they are "problems" or "troubles" and by implication undesirable qualities without which the child would be better off. In addition, naming, labeling, and talking about unpleasant subjects reduces their anxiety-provoking potential. The child often anticipates that revealing defects will result in scorn, punishment, derogation, and/or other very unpleasant reactions from the therapist and/or parents. When the expected condemnation is not forthcoming, the child has what F. Alexander and T. French (1946) referred to as a "corrective emotional experience," and the feelings of self-loathing and anxiety that surround the symptoms may be reduced. Generally, the advantages of the open discussion more than compensate for the child's embarrassment. Those who avoid such confrontations deprive the child of these benefits.

It is important to concentrate on the child's assets, accomplishments, skills, and hobbies at this time. This serves to counterbalance the ego-debasing material that has been thus far focused upon. By necessity, therapy must concern itself, either directly or indirectly, with the problems that have brought the child to treatment. There is usually little in them that the child can be proud of and much that he or she is ashamed of. In the world beyond the consultation room, the problems may represent only a small percentage of the child's living experiences; in the consultation room, unfortunately, they represent a significant percentage if the therapy is to be meaningful. In order to counterbalance this unfortunate but necessary emphasis, therapists do well to take every opportunity to focus on ego-enhancing material. If warranted, the therapist should compliment the child on a *meaningful* accomplishment. There is no place for gratuitous or feigned praise in therapy. Interest (only if genuine) should be expressed in any activity that is a source of gratification for the child. This, too, can serve to enhance the relationship.

When the child has mentioned all the problems he or she can think of, I usually say: "Well, those are probably the worst things you can say about yourself. What are the best?" or "What are you good at?" The child must be given the opportunity to present assets in order to compensate for the probable embarrassment suffered while revealing the liabilities. An inquiry that concentrates only on defects can be ego-debasing and mortifying. If the child cannot think of any assets, I respond: "If you can't think of anything good about yourself, I'd say that that in itself is a problem." If the child still has trouble identifying admirable qualities, I enlist the aid of the parents. If they also cannot describe praiseworthy characteristics, it reflects deep inadequacy in their parental affection. I consider the healthy parent to distort *slightly* in the positive direction regarding a child's assets (Gardner, 1973b). The child who lacks such parental distortion is being deprived indeed. I am not referring to gross misrepresentations which are clearly not manifestations of healthy parental attitudes. For example, to consider the mediocre piano player to be "talented" is healthy; to consider him a "prodigy" is a delusion which can only create difficulty for the child in forming an accurate self-image. Probably more important than what the parents *say* regarding the child's laudable traits is their *feeling-tone* when presenting them. Is there the smile of pride and the warm glance, which are the hallmarks of the loving parent, or are the positive qualities described in a perfunctory way, as if they felt it behooved them to "dig up something" to bolster the child's ego? Such considerations are vital to the determination of the depth of parental affection.

The concentration on assets may also reveal the pathological do-gooder, the "Momma's boy," and others with hypertrophied super-egos. The list of their assets is long. They dote over mother when she is not feeling well; they are clean, neat, bathed, and make their beds without being asked; they rarely fight with siblings; they get straight As in conduct; they may be teacher's favorite, and so on. Other mothers say to their children: "Why can't you be like Tommy?" This constellation of symptoms is often difficult to treat because it does not produce pain or discomfort for the child or the parents, but is rather a source of pride and ego-gratification. Nevertheless, it can reflect significant difficulties.

The information obtained during this phase of the interview is the most important for making the decision as to whether treatment will be necessary. The decision should be made on the basis of *symptoms*, not on psychodynamics. The therapist must not only know the appropriate levels at which normal behavior ends and the pathological begins, but must also appreciate that everyone has psychodynamics and that having psychodynamics is not the same as having psychopathology. All children have nightmares on occasion. They are a pathological manifestation only when they are frequent.

All boys engage in hostile play. Such play is pathological when it's obsessive, dangerous, excessively morbid, or in some other way bears definite stigmata of neurosis. The projective material obtained when the child is seen alone in the next-described phase of the screening interview should be considered of secondary importance in deciding about treatment. The primary considerations are obtained in this phase when symptomatology and behavioral abnormalities are presented and described.

Conduct in the home is a poorer criterion of psychopathology than outside behavior. The home generally provides a more permissive atmosphere than the world at large. It does not assess well the child's ability to inhibit the more primitive impulses and adjust appropriately to the demands of reality. An old gym teacher of mine used to respond to the sassy or back-talking child with the invective: "Who the hell do you think you're talking to, your mother?" He knew well that mothers will often tolerate much more abuse than anyone else.

When the child has not acquired the skills and capacity to function properly in school or in relationships with friends, the presence of psychopathology is strongly implied. Good functioning in these two areas generally indicates that the child is not likely to be significantly disturbed. If not provided, I ask for information about these areas of functioning. (The questionnaire also provides information in these areas.) How does the child get along in school? What does the teacher say about his or her conduct? Does the child have a "best friend?" If so, how often do they see one another? Do children call on the child? If so, how often? Is the child invited to others' homes? Is the child in the "in-group," on the fringe, or is he or she a "loner"? Questions such as these are the most vital of the interview and provide the most meaningful data as to whether psychopathology is present.

One area of difficulty which I have not found helpful to dwell on at length is that of sibling rivalry. In my opinion, it is normally fierce, and to devote much time to its vicissitudes is wasteful because such inquiry adds little meaningful information. If the mother, for example, says that the child fights often with his brother, I'll ask her how often. If the frequency is less than ten-to-fifteen fights a day and if there is no history of dangerous trauma being inflicted then I usually say something like: "That sounds par for the course. What other problems are there?" Of course, if a sibling is having nightmares in which he screams out: "No, no, Jerry. Don't beat me!" then the rivalry is probably pathological. Also, the absence of overt manifestations of sibling rivalry suggests a family in which aggression is significantly inhibited.

At the same time that one is obtaining verbal accounts of the child's difficulties with the back-and-forth inquiry, one should also attempt to stimulate and catalyze interaction between the members of the family. It is hoped that the exact kind of interaction which takes place in the home will be reproduced. It is the unwise interviewer who attempts to squelch or circumvent arguments between family members and tries to "cool things" when an argument threatens to erupt because much of value can be learned from such encounters. Are feelings freely expressed or is the argument highly intellectualized? Who is dominant? Does the child side with any particular person? Are there tears? If so, what effect do they have? The healthy family will be somewhat embarrassed and restrained in its argument, whereas the sicker family will not be so self-conscious. The possible considerations are endless—it is a rich source of information indeed.

One thing that is important to look for in the context of the family discussion is the presence of laughter and humor. One or two humorous comments, mutually enjoyed by members of the family, speaks for a healthy element in their relationship regardless of what pathology may be present. The ability to laugh is a vital ingredient to health, whereas the humorless family is usually a very sick one. And the capacity to laugh at oneself indicates ego-strength, healthy insight, and makes one's foibles more bearable. Therapists who respond warmly, with a humorous comment at the right time, provide a setting that fosters these informative responses.

Of course, the therapist should not be party to pathological humor. The hail-fellow-well-met type, the back-slapping jokester whose humor is patently obsessive and defensive, should not be responded to in kind, for that would only encourage the utilization of this ploy to avoid honesty. The parent who uses wit in the service of expressing hostility should not be encouraged by the therapist's laughing at his or her jokes. Sarcasm, verbal scapegoatism, and laughing ridicule should be noted mentally but certainly not joined by the therapist.

If during the course of the parents' description of the presenting problems the child interrupts with comments such as, "Don't tell him that," or "I told you never to tell him that," or "You promised me you wouldn't talk about that," one might react with surprise and say something like "What! Keeping secrets from your own psychiatrist? Didn't you know that you're never supposed to keep secrets from a psychiatrist?" One might then reinforce this principle by asking the child to think about television programs he or she has seen in which this fact has been demonstrated.

During the discussion of the presenting complaints it is important to observe the various parties. One should especially observe the child's relationship with each of the parents. Glances and gestures, as well as vocal intonations, provide information about affection, respect, and other forms of involvement. Seat placement, physical contact, and direct statements to one another also give much information about the interpersonal relationships of the parties being interviewed. In fact, this aspect of the interview may be more important than the specific information about presenting problems that is ostensibly the focus.

At this point, one can proceed in a number of different ways. If the examiner suspects that there is much useful information that the parents can relate but have been hesitant to reveal in front of the child, the child might be told, "Now I'm going to speak with your parents alone, so I'd appreciate your having a seat in the waiting room. Then, I'll speak with you alone while they sit outside." To some children this might be followed by, "I'll be speaking with them about things that are personal for them. Then, when I'm with you, I'll be speaking about things that you may want to be kept personal." However, it is important for the reader to appreciate that the latter comment is not made very often. I much prefer that the atmosphere be one of an open pool of communication in which all things pertinent to the child are discussed freely with both parents and the child. The examiner may, however, see the child alone at that point, especially if the parents have stated that there is nothing additional that they wish to relate. Or, the interview with all three parties may be continued, if that appears to be the most judicious approach.

5 INTERVIEW WITH THE PARENTS ALONE

When the parents are seen alone, they should be asked about other problems that they have hesitated to discuss in front of the child. Often such reluctance is ill-advised, and the parents should be encouraged to discuss these issue(s) with the child (who is then brought back into the room). When this is not the case, and the parents are alone, one does well to get some information about the marital relationship. Time does not permit going into great detail at this point, but the therapist wants to get a general idea about its stability and whether significant problems are present. When making inquiries about the parental relationship, each side should be heard; but in the initial interview, it may not be possible to come to any conclusions regarding which party exhibits the greater degree of pathology. The examiner merely wants to obtain a list of the main problems; an in-depth inquiry goes beyond the scope of the initial consultation.

On occasion, both parents will claim that they have a good marriage and that they love one another. There are two possibilities here: One is that this is true and the other is, of course, that the parents are denying (either consciously or unconsciously) impairments in their relationship. When presented with the "happy marriage," the examiner might respond with a comment like, "Every marriage has some problems; no marriage is perfect. There are times, I am sure, when the two of you have differences of opinion. Every marriage has its fights from time to time. What are the areas of difference in *your* marriage?" When presented in this way, the parents are generally more comfortable about revealing areas of difficulty. Of course, there are marriages in which the partners never fight, but in such cases one or both generally suffers with a deep-seated anger-inhibition problem, and the "peace" they enjoy is paid for dearly with symptoms and/or character traits resulting from the pent-up hostility that inevitably arises in all human relationships. Sometimes parents who deny marital difficulties in the joint session will provide significant information about their marital problems in individual sessions. Of course, the therapist would then be negligent if he or she did not go into the reasons for the "cover-up" during the joint session.

It is desirable to get some idea about the depth and nature of psychopathology in each of the parents. The interviewer will usually already have some information along these lines from general observations. The level of tension in the initial interview is generally quite high from the outset. Strong emotions are evoked. In such an atmosphere it is likely that many forms of psychopathology will be revealed. This is especially so for such character traits as suspiciousness, dependency, volatility, low frustration tolerance, strong need to control and dominate, and seductivity. One of the easiest ways to obtain information about the parents' psychopathology is to ask whether either of them has ever been in treatment. If the answer is yes, the therapist should ask about the main problems for which the parent has been or is in therapy. A person who is in relatively good psychological health usually will not hesitate to discuss the major reasons for seeking treatment. Significant secretiveness may, in itself, represent a problem. One should not, however, expect a person in therapy to reveal every secret or personal problem in the presence of the spouse, although it is reasonable to expect that the major issues will be comfortably discussed. Time only permits an outlining of the major problems for which the parent sought therapy; more detailed information can be gained in subsequent interviews.

Before closing the part of the initial interview in which the parents are seen without the child, they should be invited to talk about anything else they consider important. If a presented issue appears to be significant, some time should be devoted to it—to a superficial degree—reserving detailed elaboration for subsequent sessions.

6 INTERVIEW WITH THE CHILD ALONE

The main object at this stage is to obtain as much information about the child in as short a period as possible, so that the interviewer can be in a better position to make definite statements about the presence of psychopathology and the necessity for treatment. Actually, the therapist should have a good idea already about these two issues, and this phase should serve to supplement what he has already learned. Although allowing the child to select the activity *he* or *she* wishes to engage in is my usual approach during at least some part of the *therapeutic* interview, in the *diagnostic* interview my inclination is to present the child with activities which are most highly calculated to provide me with meaningful psychodynamic information. If, however, the child shows a strong desire to engage in a particular activity (which is unusual), I do not stop him or her and I learn what I can from it. However, I might say: "Okay, we'll spend some of our time doing what you want, and then we'll spend the rest of the time with the games I'd like to play with you."

It is important to reiterate that at this point I am primarily concerned with symptoms and less with psychodynamics. My primary interest in this phase is to determine *if* psychopathology is present, not why or how it came about. In the context of the inquiry I observe for the presence of symptoms and am only secondarily interested in the psychodynamics which are revealed by what the child does. I look for manifestations of atypical and/or abnormal behavior, such as obstructionism, passive-aggressivity, attempts to destroy or lack of concern for my property, hyperactivity, poor concentration, speech impairment, being a "sore-loser," compulsive cleanliness, excessive questioning, inordinate need for reassurance, failure to understand directions, and so forth.

The Freely-Drawn Picture

A good way to start a meaningful interview when alone with a child is to ask the child to draw with crayons a picture of anything he or she wants. I will generally say something like, "I'd like to see how good you are at drawing a picture. Draw anything you want. After you've finished I want to see how good you are at making up a story about the picture that you've drawn. It has to be a completely made-up story, not something that really happened to you or anyone you know, not something that you saw on television or read in a book." By using the phrase "to see how good you are," I hope to enhance the child's motivation. Presumably, if the child draws a "good" picture, I will not only offer praise (which I will), but the child will feel good about him- or herself because of the accomplishment. And the same holds true with regard to the story I hope to elicit. If the child begins to draw something that looks like a design, I will ask what it is. If the child confirms my suspicions, I will say, "It's against the rules to draw a design. The rules of the game are that you have to draw something about which you can tell a story." Of course, the child is under no real compulsion to "follow the rules." Most children, however, will overcome the resistances that contributed to their drawing the design and provide a recognizable drawing.

It is important for the examiner to appreciate that only limited pressure, cajoling, and other forms of "encouragement" should be utilized in this phase of the evaluation. At worst, the child will refuse to draw. The only result of this will be that the examiner would be deprived of some information. In the extreme, the child will absolutely refuse to become involved in any of the diagnostic activities. If such is the case, the child will not become a patient. If the therapist considers this to represent a lack of professional ability, then it is likely that he or she will place undue pressures on the patient. As mentioned, the therapist should take the position that he or she did not cause the pathology—it is often generations in the making—and although it is important to *try* to help the patient, it does not behoove the therapist to bring about any kind of alleviation of the presenting problems. Psychopathology is most often complex and we are only at the most primitive levels of our understanding. Considering our ignorance, it is even a bit grandiose of therapists to take the position that help can be given to more than a small fraction of all those who come our way. With this more modest and realistic position, examiners are less likely to place undue pressures on themselves and their patients.

As is true of many aspects of psychodynamic theory, there is little that one can say with certainty. But even within the analytic framework, one must be aware that a psychological interpretation based on a child's picture itself is a very risky business. For example, a boy may draw a picture of a happy scene: a house, a brightly shining sun, and beautiful flowers all around. From the appearance of the picture one is likely to conclude that the boy is a happy child who has an optimistic view of the world. However, one must consider the possibility that the picture represents a reaction formation against depression, hostility, pessimism, or various other unpleasant feelings. Accordingly, one is in no position to make any statements about a picture in isolation from the child who draws it. The more knowledge the therapist has about the child, the better able he or she is to understand the meaning of the picture. In addition, isolated interpretations are likely to be far less valid than persistent themes that exhibit themselves in many different ways. Thus, if the boy who drew the aforementioned scene was clinically depressed, had a generally "sourpuss" attitude, and had few friends, it is likely that the picture is reaction formation. And this would be supported if he exhibited both clinically and through projective material other manifestations of denial and reaction formation. This caveat about interpreting the child's projections cannot be emphasized too strongly.

The examiner should also appreciate that many age-appropriate, stereotyped pictures may appear to have complex psychodynamic significance when a simpler explanation will suffice and be far more accurate. For example, an eight-year-old boy who draws pictures depicting ships and airplanes in combat should not automatically be considered to have excessive hostility that is being released vicariously through the vehicle of the drawing and its associated war story. All individuals have pent-up anger that they cannot release directly. All of us must utilize various socially acceptable vehicles for vicarious release. Release through space-war fantasy is presently in vogue among children, and the child's utilization of it, to a reasonable degree, is normal and healthy. Accordingly, one should not impute too quickly pathological motives in this book.

What has just been said regarding interpreting the meaning of a picture is also applicable to analyzing the self-created story for its psychodynamic significance. Some children will tell a relatively mundane story depicting events of the day. This is usually a resistance against the expression of more revealing material. Others will tell extremely elaborate stories, sometimes to the point where the examiner will have to interrupt because they appear to go on endlessly. These can also serve the purposes of resistance. However, the therapist may detect one or two themes that are repeated over and over. Such repeated themes may be significant. The repetition may serve the process of working through, in that reiteration and desensitization are central to that process. It is beyond the scope of this chapter to discuss in detail the wide variety of psychodynamic themes that may be revealed in children's stories.

Draw-a-Person

During the initial interview many examiners ask the child simply to "draw a person." It is preferable to make this request after the child has drawn the free picture because asking the child to draw a person restricts fantasy significantly. From the universe of possible things a child can draw, selecting a person considerably narrows the child's options. However, there is still a universe of possible drawings and associations (a universe within a universe so to speak), and so the drawing is still fairly useful as a projective instrument. One should not ask the child to draw a person of a specific sex because that may further narrow the possibilities and restrict associations. *After* the child has drawn a figure of a particular sex, one can then ask for one of the opposite sex. Generally, the age and sex of the figure drawn is revealing. If a boy, for example, draws a picture of a girl and, in addition pays significant attention to such details as eyelashes, coiffeur, fingernails, jewelry, and other attributes generally of great concern to females in our society, one should consider the possibility that this boy has a sexual identification problem. This would especially be the case if most observers, not knowing the sex of the child, would consider it to have been drawn by a girl. If, however, a boy draws a picture of an older woman, it is likely that the mother or her surrogate is being depicted.

By looking at the picture, the therapist can sometimes learn some important things about the child. However, the reader should be warned that such interpretations are highly speculative and interexaminer reliability is quite low. This drawback notwithstanding, useful information can still be obtained. This is especially the case if speculations from projective material are substantiated by clinical assessment. Placing the feet of a figure flush against the bottom of the paper may connote feelings of instability with a need to anchor or secure the body to a stable place. Children with marked feelings of inferiority are more likely to draw their picture in this way. Significant blackness, especially when drawn frenetically, sometimes symbolizes great anxiety and a view of people as threatening. This kind of picture is more frequently drawn by children who are clinically anxious. Large shoulders and other accentuations of traditionally "macho" features may represent a boy's attempt to compensate for feelings of weakness. This is especially likely in the adolescent with feelings of masculine inadequacy. The way in which the child deals with breast outline may provide information about the child's sexual feelings and attitudes. Family attitudes toward sexuality will often provide clues as to whether the examiner's interpretation in this area is valid. The way in which the child draws the eyes may provide information in a number of areas. Shy children and those prone to use denial mechanisms to a significant degree may draw a figure with the eyes averted. Staring eyes have generally been interpreted to connote suspiciousness and sometimes even paranoia. Again, the examiner does well to make such interpretations cautiously and to use clinical data for support or refutation of these speculations. Machover (1949, 1951, 1960) has written extensively on the psychological interpretation of children's drawings.

The examiner should try to get the child to tell a story about the picture. One can begin the process by asking for specific information about the person depicted. Some start with the general request that the child tell a story, and then only resort to specific questions if the request is not or cannot be complied with. What has been said about interpreting stories told in association with freely drawn pictures holds for the human-figure drawings as well. The therapist does well to differentiate between age-appropriate stereotyped stories (which are probably normal) and idiosyncratic ones. The latter provide the more meaningful information. But here again there is much speculation.

After drawing the first picture, the child should be asked to draw a picture of a person of the opposite sex. One should take care not to specify whether the picture should be of a child or an adult, lest the universe of possibilities be reduced. One might say, "Now that you've drawn a picture of a male, I want you to draw another picture. This time I want you to draw a female." Or, for the younger child, one might say, "Now that you've drawn a picture of a boy, I want you to draw a picture of either a girl or a woman." After as much information as possible has been extracted from the pictures, the examiner should ask the child to draw a picture of a family. Because of time limitations, it is prudent not to require the child to spend too much time on the details of the various family figures. Here, the therapist is primarily interested in the number and sexes of the figures chosen, their relationships with one another, and the story the child tells about the family. Stories elicited from the family picture are generally less revealing than those from the individual pictures. More frequently one obtains stereotyped stories about family excursions or day-to-day activities. These are usually resistance stories and provide little if any psychodynamic information. Of course, at times, one does obtain rich and meaningful stories.

The Make-a-Picture Story Test

The Make-a-Picture Story test (MAPS) (Schneidman, 1947) is particularly useful for eliciting psychodynamic material from children, especially from those who may not be free enough to reveal themselves through the aforementioned less-structured methods for gaining psychodynamic material, namely, the freely drawn picture, the mutual storytelling technique, and the Draw-a-Person and Draw-a-Family tests. The equipment consists of a series of cards, each of which depicts a scene without human or animal figures, and the child is provided with a collection of figurines (cut from thin cardboard) representing a wide assortment of human and animal figures. The child is simply requested to select one of the cards and one or more of the figurines, put the figurines in the scene, and then make up a story.

Although there is a similarity between the Make-a-Picture Story test and the more commonly used Thematic Apperception Test (TAT) (Murray, 1936), there are definite differences—differences that, in my opinion, make the MAPS a superior diagnostic instrument. First, the scenes depicted in the TAT, although designed to be vague, are still definitely identifiable and have figures with recognizable sex and age. In the TAT these specific figures are placed in specific scenes. In the MAPS the child decides which figure(s) shall be in which scene, thereby increasing almost infinitely the number of possible stimuli for storytelling. In the MAPS the child is much more the creator of the facilitating stimulus. Furthermore, having more of a say in what the picture will be like and playing an active role in determining what picture to create, the child is generally more motivated to associate stories to it.

Another advantage that the MAPS has over the TAT is that the TAT cards are primarily designed for diagnostic work with adults. Although some of the TAT cards do depict children, most depict grown-ups. The adult scenes will certainly elicit fantasies around family life, especially the parents; however, the paucity of children is a definite detriment if one wishes to draw out stories from children. While some of the TAT cards are specifically designated as relevant to boys and girls, the author's experience has been that the child's opportunity to select the figures in the MAPS creates a situation in which more child-type fantasies are likely to be evoked.

Additional Diagnostic Instruments

The stories that the child tells in association with the freely drawn picture, the Draw-a-Person Test, and The Make-a-Picture Story cards, can sometimes be used as a point of departure for an informal introduction into the mutual storytelling technique. I say sometimes because time limitations may not permit the examiner's responding with stories during the two-hour consultation. But more important, presenting responding stories during that early stage may be injudicious and even risky. The creation of a responding story is best done in circumstances in which one has extensive information about a child, especially after a thorough and intensive evaluation of the child and family members. However, there are times when the meaning of the child's story is so obvious, and the pathological adaptations contained therein so blatant, that the examiner may be in a good position to provide a reasonably accurate responding story. Under such circumstances, the examiner does well to respond with his or her story and take some time discussing it with the child.

There are other projective instruments that the examiner can utilize in the initial screening interview. Whether or not these are used depends primarily on the amount of time available. The three wishes question certainly does not take much time, unless elaborate discussions have been spun off from the child's responses. I generally try to get the child to tell me not only what he or she would wish for but *why*. However, I have not usually found this series of questions useful. Most often children provide relatively stereotyped and nonrevealing responses. A common response is, "All the money in the world" or some huge amount of money, like "a billion trillion dollars." When I then ask children who respond in this way what they would do with all the money, they generally provide a list of toys and other material possessions. (I have yet to interview a child who utilized the money philanthropically.) Another common response is, "My first wish would be that I could have as many wishes as I wanted." This response is usually provided as a "joke," but it is obviously also a resistance.

Another instrument that may be utilized in the initial interview for obtaining useful psychodynamic information is a series of questions described by N.I. Kritzberg (1966). The child is asked the question: "If you had to be turned into an animal, and could choose any animal in the whole world, what animal would you choose?" After the child responds, he or she is asked the reason for that choice. Following this, the child is asked for his or her second and third choices and the reasons why. Then the child is asked what three animals he or she would not want to be, and the reasons why. There are a series of similar type questions that I will describe in detail in the next chapter. Generally, time only permits the presentation of the aforementioned in the initial screening interview.

Generally, time does not permit my introducing *The Talking, Feeling, and Doing Game* (1973a) in the initial screening interview. However, there is occasionally a child who is so inhibited that no meaningful material has been obtained from the aforementioned projective instruments. Under such circumstances, I will devote some time to playing the game with the child. This not only may provide me with information that might not have otherwise been obtained, but gives me a hint as to whether the child is a possible candidate for therapeutic involvement. The inability to provide projective material certainly speaks poorly for therapeutic involvement, but *The Talking, Feeling, and Doing Game* may still be a viable instrument for utilization for such children.

The tests discussed are used with the child whom I suspect to be suffering with psychogenic difficulties. If, however, on the basis of information obtained from the parents and the questionnaire, I strongly suspect that a neurophysiological disturbance is present (GMBDS), I do not devote much time to projective instruments but rather administer some of the tests on my GMBDS screening battery (Figures 6.1–6.3). Obviously, in the 60–75 minutes during which time the child is seen alone, it is not possible to administer all of these instruments. Rather, I select a few that are most likely to assess functioning in areas in which clinical deficiencies are described. For example, if the parents describe hyperactivity, I will administer *The Steadiness Tester* (R.A. Gardner and A.K. Gardner, 1978; R.A. Gardner et al., 1979). If they describe "dyslexia" as manifested by a high frequency of letter and number reversals, I will administer the three sections of *The Reversals Frequency Test* (R.A. Gardner, 1978, 1979b; R.A. Gardner and M. Broman, 1979). If an attentional impairment is described, I will administer the Digits Forward and Digits Backward sections of the *Digit Span* subtest of the *Wechsler Intelligence Scale for Children—Revised* (WISC-R) (D. Wechsler, 1974). If an eye-motor or visual-perceptual problem is described, I will administer the *Developmental Test of Visual-Motor Integration* (K.E. Beery and N.A. Buktenica, 1982).

Generally, it is in the intensive evaluation that I will have the opportunity to assess in depth the neuropsychological deficits of these children, not only with regard to the administration of my full screening battery but to the administration of other instruments that may be warranted for proper diagnosis. Because it is the primary purpose of this book to discuss the diagnosis and treatment of children with *psychogenic* disorders, I will not be devoting significant discussion to GMBDS childrens' diagnosis here. Elsewhere (Gardner, 1979b) I have presented in detail the instruments I utilize for the objective diagnosis of these childrens' difficulties.

Figure 6.1   The Group of Minimal Brain Dysfunction Syndromes

Screening Diagnostic Battery

Diagnostic Instrument	Primary Information Provided	Additional Information Provided	Age Range
WISC-R: Information (Wechsler)	auditory linguistic reception long-term memory fund of inforation linguistic expression	intellectual curiosity	6-0 ———— 16-11
WISC-R: Similarities (Wechsler)	auditory analogous logic auditory conceptualization abstraction	auditory linguistic reception linguistic expression long-term auditory memory	6-0 ———— 16-11
WISC-R: Arithmetic (Wechsler)	arithmetic logic auditory and visual conceptualization abstraction	auditory concentration short- and long-term auditory memory long-term visual memory	6-0 ———— 16-11
WISC-R: Vocabulary (Wechsler)	auditory linguistic reception linguistic expression	long-term auditory memory intellectual curiosity	6-0 ———— 16-11
WISC-R: Comprehension (Wechsler)	social judgment common sense conscience		6-0 ———— 16-11
WISC-R: Digit Span, Digits Forward (Wechsler, Gardner)	short-term auditory sequential memory	auditory concentration	5-0 ———— 15-11
WISC-R: Digit Span, Digits Backward (Wechsler, Gardner)	short-term auditory sequential memory short-term visual sequential memory	auditory concentration visual concentration visual scanning	5-0 ———— 15-11

Age Range: 2 4 6 8 10 12 14 16 18 A

Figure 6.2

Diagnostic Instruments	Primary Information Provided	Additional Information Provided	Age Range
WISC-R: Picture Completion (Wechsler)	long-term visual memory	visual Gestalt	6-0 ———— 16-11
WISC-R: Picture Arrangement (Wechsler)	social judgment, common sense, visual organization, visual Gestalt, long-term visual sequential memory		6-0 ———— 16-11
WISC-R: Block Design (Wechsler)	visual analysis, visual-motor synthesis, visual-motor organization, visual-motor Gestalt	dyspraxia	6-0 ———— 16-11
WISC-R: Object Assembly (Wechsler)	long-term visual memory, visual-motor organization, visual Gestalt, visual conceptualization	visual concentration, persistence	6-0 ———— 16-11
WISC-R: Coding (Digit Symbol) (Wechsler)	visual concentration, visual-motor integration	short-term visual memory, visual discrimination	6-0 ———— 16-11
WISC-R: Mazes (Wechsler)	impulsivity	visual concentration, planning and foresight, visual-motor coordination	6-0 ———— 16-11
Reversals Frequency Test: I, Execution (Gardner)	long-term visual memory		5-0 ———— 14-11
Reversals Frequency Test: II, Recognition (Gardner)	long-term visual memory		5-0 ———— 14-11

Age Range scale: 2 4 6 8 10 12 14 16 18 A

Figure 6.3

Diagnostic Instrument	Primary Information Provided	Additional Information Provided	Age Range 2 4 6 8 10 12 14 16 18 A
Reversals Frequency Test: III, Matching (Gardner)	visual discrimination	visual concentration	5-0——8-11
Purdue Pegboard (Gardner)	visual-motor coordination	fine motor coordination	5-0————15-11
Balls and Basket Test (Gardner)	gross motor coordination		5-0————15-11
Developmental Test of Visual-Motor Integration (Beery and Buktenica)	visual-motor coordination, constructional dyspraxia, visual Gestalt	visual discrimination	2————15
Steadiness Tester (Gardner)	hyperactivity, concentration, motor impersistence	tremors, choreiform movements	5-0————15-9

Final Comments

At this point therapists should direct their attention to an issue that is second in importance only to the question of whether the child is in need of treatment. They should ask themselves the simple question whether or not they *like* the child being evaluated: "Can I relate well to him(her)? Does the child appear to be relating well to me? Have we established rapport? Is there some mutual emotional resonance?" If the answers to these questions are for the most part *no*, and it does not appear that there is a potential for improvement in the relationship, then the therapist should have serious reservations about treating the child. As stated already, *we cannot treat everyone*. We should not expect ourselves to establish a meaningful therapeutic relationship with all of those who seek our help. If this is truly to be a "screening interview" we must not indiscriminately try to treat all those who need it. We must try to treat all those whom we think might profit from working with us. There is a vast difference.

I cannot present specific criteria for making this discrimination, because the decision must be made primarily on the basis of the subjective feelings therapists have toward the patient and what they *surmise* the patient feels about them.

For example, I once saw an eight-year-old boy and his paternal grandmother with whom he was living (He had been abandoned by his parents). During the interview the grandmother showed me a bottle of pills which her pediatrician had prescribed. I considered them to be contraindicated for this boy's condition and suggested that she hold off giving him any further medication until I had had a chance to talk to the pediatrician. At this point, the child grabbed the bottle out of his grandmother's hands and quickly gobbled down two pills, looking at both of us with a victorious smile of defiance. Such blatant contempt in the first interview spoke quite poorly for his ability to establish a meaningful therapeutic relationship with me. But more important the act produced in me a strong feeling of aversion for this child and I suspected that I would probably be a poor choice of therapist for him. During the remainder of that interview and in two more he continued to exhibit passive-aggressive behavior, which frustrated my attempts to involve him in a friendlier relationship. I found myself becoming increasingly irritated with his obstructionism, to the point where I found him obnoxious, and so I recommended him to someone else. I must emphasize here that I appreciate that my anger might have been inappropriate. Whether appropriate or not is less important than the fact that after three sessions I was still unable to like this child. If the therapist, in the work with such a child, can express and/or otherwise utilize such resentful feelings—and thus successfully reduce them as well as the irritating behavior that provokes them—then treatment may still be salvaged. My attempts to do this with this child were unsuccessful.

In summary, what I am saying is: Don't treat a child you don't like. If you cannot bring about a change in such negative feelings then recommend someone else. Generally, during the first interview I am able to come to a decision regarding this issue. If not, I may suggest a second (and sometimes a third) session. If by then I feel there is hope for the formation of a good relationship with the child, I will suggest the full intensive work-up. If not, I save everyone time and trouble and either refer to someone else or, if the child has already been given up as untreatable by a few previous therapists, I suggest no treatment at that time and consider alternative recommendations.

7 CRITERIA FOR DECIDING WHETHER TREATMENT IS WARRANTED

There are four areas of inquiry useful in helping the examiner decide whether a child needs treatment. Before elaborating on these, it is important to emphasize that transient symptomatic manifestations are extremely common in children. Practically every child exhibits occasional tics, short-term phobic reactions, temper tantrums, occasional stealing episodes, lying, bribing, sleep difficulties, and so on. An example of this kind of situation would be the child whose parents have recently announced that they are going to separate and then get a divorce. It is normal for such children to exhibit transient symptoms such as depression, impaired school curiosity and motivation, crying spells, psychosomatic complaints, withdrawal from friends, and antisocial behavior. The examiner should recognize this point and not quickly recommend therapy. It is only after these symptoms persist more than a few months that treatment is warranted.

Of course, some counseling with the parents may be useful during this period. It is often difficult to ascertain that level of symptomatology at which the normal frequency ends and the pathological begins. Also, it is only when atypical, inappropriate, or pathological behavior exhibits itself over time that one should consider therapy. Also, it is difficult, if not impossible, to provide a sharp cutoff point regarding how long symptoms should be present before treatment is warranted, but a few months is certainly reasonable. This important consideration is taken into account in the latest diagnostic and statistical manual—DSM-III (1980).

School

The school is the most important area of inquiry for determining whether or not a child requires therapy. The child is born a primitive infant. It is the role of parents, during the earliest years, to make every reasonable attempt to transform these primitive human beings into individuals capable of functioning in society. The school can be viewed as the first "testing grounds" as to whether they have been successful in achieving this goal—to the degree required for functioning in nursery or kindergarten. It is there that children must restrain their primitive impulses most consistently and predictably. The home is a much more relaxed atmosphere, and its toleration for atypical behavior much greater. In addition, parental denial of difficulties may also leave psychopathology undetected. It is in the school, however, that the teacher can compare more objectively the child with others his or her own age and ascertain whether atypical behavior is manifesting itself.

There are two areas of inquiry that most sensitively assess school adaptation, namely, academic performance and behavior. If the child is not reaching what the teacher reasonably considers to be his or her academic potential, then psychopathology may be present. In addition, one wants to know about the child's relationship to the teacher, especially with regard to cooperation, respect for the teacher's authority, and general willingness to comply reasonably with classroom routine. Inquiry into the child's relationship with classmates is also important. Children who are functioning well with regard to these classroom functions are not likely to have serious psychopathology.

However, there are occasional children with psychiatric difficulties who do well in school, both in the academic and behavioral areas. They may be over compliant and passive children who are quite fearful of any manifestations of defiance or failure to follow usual routines. They may be viewed by the teachers as "a joy" and may be an immense source of pride to their parents. Their "uptightness," however, will probably get them into trouble in some areas, especially when self-assertion is warranted. But these children represent a small minority and the basic principle still holds, namely, that the child who is doing well in school in both the academic and behavioral realms, in realtionships with teachers and peers, is not likely to be suffering with significant psychopathology.

Neighborhood

The second most important area to consider when deciding whether a child needs treatment is relationships with peers in the neighborhood. Whereas peers will tolerate more atypical behavior than teachers, they will not tolerate more than the child's parents. Accordingly, maintaining friendships does not require a degree of integration that successful school performance necessitates. In order to maintain good relationships with neighborhood friends, children must have learned to share, to consider the rights of others, to wait their turns, to adhere to the rules of games, and they must have developed a wide variety of other interpersonal accommodations that will enable them to maintain friendships. The therapist does well to inquire as to whether the child actively seeks friends and is sought by them. Does the child invite others to the home and do other children come around in order to play with the patient? One wants to know the kinds of children the patient plays with. Are they reasonably normal, healthy, and well integrated children or are they in the fringe groups, the atypical, the antisocial, or those who have such personality disturbances that most of the children do not want to involve themselves with them? If the latter is the case, then psychopathology may very well be present in the patient. But even this child may be healthier than those who have no friends at all.

Home

Home behavior is the least valuable area for ascertaining whether or not psychopathology is present. There, the consequences of atypical behavior are the least (when compared to school and neighborhood certainly), and the mechanism of parental denial may also operate to compromise the parents' capacity to ascertain whether or not behavior is atypical. Children normally do not behave as well in their homes as they do in the homes of their peers and in school. They often follow the rules applicable to each situation, and the rules at home are generally most lax and the consequences for breaking them most lenient. It is well to assume that children "get away with as much as they can" in each situation.

If a mother, for example, complains that her son fights frequently with his brother, I will often ask how many fights a day she observes. Often she will respond along these lines, "I really can't tell you, Doctor. There are so many, I can't keep count. Maybe it's 20 to 30 times a day." I will then ask her if the brother still has two eyes, two ears, one nose, one mouth, two arms, two legs, and whether other body parts are intact. She will most often respond affirmatively. I will then ask her if the brother wakes up in the middle of the night screaming, "No, no, Joey. Don't beat me!" If she responds that no such dreams have taken place, I will reassure her that the sibling fighting is probably within the normal range—so fierce is the usual degree of sibling rivalry. It is only when there is no fighting that one might consider there to be psychopathology in that one or both children are probably significantly inhibited in expressing the normal sibling rivalrous feelings.

It is reasonable to say that when the second child appears on the scene, the first child is going to often exhibit severe jealous reactions. After all, prior to the appearance of the second, the first child has been "king (queen) on the throne." Now, the newborn infant doesn't just take half of the parents' time, but maybe three-quarters or even more. One can compare the appearance of a new child in the family to the situation in which a husband, for example, comes home with another woman, introduces her to his wife, and says something along these lines: "Darling, I'd like you to meet Jane. She's going to be living with us from now on. She's a wonderful person, both in and out of bed, and I know you're going to like her. So give her a big kiss."

Parents will often complain that a child does not cooperate at home doing the usual chores and assisting in the household routine. For example, a mother may say that she has a hard time getting Billy to take out the garbage, and he always dawdles, finds excuses, or just flatly refuses to do it. My views on this are that there has probably been no child in the history of the world who ever wanted to take out the garbage. In fact, even garbage men generally don't like taking out garbage, although they are often paid quite well for these services (most often even more than the child's teachers)! It is the child who *wants* to take out the garbage who may be exhibiting difficulties. This is especially the case if the child wants to make sure that the garbage cans are completely clean, that there isn't a speck of dirt, and that every coffee grain is completely removed. Obviously, such a child is suffering with some moderately severe obsessive-compulsive symptomatology. I would go further and say that the child who does *not* occasionally exhibit uncooperative behavior probably has difficulties.

I recall, as a student at The Bronx High School of Science, a teacher named Mr. Levinson who was the school disciplinarian. If a child was sassy to him he would often respond, "Who do you think you're speaking to? Your mudda?" Mr. Levinson recognized well that children are likely to be more disrespectful of their parents (especially their "muddas") than their teachers. A child who exhibits similar disrespect to teachers has not "learned the rules" and is thereby atypical. Parents, like siblings, serve well as scapegoats, as targets for much of the pent-up hostilities of the day that cannot safely be released elsewhere.

The repercussions for "unloading" one's pent-up anger on one's family are far less than directing them toward their original sources. I am not stating that this is a "good" thing, nor am I recommending it. I am only stating that it is a widespread phenomenon and that examiners do well to appreciate it when assessing for the presence of psychopathology. It is extremely difficult, however, to differentiate between normal and pathological degrees of disrespectful and uncooperative behavior in the home. The level at which the normal ends and the pathological begins is very blurred. This is an extremely weak area of inquiry for determining whether or not a child needs treatment. However, it is not an area that should be ignored totally. If the child *rarely* cooperates, if sibling rivalry is so fierce that the fighting is almost incessant, if turmoil and conflict is the *modus vivendi* in the home, then psychopathology is probably present.

DSM-III

If a child exhibits no difficulties in the three areas, school, neighborhood, and home, it is unlikely that a DSM-III diagnosis will be applicable. However, on occasion, a child will exhibit such symptoms and still function well in the aforementioned areas. This would be the case for a child with obsessions and/or compulsions that do not interfere significantly in daily life. Or, other symptoms such as phobias, depression, and psychosomatic complaints may be present without significant compromises in these three areas of functioning. The main reason for this is that most children come to treatment with interpersonal, rather than intrapsychic, conflicts. The problems lie not so much *within* themselves but *between* themselves and significant figures in their environment, especially parents and teachers.

8 PRESENTING THE INITIAL RECOMMENDATIONS

By this time about one-and-a-half hours to one-and-three-quarter hours of interviewing have taken place, and the examiner should generally have enough information to decide whether or not treatment is warranted. Although little information may have been obtained about the underlying psychodynamic factors that have brought about the presenting symptoms, the *symptoms* are the important things to focus upon in deciding whether or not therapy is warranted. This is an important point. All behavioral manifestations have psychodynamics. And sometimes the psychodynamic patterns include pathological adaptations. Treatment should only be recommended if the symptomatic manifestations are interfering *significantly* in the major areas of functioning. I have emphasized the word *significantly* because all individuals exhibit, at times, transient pathological manifestations and even pathological manifestations that may be ongoing. Treatment should be recommended only when these are interfering in the patient's life to a significant degree. It is only then that the time, effort, and expense of involvement in treatment is warranted. At this point the parents should be brought back into the room and the examiner's findings and recommendations discussed with them.

Should the Child Be Present?

The question regarding whether the child should be present at the time of the presentation of the initial conclusions and recommendations is sometimes of significance. My general preference is that the child be present. As mentioned, children are not renowned for their insight into the fact that they have problems, and being witness to the presentation may contribute, admittedly in a small way, to the child's gaining some insight. Furthermore, not permitting the child to be party to the discussion may contribute to a compromise in the therapist-patient relationship because the child cannot but be aware of the fact that things are being spoken about him or her, "secrets" that the child is not being permitted to learn about. This engenders distrust in the therapist and the parents and thus compromises relationships with both.

There are situations, however, when it is probably judicious to have the child sit in the waiting room at this point. For example, if the parents have advised the therapist during their time alone with him or her that a separation is impending—but the child has not yet been told—the therapist should not be the one to divulge this to the child. Rather, I generally recommend that the parents be the first ones to tell the child. For the therapist to do this compromises the parents' capacity to deal with the residual reactions that inevitably will ensue. (This issue is discussed in greater detail in my *The Parents Book About Divorce* [1977, 1979a].) Retarded children and those with borderline intelligence are probably best left outside the waiting room because of the likelihood that they will misinterpret significantly what is being said. A child with a severe physical disease such as leukemia might be psychologically traumatized by such a discussion, and so it is preferable that such a child remain in the waiting room at this point. There are other situations which would warrant a child's remaining in the waiting room, but these are relatively rare. My experience has been that, in the overwhelming majority of situations, I have the child present at the time of the presentation of my initial findings and recommendations.

When Therapy Is Not Warranted

On occasion, I have concluded that treatment is not warranted. Sometimes the parents have been overly concerned about the child and have not appreciated that the behavioral manifestations that have been a source of concern are within the normal limits. Sometimes these parents may need some counseling themselves; other times they just need some reassurance. This is more often the case with first-born children. With subsequently-born children the parents become more knowledgeable and less anxious and so are not as likely to seek unnecessary consultations. In some cases the child has been "cured" between the time that the appointment was made and the time of the consultation. Merely having been informed of the fact that an appointment has been made may result in a significant reduction and even complete alleviation of symptomatology. I refer to this as "threat therapy."

One could argue that treatment in such cases is still warranted because the underlying problems have not been resolved. Classical psychoanalysts, especially, would take this position. I generally do not embark on treatment or even continue therapy with anyone who is asymptomatic. The symptom gives me the "handle" for the therapeutic work. Our theories about psychodynamics are extremely theoretical and speculative. If the underlying processes that have originally caused the symptomatology are still present to a significant degree, they will erupt once again and bring about symptoms once more. Then, I will be in a better position to treat. I have even had situations in which a parent will call me a few days before the initial consultation and state that since the child was informed of the appointment, the presenting symptoms have disappeared. I will express my pleasure and advise such a parent not to hesitate to call me again if the situation has changed. Sometimes a new appointment is set up in the future and sometimes not.

I generally take a conservative approach with regard to recommending therapy. Recommending that the parents embark on the intensive evaluation (to be discussed in detail in Part Two) is an expensive and exhausting proposition. I do not recommend it lightly. Furthermore, therapy may be extremely expensive and extended—even more reason to be cautious about recommending it. In spite of what I have said, the vast majority of children who come for initial consultations do require therapy. One reason for this is that there may have been a long period of denial and refusal of treatment and, by the time the child does come, things have built up to the point where treatment is definitely warranted. This is especially the case when a school has recommended therapy. Schools will generally tolerate significant degrees of atypical behavior before recommending treatment. By the time they do so, it is likely that it is warranted.

When A Decision Regarding Therapy Has Not Yet Been Made

There are times when the two-hour consultation does not prove adequate to make a final recommendation. On those occasions I will recommend one or more further sessions for data collection. I will not allow myself to be pressured into coming to conclusions and making recommendations in a specific period. My experiences in the military taught me that such restraints are antitherapeutic. In the military, "orders is orders" and the psychiatrist may have little choice. Since that time (now 25 years) I have never permitted such constraints to be placed on me. When the parents are brought in I tell them in a matter-of-fact way, without any embarrassment or apology, that the situation is a complex one and that I have not been able to come to any definite conclusion at that point. I then advise them what further data collection will be necessary. Sometimes one or two sessions with child and/or parents is all I anticipate will be required. On some occasions I will need more information from the child's teacher, and this is preferably done by directly speaking with her. Sometimes the child has exhibited significant resistance during the initial session. Although psychiatric problems are present and warrant treatment, the child's resistance has been such that I cannot reasonably make a recommendation for therapy because there would be no patient to involve meaningfully in the process. I may recommend under these circumstances one or two more sessions with the child in the hope that I might then engage him or her. If this also proves unsuccessful, I discontinue my work with the child. I may provide some parental counseling, generally over a few sessions. On occasion, I might recommend that the child needs speech therapy, summer camp, organized recreational experiences, or treatment by a pediatrician or a neurologist. Under these circumstances, no further work with me is warranted.

When Psychotherapy Is Warranted

Most often, psychotherapy is indicated. I then outline to the parents what I consider to be the major problems, at the symptomalogical level as well as the family factors that may have contributed. I emphasize that these are my *initial* conclusions and that it is only with further experience with the family that I will be able to be more certain about the factors that are contributing to the child's difficulties. I advise them that it is going to be necessary for me to get to know each of them better if I am to work optimally with the child. In order to do this I will need to see each of the parents once or twice individually to get background information from them. Following the individual interviews with each of the parents I will want to see them together because I will often get conflicting information about what is going on between them. If there are older siblings I will often recommend a family interview. I also advise them that I will want to see the child two or three times more in order to collect more information from him or her. At times psychological tests will be indicated, and these will be administered concurrently with the intensive evaluation. I advise the parents that during the intensive evaluation I will be interviewing them as if they themselves were coming to me for a psychiatric evaluation. I then tell them that, when all the information is collected, I will review the material and present my findings and recommendations to them. I impress upon them the fact that I only recommend the intensive evaluation when treatment is warranted and that it serves as a foundation for my therapy.

It is important that the therapist invite the parents at this point to ask any questions they may have about the proposal. They have to appreciate (if they do not already) that, in the private practice setting, it is expensive and time consuming but that it is the optimum way to proceed. My experience has been that many parents do not "hear" me at this point. They may have come with the idea that I will give them a recommendation and send them on their way and that is all that treatment involves. Although there was nothing in the face letter to my questionnaire to suggest this, their wishes that this were the case or their misinformation about what treatment entails has led them to this conclusion. In such cases I try to impress upon the family the fact that the child's problems are complex and that they cannot be understood very easily.

Some parents at this point will ask my opinion regarding how long the treatment will take. As mentioned, I hesitate to use words like *always* and *never*. However, I have no hesitation in advising therapists that they should *never* speculate on how long treatment will take. This is one of the most foolish things a therapist can do. One cannot know how successful one will be in engaging the child, nor can one predict how successful one will be with regard to involving the parents. One cannot predict how slowly or rapidly the difficulties will be alleviated; in fact, one cannot even know whether or not one will be successful at all. Often significant social and cultural factors are operative in bringing about the problems and these are completely beyond the therapist's control. Accordingly, I firmly state to the parents that I cannot predict how long treatment will take and that it would be foolish on their part to put any circles on their calendars. I try to explain to them what I have just said about those factors that contribute to the unpredictability of the process. Such a statement also gets across the message that *their own participation* will play an important role in how rapidly or slowly therapy proceeds. I cannot emphasize this point strongly enough. If the parents view the treatment as a process involving their dropping the child off at the therapist's office, and then picking him or her up after a prescribed period of time, and then after X number of sessions, all will be well, they have a very misguided view of the process. This may work well for many forms of medical treatment, but it is completely ill-suited to the treatment of a child's psychiatric difficulties. The discussion at this point provides the therapist with an opportunity to get across this point.

I emphasize to the parents that I would not be making a recommendation for the extended evaluation if I were not certain that treatment was indicated. However, I may not be able at that point to be more specific about exactly how I am going to proceed. I may say that I would anticipate one or two sessions per week (my usual frequency), but that I cannot say at this point who will be involved. Perhaps it will be primarily the child, perhaps primarily the parents, perhaps a combination of both. It will only be after I have had the opportunity to collect more data that I will be in a better position to ascertain what the optimum therapeutic program will be. Here again, the examiner is foolish if he or she allows the parents to extract a specific statement at that point regarding exactly what the therapeutic program will be. Of course, there are times when one can state it with certainty at that time and, under such circumstances, there should be no problem in doing so. My own usual procedure at this point, however, is to inform the parents that even after the evaluation, my proposed therapeutic program will be the one that seems most propitious *at that time.* It may be that new situations will arise that will warrant an alteration of the therapeutic program. As mentioned, therapy is a slice of life. And like life, things are always happening that will warrant a change in one's plans.

Discussion of Fees

And now to the delicate subject of money. Although the face letter of my questionnaire indicates my fee policy, the subject may still come up. This is especially the case if the parents wish to discuss with me the question of whether they should be given a lower fee than my standard. Whereas Freud's patients in Victorian Vienna were inhibited in discussing sex, most adult patients today reveal freely their sexual activities to their therapists, but are quite restrained when discussing financial matters. Some therapists may, indeed, share their patient's inhibitions in this area. The problem is complicated for the child therapist because the person paying for the treatment is not the one receiving the treatment. The adult in therapy is available to discuss his or her reactions to the payment of fees; the parent of a child in treatment is often unavailable or unmotivated for such an inquiry. Accordingly, one cannot easily ask what the parents' income is. Even if one were to do so, and even if one were to obtain a figure, one is still not in a position to know exactly whether a fee reduction is warranted because gross income is only one part of the information one needs to assess properly a person's capacity to pay one's fee. One must also know about expenses, debts, and other financial obligations. In many situations one would have to have the expertise of an accountant to know whether or not a parent can afford the standard fee or whether a reduced fee is warranted. Even then, a question of family priorities must come into play, that is, what the parents want to spend their money on, and the examiner is in no position to make decisions in that realm.

What I do then is to proceed as if the standard fee will be paid and ask the parents if they are clear on my policy of payment, namely, that payment is due at the time of each session and that my secretary will be available to assist with insurance forms and payments from third parties. It is important for the reader to appreciate that my policy of requiring payment for each session is the one that I utilize for parents of children in treatment, but I do not use it for adults who are in therapy themselves. Asking a patient to pay for each session is essentially saying to the patient that there is no trust. Up until about five years ago I did indeed trust parents to pay each month for the treatment of their children. However, I believe that our society is becoming progressively more psychopathic and my former policy resulted in a significant percentage of defaulted payments. Accordingly, I have changed my policy and require parents to pay at the time of each session. This has not compromised my relationship with the child because he or she is generally oblivious to this aspect of the treatment. With adult patients, however, I have still maintained my original policy of their paying at the end of each month. To require the adult to pay at the time of each session is essentially extending the "no trust" communication to the patient him- or herself. And this cannot but compromise the therapeutic relationship. If, however, a patient does exhibit difficulties in paying promptly, then I may very well, after therapeutic discussion, institute a policy of more frequent payments after each session. Under these circumstances, the patient has so acted that my distrust is warranted, and to trust a patient under these circumstances is not only naive but antitherapeutic.

With regard to the question of a reduction to a lower level on my fee range (as originally described in the face letter of the questionnaire), I generally take a somewhat passive position when discussing this issue. It is preferable for the patient to step forth and make the request. And it also behooves the patient to present the information that supports his or her position. Otherwise, the examiner compromises him- or herself by becoming beholden to the parent to provide the information. In the context of such a discussion I might ask if the parents have insurance and exactly what coverage they have. If they cannot answer specifically these questions, then I reserve a decision until the information becomes available. If it is provided, and the examiner is still not in a position to ascertain whether a reduction is warranted, I might ask for other reasons why the parent feels a reduction is warranted. It is beyond the purposes of this book to go into details of such discussions. The examiner must be aware that there are some parents who pride themselves on their bargaining acumen, in the context of which guiltless duplicity is the rule. There are others who are ashamed to come forth with a statement of their difficulties in paying the higher fee. If the examiner suspects that such is the case, it behooves him or her to initiate the discussion of a lower fee. Some masochistic people may stay with the higher fee because of the self-destructive gratifications that it offers. Others may assess the value of the therapy with the level of the fee and would consider themselves to be getting less valuable treatment if they were to take a lower fee or even consider the therapist to be less adequate if he or she were to treat for less. Some parents feel a sense of superiority from paying the "top fee." Some may be too passive to request a lower figure or may feel that the reduced-fee patients get inferior treatment. A divorcée, whose former husband is paying for the treatment, may welcome a high fee as another weapon against her former spouse.

What I have said thus far regarding fees relates to the initial fee at the outset of treatment. A fee may be reduced (even below my minimum) when a patient, in treatment for a significant period and committed to the process, suffers financial reverses which are not related to the patient's psychopathological processes. (I use the term patient here to refer to an adult patient in treatment or the parents of a child in therapy.) Under such circumstances I will discuss a reduction, but never to the point where no fee at all is charged. It may even be a few dollars taken from a welfare check, but I do not give "free therapy." Patients who receive free therapy often get exactly the value of what they are paying for.

The Question of Payment for Missed Sessions

The question of charging for missed sessions is a difficult one. With adults, advance notice of cancellation varies from many months to no notice at all (the patient just doesn't show up). The reasons for missing can fluctuate from the most realistic (patient in the hospital) and appropriate (household emergency requiring the patient's presence) to the clearly psychopathological and/or acting out ("I forgot"—"I just didn't feel like coming"). The intermediate situations are probably the most common ("I had a bad cold"—"My bursitis acted up"). A physical illness may not be the patient's "fault," but psychological factors clearly play a role in the degree to which the patient is incapacitated.

Some therapists do not charge for missed sessions. Missing sessions and/or witholding fees may be among the most common ways in which patients act out with their therapists. Not charging for missed sessions may serve to encourage such behavior, and thereby entrench pathology. One approach is not to charge when the therapist is able to fill the session. Some charge if the session has not been filled *and* the absence was due to pathological behavior, e.g., "forgetting," or a voluntary decision that something else had priority, e.g., "an important business meeting." This approach has intrinsic defects which led me to abandon it after using it for a few years.

I prefer to charge my patients for *nonfilled* missed sessions *regardless* of the reason for the absence. Patients are informed that the time is reserved for them. They are told that if I am given advance notice I can usually fill the hour. In such cases there is no obligation to pay for the session.

In child practice, this approach is helpful. At one time I was proponent of the "no fee for illness policy." I would be called by a mother who would inform me that her child was sick and could not keep an appointment. In the next session the child would tell me about the wonderful time she had at a birthday party on the afternoon of the missed session. What does the therapist do in such a situation? Another mother is getting over "the grippe" and can't bring the child; another says that a sibling is sick and she can't get a babysitter. It was amazing how the frequency of such missed sessions diminished once I began charging. When describing my missed session policy, I inform the parents that I have found that when a child has to miss a session, seeing one or both parents instead has often been helpful.

When telling parents about my missed-session policy, I emphasize the fact that there is *no specific cutoff point* to determine whether or not they will be charged. I emphasize that the more advance notice I have, the greater will be the likelihood of my filling the appointment and, conversely, the shorter the notice the less the likelihood of the sessions's being filled. I strictly avoid mentioning any numbers, even in the negative sense. To do so is injudicious. For example, if I were to say, "I have *no* cut-off point, such as 24 hours. The determinant of whether you will be charged is purely whether or not I can fill the session." It is likely that that number 24 will be branded in that parent's brain as the cut-off figure. In fact, even though I studiously avoid mentioning numbers in presenting my policy, on a number of occasions, parents have quoted me as giving the 24-hour figure, and may even swear that they heard me say it.

In child practice, with many children going off to summer camp for two months and the therapist usually taking one, I inform patients that between July 1 and Labor Day there will be no charge for missed sessions for *pre-planned, out-of-town vacations* about which I am told in advance. I tell them the dates of my own vacation, and advise them that I will be available for treatment during the other weeks of the summer.

9 CONCLUDING COMMENTS

Before the family leaves, I generally give the child a complimentary copy of my book, *Stories About the Real World*, Volume I (1972). I will often inscribe the book with a little message to the child such as "I hope you find this book useful" or "I hope you enjoy reading these stories." I also tell the child that he or she has to read the book as a homework assignment, and I'll be asking him or her about these stories during the next session. My purpose in giving the book is twofold. First, the present helps establish a good relationship, in that the overwhelming majority of children enjoy receiving presents. In addition, the material contained in the book is generally applicable to most if not all children's treatment. And, when the child returns for the intensive evaluation, I will often inquire whether the child read the stories and am particularly interested in knowing which ones produced special reactions.

If, at the time of the final discussion, the parents express ambivalence or hesitation, the examiner does well to invite them to discuss further their reactions. At times, it is judicious to suggest that the parents think over what has been said, rather than make a decision at that point. This is a most judicious policy. Sometimes, a parent will have deep reservations but will not express them at the time of the consultation. Such a parent might even then accept subsequent appointments, only to cancel them on short notice. It is very difficult to charge people who have indicated that they wish to discontinue treatment entirely. In fact, it might be unethical in spite of the aforementioned verbal agreement. Accordingly, for the sake of the parents as well as the therapist, it is wise to invite ambivalent parents to think about their decision before making appointments.

For those who say they wish to go ahead, I generally set up three appointments: one for the child, and one for each of the parents. Whereas my initial consultation is generally two hours, my subsequent sessions are generally 45 or 60 minutes, depending upon which appears to be most useful and judicious. Some patients (adults as well as children) use the full hour quite expeditiously; others find 45 minutes to be optimum. People who travel greater distances often prefer the full-hour session. One does well to clarify this issue before closing the initial session.

At this point, the reader may conclude that it is not likely I can accomplish all that has been covered in this chapter in a two-hour consultation. This conclusion is not completely unwarranted. Actually, I have tried to cover in this chapter many contingencies, all of which are not likely to come up with the same family. Accordingly, I generally am able to accomplish most of what has been presented in this chapter during the initial consultation. But, as mentioned, if I cannot, I have no hesitation requesting a third or even a fourth appointment.

Part Two

The Intensive
Diagnostic Evaluation

Nam et ipsa scientia potestas est.
Indeed Knowledge itself is Power.

Francis Bacon

In the Greek language, the word *diagnosis* means *to know thoroughly* or *to know in depth*. Accordingly, when we use the term as a mere label we are not using it in the true spirit of its meaning. The initial two-hour consultation may enable us to provide a diagnosis in the superficial sense, but it does not enable us to provide a diagnosis in the true sense of the word. It is the purpose of this chapter to describe the techniques I utilize to provide me with a bona fide diagnosis, in accordance with the original meaning of the word.

This is being written at a time when shorter forms of treatment are increasingly in vogue. Many time-limited therapy programs provide a fixed number of sessions, ten or twelve not being uncommon. Considering the complexity of the problems with which we are dealing, it takes that number of sessions to understand what the basic problems are. The patients, therefore, are being discharged at just about the time when the therapist is beginning to understand what the fundamental problems are. To me such treatment can be compared to the surgeon who opens the abdomen, isolates the source of disease, and then, without doing any further operative procedure or closing the abdomen, discharges the patient from the hospital. I am not claiming that therapy cannot possibly take ten or twelve sessions; I am only claiming that one can generally not predict in advance how long it will take, and it usually takes longer than that. Time-limited therapy is generally appealing to those who want quick solutions to complex problems. It is particularly attractive to administrators and those who are supporting treatment for large numbers of patients. Accordingly, I consider it most often to be a rip-off of the poor; rich people (unless they are naive) generally do not have to accept time-limited therapy.

Here I present what I consider to be the judicious kind of evaluation, an evaluation that enables the examiner to learn in depth what the patient's basic problems are. The evaluation here serves as a foundation for subsequent treatment. The knowledge so gained puts the therapist in the best position to proceed most effectively with the therapeutic program.

10 THE EVALUATION OF THE MOTHER

I generally find it useful to begin with an interview with the mother alone. My experience has been that, of the three parties, she is the one who is most likely to give me important background information. Obviously the child is the least capable of the three because of his or her immaturity and ignorance of the processes that may be contributing to the difficulties. Fathers, unfortunately, are generally less receptive to "opening up." I believe this, in part, relates to the general pattern in our society that fathers are supposed to maintain a "macho" image and not admit weakness or deficiency. Discussing problems with a therapist is viewed by many fathers as being a sign of weakness. Another factor probably relates to the fact that, in the traditional home, the father is less likely to be knowledgeable about all the details involved in the child's life. He may also be more reluctant to admit difficulties in the marital relationship. Although these reasons are speculative, I am convinced that my generalization is a valid one, namely, that fathers are less likely to provide me with important background information than mothers. Accordingly, I find it judicious to interview the mothers first in the intensive evaluation. However, I am not rigid with regard to this and, if scheduling of the child or father first is more readily accomplished, I will certainly depart from this principle.

The Initial Inquiry

I generally begin the interview with the mother with an open-end question such as: "Is there anything special on your mind that you would like to say to me at this point, before I proceed with my questions?" The question is purposely vague and is designed to provide the mother with the greatest freedom to discuss any issue that she considers pertinent. I want to know here what is at the forefront of her mind, especially things that may be upsetting her, things that may be pressing for release. To ask a specific question at this point may deprive the examiner of this important information. Sometimes the mother's comments may suggest ambivalence for the intensive diagnostic program. It is important for the examiner to appreciate that bringing a child to treatment is generally viewed as an indication of the parents' failure to have raised a psychologically healthy child. The examiner's conclusion that treatment is warranted may then be viewed as confirmation that the parent is indeed deficient. In such cases I usually try to reassure the mother that I am convinced that she loves the child deeply and that, at every point, she did what she considered to be best for her child's healthy growth and development. I emphasize the point that the fact that she is coming for treatment for the child, and is willing to make the sacrifices of times, money, and energy for the child's welfare, is a statement of parental strength and commitment. Comments along these lines sometimes reduce the parental feelings of failure. Of course, it is not proper for the therapist to make such a statement if it is untrue, and there is severe maternal deficiency. However, mothers who are willing to bring their children for treatment do not generally fall in that category.

Some mothers will express guilt at this point. They may express the feeling that the child's illness was related to some minor indiscretion or lapse in parenting capacity. Many in the classical psychoanalytic school are quick to consider such guilt to be related to unconscious hostility toward the child and the parents' view that the child's illness represents the magic fulfillment of the parent's hostile wishes. I am dubious about this explanation. I believe that for most parents it represents a magic need to control, to undo, and/or to have prevented the illness. The element of control is intrinsic to the notion: "It's my fault." There is an element of validity in this guilt, because the child's pathology is often related to the parents' child-rearing practices; if the child had not been exposed to the parents' inappropriate behavior, he or she might not have developed the psychiatric difficulties. The issue of guilt in such parents is a complex one, and I have directed my attention to its psychodynamics in other publications (1969, 1970). To the mother who describes such guilt I will often make comments along the following lines:

> I'd like to say a few things to you about the guilt which most parents in your situation have. I recognize that it's a very painful thing to have to bring your child to a psychiatrist. Most parents look upon it as a grave sign of personal failure and wonder how and where they went wrong. I know enough about you already to know that, at each point, you did what you thought was best for your child and your bringing him(her) here today is just another example of this. I'm sure you basically love him(her) and want the best for him(her). However, it's clear to all of us that mistakes were made or else he(she) probably wouldn't be here today. So, in a sense, the illness is partially your responsibility. I say *partially* because we still don't know enough about all the factors that brought it about.
>
> Also, it's important that you distinguish, as the law does, between two kinds of guilt: guilt by commission and guilt by omission. Let me give you examples. Compare the man whose car runs over someone because of a factory defect in the brake system with the one who, in a calculating and premeditated manner, hits someone with his car. The first man is guilty by omission and is generally not punished. The second is guilty by commission and is usually punished. You people are certainly in the first category. You acted with the best of intentions, but because of your own blind spots—many of which you don't appreciate—you've contributed to the child's difficulties. Flagellating yourself over the past will accomplish nothing. Directing your efforts, as you are now doing, into learning about what went wrong and trying to change the situation is your best way of feeling less guilty. And I will be actively enlisting your assistance in the treatment. Now, is there anything you would like to ask me about this?

Generally, these comments are successful in alleviating some of the parent's guilt. One of the things I am doing here is to lessen the guilt by giving the parent a sense of control. Because an element in the formation of the guilt relates to the sense of impotence associated with the child's having developed the illness, my inviting the parent to participate actively in the treatment provides for the opportunity for gaining some control over what was previously considered to be an uncontrollable situation.

If the mother has not offered any responses to my initial open-ended question, I will ask, "I'd like to know what reactions you had to our meeting last time." Or, if she has given no response along the lines just discussed, I might ask, "Are there any other reactions you had to our meeting last time?" In both cases, I direct my attention specifically to the two-hour consultation. This question also enables me to learn about feelings about the treatment, both positive and negative. As I will discuss in detail in Chapter Seven, it is crucial for the therapist to have a good relationship with the parents if child therapy is to be successful. The answers to these questions at this point in the initial interview with the mother can provide information about the kind of relationship that is starting to develop between the mother and the therapist. It is the best opportunity for "nipping in the bud" difficulties that may already be starting to exhibit themselves.

I will then ask the mother what the child's reactions were to the interview. Here again there are a wide variety of responses. If the child's reactions have been negative, I will try to ascertain what the issues were that caused the reaction. If positive, I will want to learn what things attracted the child. If the mother states that she did not make inquiries in order to respect the child's "privacy," I will impress upon her the fact that my general therapeutic approach is to encourage all concerned parties to discuss the therapy as much as possible and she should err on the side of "invading the child's privacy." I do not recommend that she be intrusive here, only that she err on the side of being so and to let the child's own defenses and desire for privacy be the determinants of how much and how little the child will reveal. Such "respect" for the child's privacy often works against the aims of treatment in that it reduces the open communication that the therapist is trying to achieve in the family. Open communication among family members may be one of the most therapeutic experiences the therapist can provide. All too often psychological problems within families are the results of conspiracies of silence, suppressed and repressed thoughts and feelings, and other "skeletons in the closet." Therapy must open Pandora's boxes, and facilitating open communication is a step toward this goal.

The mother may, for example, say that the child told her something but made her promise not to divulge it to me. Here I will advise the mother that it was an error on her part to have agreed to keep a secret from me and that she would have done better to have said something like: "There must be no secrets from Dr. Gardner and I won't promise not to tell him." The mother may respond that if she were to say such a thing, the child might not give her the information. My response to this is that it is better that the child not provide the information than for her to be a participant in a conspiracy in which she and the child join forces to keep secrets from me. Also, I reassure her that important issues are likely to come out anyway and she need not fear that the nondivulged secret will compromise the treatment.

I will then ask the mother what her husband's reactions were to the initial consultative interview. As mentioned, mothers are generally more candid to me than fathers, and so she might provide me with information about his reactions that the father himself might not so readily reveal. Often his comments relate to the financial aspects of the treatment, which may then open up a discussion again of the fee and the payment. If the husband has expressed negative reactions, I encourage the mother to tell her husband to express these directly to me. I use this as a point of departure to impress upon her that a common cause of disruption of treatment is parental discomfort regarding the expression of their grievances, disappointments, disagreements, and so on.

Inquiry into the Causes of the Child's Difficulties

At this point I will make the following statement to the mother: "I know that you're coming here to get my opinion about why your child has problems. However, it's important for you to appreciate that, at this point, you probably know more about the reasons why your child has to come to therapy than I do. After all, you've lived with the child all his(her) life. You have been observer to thousands of events that I have not witnessed. Accordingly, I'm sure that you can provide me with the very important information relevant to the question of why your child has difficulties." Most mothers will come up with some explanations at that point. And, interestingly, the issues they bring up are often extremely valuable and very much on point. Although not specifically trained in psychiatry or psychology, the mother's "guesses" are most often valid explanations and provide the examiner with extremely important information about the sources of the child's psychopathology.

I cannot emphasize this point strongly enough. Although the mother may never have gone to graduate school, she knows the child better than the examiner and her hunches regarding why the child has difficulties (her denial mechanisms notwithstanding) may be better than the examiner's. If the mother cannot come up with any explanations, I will often urge her to "guess" or "speculate." I encourage her to do so with the advice that her guesses may still provide me with valuable leads as to what is going on with the child. Again, these "wild" guesses are often valuable sources of information.

Inquiry Regarding Parental Dealings with the Child

My purpose here is to get more specific information about the way in which the parents have raised the child, with special focus on detrimental exposures and experiences. There are a number of ways of getting information in this area. I sometimes ask the mother to describe what she considers to be her strong points and weak points in the child-rearing realm. By presenting the question in this balanced way, one is likely to obtain information related to maternal weaknesses that the mother might otherwise have difficulty admitting. It is usually useful to ask questions in this area in such a way that guilt or embarrassment is reduced or obviated. For example, if the examiner were to ask: "Do you hit your child?" an accusatory finger is implied. But, if the examiner says: "All parents find. at times, that their backs are up against the wall and the child's behavior is so irritating that they feel that the only thing they can do is to give him(her) one. Then the child has a good cry, gets it out of his(her) system, and all is again well with the world. How often have you found this to be the case with your child?" Obviously, when the question is posed this way, the examiner is going to be in a better position to find out exactly how much (or how little) corporal punishment was utilized.

The same principle holds for questions in other areas. For example, if one says to a mother: "Did you like cuddling your child?" the answer is likely to be yes in that the mother generally recognizes that not to have done so represents a parental deficiency. One is more likely to find out what really went on with a question such as: "When they're born, some babies love cuddling and others do not. How was Billy when he was born?" Actually, there is a small element of duplicity in this question. The realities are that there are indeed some babies who do not like cuddling when they are born, but they are relatively rare. They are mainly children who are born with serious physical illness, congenital defects, mental retardation, autism, and other severe disorders that manifest themselves at birth. Children who are not in these categories not only love to be cuddled at birth, but the deprivation of such may ultimately prove lethal. Because I know that Billy is in none of the aforementioned categories, I know that he would have wanted cuddling at the time of his birth. If his mother responds that he was not that kind of a child, it generally suggests that she herself had some deficiency in providing cuddling and her motivation for doing so was impaired.

One could ask the question: "Did you like to have Janie cuddle with you in the morning when she was a toddler?" Again, most mothers will say yes, even though the response may not be an honest one. However, if one asks: "Some children, when they're toddlers, love to come into their parents' bed, especially on weekends. How was Mary when she was that age?" By presenting the question in such a way that there are two categories of children, some who like cuddling and some who don't, it becomes easier for the mother to state that Mary was not in the cuddling category. Again, the implication here is that the deficiency lies in the child and not in the parent.

Another useful question: "What are your husband's feelings about the way you've raised Bobby? What does he consider your strong points to be and what does he consider your weak points to be?" It is generally easier for the mother to talk about deficiencies about herself if they originate from someone else because she has the opportunity to present disagreements if she wishes to do so. The examiner does well to review the list of the father's reported descriptions, both positive and negative.

An important area of inquiry to ascertain maternal capacity is the mother's involvement in school activities. In fact, this may be the most important area of inquiry if one is looking for manifestations of parental deprivation of affection. I first begin with a general question about the mother's involvement in school activities and encourage her to provide me with a general description. Following that, I ask specific questions that give me information about the mother's participation in the PTA, attendance at conferences with teachers, and involvement in the child's extracurricular activities such as school plays, recitals, sporting events, et cetera. The latter area is extremely important. The healthy involved mother finds attendance at such performances extremely gratifying. It is a grand moment when little Susie comes out on the stage dressed as Cinderella. Tears well up in the mother's eyes and her heart swells with pride. The parent who knows no such joy is not only missing out on some of life's greater moments but, for the purposes of the interview, has provided the examiner with important information regarding maternal capacity. In the context of this discussion, I ask the mother about the father's participation in school activities. Does *he* attend teacher conferences? Does *he* attend the school performances and does he exhibit joy and pride at them?

One wants to know about who the child goes to in the middle of the night when he or she wakes up with nightmares, croup, or physical illness. One wants to find out about who takes the child to the pediatrician, especially during emergencies. Inquiry about what goes on during the evening, when both parents are home, is also important. One should inquire about homework and who helps the child with it. Does one parent do better than the other? One wants to know about parent's comfort with and patience with sitting on the floor playing childhood games. One should inquire into who puts the children to sleep at night, reads the bedtime stories, and has more patience for dawdling.

A concept that I have found useful in assessing parental capacity is what I refer to as "Grandma's criteria" (Gardner, 1986). These are the criteria Grandma's ghost would use if she were to be roaming invisibly around the house collecting data about parental capacity. Because she doesn't have a Ph.D. in psychology she would be using more traditional criteria for assessing parental capacity, criteria related to the involvement of the parent in the everyday activities of the child-rearing process. Accordingly, the examiner does well to go through the course of a typical day with the mother, from the time the children wake up in the morning until the time they go to sleep at night, and find out exactly what each parent does with each of the children, especially the patient. One is especially interested in who takes on the more unpleasant tasks and who has the greatest willingness to make sacrifices. Because she knows nothing about unconscious processes, Grandma will be focusing on these more valid criteria for assessing parental capacity.

The reader who is interested in more information about assessment of parental capacity does well to read pertinent material in my *Family Evaluation in Child Custody Litigation* (1982). Because the assessment of parental capacity is so important to the custody evaluation, my discussion of this area is quite detailed in that volume.

Description of the Marriage

I will then ask the mother the general question: "Tell me about your marriage?" Of course, I may have gotten some information about this during the initial two-hour consultation; however, here I want to get more details, especially as they relate to the child's difficulties. This is an important area of inquiry. Children exposed to ongoing marital animosity are likely to be deprived, and such deprivations may contribute to the development of their symptomatology. And, if the children become actively embroiled in the parental conflict, there is even a greater likelihood that psychopathology will develop. It is reasonable to say that many (but certainly not all) children who develop psychological difficulties do so because of problems in their parents' marriages. If the mother describes difficulties, I will go into detail, especially with regard to those problems that the child is either aware of or exposed to. Some parents naively believe that children are in no way affected by parental problems that they are not directly exposed to or aware of. I attempt to impress upon such parents the fact that the effects of marital discord tend to filter down to children, even without the awareness of the concerned parties. I try to impress upon them that, if parents are depressed or otherwise unhappy over difficulties in the marital relationship, this is going to compromise the care of the children.

Some mothers routinely state that their marriages are good ones. This is their automatic response, and they may consider it the socially acceptable thing to say. Along with this, they will often say, "I love my husband." In some cases the marriages are quite poor, but denial mechanisms have resulted in both parents maintaining a façade that they have a "good marriage." In such cases, I might say, "You know, no marriage is perfect. Every marriage, like every human relationship, has strong points and weak points. In every relationship there are things that you like about the other person and things that you don't. There is no marriage in which there aren't occasional fights. What I want you to tell me now are what the strong points of your marriage are and what are the weak points. I'd like to hear about the things you agree on, and the things about which you don't agree." When the question is posed this way, it becomes more socially acceptable for the mother to reveal deficiencies in the relationship. When one begins with a discussion of the positive aspects of the marriage, it becomes easier to talk about the negatives. Because mothers are generally more comfortable talking about deficiencies in the marriage than fathers, the information obtained here will be useful to the examiner during the interview with the father.

Some mothers will describe the marital difficulties but state that their husbands have strictly warned them not to talk about them to me. There are many women who comply with this wish and I never learn about the marital difficulties. This, of course, compromises my evaluation. Other mothers tell me the problems, but request that I not tell their husbands that they revealed the information to me. Sometimes I am successful in my attempts to get such mothers to assert themselves and advise their husbands that they have provided me with this information. Others fear doing so and when I meet with the husband it becomes apparent that their wives have never revealed that they have disclosed the details of the marital problems to me. Sometimes I am successful in "smoking this information out" during the joint interview with the husband and the wife; and other times the mother is so frightened of "rocking the boat" that she continues to withhold the information. Such mothers are serving as models for passive submission to their husbands and this, of course, is likely to contribute to the child's difficulties. I believe that refusal to discuss marital difficulties is one of the most common reasons why parents do not agree to embark upon the intensive evaluation or, if they do so, it is one of the most common reasons why they interrupt it. Therapists who confine themselves to working exclusively with children, and do not delve deeply in the marital and/or family situation, are likely to attract such parents. However, I believe that the therapy is likely to prove useless.

Sometimes the marital conflict may center directly on the child. A mother may say, for example, "The only fights we have are over how to deal with Tom. I believe that if things went well with him, we wouldn't fight about anything." There are two possibilities here. One is that the statement is true, and the marriage is basically a good one with the child's problems the main source of parental friction. The other possibility is that the child is being used as a weapon or tool in the parental conflict and that differences over management are being utilized in the service of less noble goals. It behooves the examiner to inquire further into this issue in order to ascertain which of the two possibilities is the more likely one. When parents are involved in divorce, the second possibility is generally the more likely. Because divorced parents are living separately, they do not have direct access to one another to vent their rage. The children, who move back and forth freely between the two households, become good candidates to be used as weapons, spies, and tools in the parental conflict (Gardner, 1976, 1977, 1979a).

History of Psychiatric Treatment

I will then ask the mother whether she has ever been in treatment. If so, I want details about the phases of her life when she had therapy, the names of the therapists, the reasons for having entered into treatment, and what she recalls of the experience(s). This is a good way of getting into the question of the mother's own psychopathology. Simply to ask the question, "Do you have any psychiatric disturbances?" may produce defensiveness. However, a discussion of previous therapeutic experiences is more likely to provide useful data in this area. I am often amazed at how little people remember of their therapy. I am rarely surprised when an adolescent has little recollection of early childhood therapeutic experiences with me. But it does amaze me how little adults remember of treatment that took place 10 or 15 years previously, treatment that may have occurred while they were adults. They commonly do not even recall the name of the therapist. I am particularly interested in any marital counseling or conjoint therapy that the mother may have involved herself in with the father. This is another way of learning about marital problems. I often try to get information about what the therapist said, especially with regard to each party's contribution to the marital difficulties.

Background Information

Family Background   It may come as a surprise to some readers that my discussion of the acquisition of background information about the mother comes so late in this section. It is important for the reader to appreciate that we are not dealing here with the mother's psychoanalysis, but her involvement with her child—especially with regard to maternal capacity. Were we interested in psychoanalyzing the mother we might be much more interested in her early developmental life, her relationships with her parents, and the influences in her development that played an important role in shaping her present personality. Although I am interested in these subjects (and will discuss them in this section), I consider them to be less important than the areas of inquiry discussed thus far.

I begin with questions about the mother's date of birth, place of birth, and list of places where she has lived during her life. If the mother has moved frequently, especially during the child's own lifetime, then I may have a clue to a factor that may have contributed to the child's difficulties. Children who shift around from location to location during the formative years, especially if this involves frequent changes of schooling, may suffer psychologically from the disruptions. I then ask the mother about her own mother, whether she is living or dead, and where she lives at the present time. If dead, I want to find out about the cause of death. If the information hasn't been obtained already, I want to know about the ethnic and religious background of the maternal grandmother. Ethnic factors often play a role in the development of psychopathological processes. I want to know about the maternal grandmother's religion and how religious she was (or is). I am especially interested here in fanaticism or dogmatic religious beliefs that may contribute to the development of psychopathology. I ask the mother to describe the kind of person her mother was and the kind of relationship the mother had with the maternal grandmother during the mother's childhood. I am particularly interested in the kind of maternal care that the maternal grandmother provided the mother.

I also want to know whether the maternal grandmother worked or was a homemaker. If she worked, I want to know about her occupation and whether or not she was mainly out of the home or was actively involved in the mother's child rearing. This may provide informaton about the mother's own maternal capacity, in that if the model she had as a child was a good one, it is more likely that she is providing good maternal input into the patient. And the opposite is the case if the maternal grandmother was deficient in this regard.

I also want to know about the maternal grandmother's relationship with the mother's husband. If there is dissension between the maternal grandmother and the child's father, it may play a role in the child's difficulties. I am particularly interested in how much grandparental input the maternal grandmother has with her grandchildren, especially my patient. Good grandparenting can play an important positive role in a child's psychological development. The exaggerated high esteem that grandparents often have for their grandchildren can serve as a buffer for the criticism and the undeserved negative feedback that children (like the rest of us) often are subjected to in life. I also ask about the maternal grandmother's psychiatric status, whether she has ever been in psychiatric treatment or has suffered with unusual medical illnesses. I then ask the mother if there is anything else that she can mention about her mother that might be of importance to me.

Next, I ask the mother similar questions about her father. I ask about her father's occupation, especially with regard to how much time he had for input into the mother's own upbringing. Information about the mother's relationship with the father may provide useful data about the mother's relationship to her husband. The female-male relationship patterns laid down in childhood tend to repeat themselves in our subsequent lives. Here too I am particularly interested in the relationship between the maternal grandfather and the patient. This is especially important if there are deficiencies in the relationship between the mother's husband and her child.

I then ask the mother about the relationship between her parents. The model of the relationship between the parents that the mother observed during her formative years (whether good or bad) is often the model which is being repeated in the mother's present marital relationship. I am not saying that this is invariably so, only that it is quite a common phenomenon. If a mother, for example, frequently observed her father to be hitting her mother, it is more likely that she will marry a man who will treat her similarly—her vows never to marry such a man notwithstanding. If the mother's whole extended family operates in this way, it is even more likely that she will repeat the pattern in her own marriage. One could say that it is the only lifestyle she knows and that such a mother would be uncomfortable during the dating period with young men who treated her more benevolently. She would be like "a fish out of water" in such relationships and would find them strange and uncomfortable. She might even provoke men into maltreating her or always anticipate maltreatment—even though there is no evidence that it would be forthcoming. And this pattern is likely to transmit itself to a third generation and exhibit itself in the child, at a level commensurate with its level of development.

Sometimes, there may have been divorce in the mother's home during her childhood. In such cases I want to know about the reasons for the separation and whether or not there were remarriages.

If stepparents were involved in the mother's upbringing, I want to know about them and the nature of the relationships between the mother and stepparents.

I then ask the mother to list each of her siblings and get brief information about their age, occupation, and marital status. I am particularly interested in whether or not any of the siblings had serious psychological difficulties and, if so, the nature of them. Because genetic factors often play a role in various psychopathological processes, I want to know about the appearance of such difficulties in the child's aunts and uncles as well as the child's maternal grandparents.

The First Memory Question   I sometimes find the first memory question to be useful. I generally pose it in this way: "Go back as far as you can and tell me what the first memory of your life is. I'd like you to go further back than the begining of school if you can." Psychoanalysts, especially, are very interested in this question. Although it may not provide useful information, sometimes it serves as an epitomization of many factors that have played a role in the patient's lifetime. When it does, it can often provide valuable clues about central psychological themes in the mother's lifetime, themes that began in childhood and exist to the present time. Sometimes the actual memory is false and the incident never occurred. However, because the mother believes fully that it did, the response can still be a useful source of information. At this point I will present a few examples in order to impress upon the reader the value of this question.

One mother gave this response:

> I was about three years old. I remember my brother and my father urinating. I wanted to do what they did and I tried, but I couldn't.

This mother was an extremely domineering and aggressive individual. She was married to a man who was submissive and passive. This memory clearly reflects the desire to assume the masculine role, and it was certainly the case that she had done so in her marriage.

One mother responded:

> I was three years old and my mother and father and sister were fussing over me because of my dancing.

This woman was an extremely histrionic, hysterical individual. She was markedly exhibitionistic. As a child, she had been an actress and a model. But throughout her life she continued to exhibit her talents, which were probably much less than she professed. She was so self-centered that she gave little attention to her son, who was significantly deprived. It was this deprivation that played a role in the development of his symptomatology.

Another mother responded:

> I was two or three years old. I climbed out of my crib, fell, and broke my arm.

The memory reveals the mother's basic feelings that if she removes herself from a protected environment (a crib) she will be traumatized. The mother was basically an extremely dependent individual who did not view herself as capable of handling many of life's situations and anticipated that if she were unprotected by her husband and her parents, she would indeed meet with disaster. One could argue that the arm fracture incident was a psychological trauma which deserved to be remembered. My response is that this does not negate the aforementioned explanation. There were probably many other falls, accidents, and psychologically traumatic incidents in the mother's life. The fact that she remembered this one—after so many years—is a statement that it lent itself well to epitomizing themes in her life that were central to her personality.

One mother responded:

> After I was two years old, if I misbehaved, I would be tied to a table and spanked and kept there. These are the earliest memories of my childhood.

This mother was an extremely masochistic and martyristic individual. She constantly reminded her children about how much she sacrificed herself for their benefit. She stated that at times she did twenty hours of work a day in order to devote every spare moment to philanthropic work. She constantly reminded those she served (her children and others) how much they were in her debt for her benevolence. The seeds of her masochistic-martyristic tendencies are clearly present in this first memory. This mother worked on the principle that the only way she could get affection from others was to suffer pain. She also used her martyrdom as a mechanism for expressing hostility. She would get people to feel guilty over how ungrateful they were for not appreciating her suffering on their behalf.

Another mother's response:

> I was about three or four years old. We were taking family pictures and I was very shy. I didn't want my picture taken.

The memory reveals the mother's fear of exposing herself and her basic feelings that if she is "seen," the observer will be critical or rejecting of her. And she assumes that others share her own low opinion of herself. These personality qualities were playing a role in her son's difficulties in that he too was shy, submissive, and excessively dependent upon the opinions of others. These were qualities that he acquired by identification with his mother.

Another mother's response:

> I was about three years old. It was in Atlantic City. We had gone there on vacation. I was all sunburned and my mother made me put on a starched dress. It hurt my arms and I was crying.

This mother grew up in an upper-middle-class home where there was significant emphasis on propriety, attendance at the "proper schools," and appropriate manners and dress. Otherwise, her parents were not particularly interested in her, and her upbringing was given over to various housekeepers and maids. Although the memory suggests that the mother was resentful of this treatment by the maternal grandmother, she was actually reproducing the pattern in the upbringing of her own daughter. The mother worked full-time in order to send her child to the best private schools and gave little meaningful care and attention to them while she was at home.

One more example:

> Two memories come to mind. Both when I was about three or four years old. I remember being fed hot peppers by a little boy who lived next door. I thought he was giving me candy. In a second memory I remember being burned on the bottom as I backed into a gas heater.

This mother, although in analysis with another therapist, had never analyzed her earliest memories. I discussed with her their possible psychological significance and suggested that she try to analyze them. She responded:

> I come from a long line of masochists. In both of these memories I'm getting harmed. In the first I was tricked. It really wasn't candy but pepper. I still think men are untrustworthy. When they say they're gonna give you something sweet, it turns out that it isn't. The second one makes me think that I wasn't adequately protected by my parents. I feel they should have protected me.

This mother's analysis agreed with my own guesses as to the psychological significances of these first memories. In both she is harmed. In the first she is harmed by another's duplicity (being fed hot peppers) and in the second she brings about her own misfortune (backs into a gas heater). Both suggest the propensity to being hurt either by gravitating toward those who would maltreat her or by participating in behavior that would result in her being harmed. And these tendencies reflected themselves well in her life in that she married a man who, although superficially loving and benevolent, actually turned out to be an extremely hostile individual who subjected her to vicious litigation at the time of their divorce.

My presentation of these many clinical examples was done in the hope that it would impress upon the reader the great value of this question. Although I am often critical of psychoanalytic theory and technique, it would be a mistake for the reader to conclude that my criticism is so vast that I do not appreciate the benefits to be derived from certain aspects of classical psychoanalytic theory. In fact, I believe that much in this book is still very much within the psychoanalytic model, the alterations and modifications notwithstanding.

School Life   I then ask the mother about her elementary school experiences, both in the academic and behavioral realms. I ask about friendships during this period as well as things that might have been going on in her home that might have affected her personality. Similar questions are asked about the junior high school and the high school periods. Just as information about school and neighborhood can provide vital data about the child, the same questions about the mother can be useful in determining whether or not she has psychopathology. With regard to high school, I am particularly interested in whether the mother dated and, if so, what kinds of experiences she had. I ask about academic and/or emotional problems.

Work History   Next, I ask the mother what she did following graduation from high school. If she went to work, I get details of her work history, particularly with regard to how well she got along with colleagues and superiors. If she had numerous jobs, I want to know the reasons for the various changes, especially if she was repeatedly fired. If she is still working now, I want to know the nature of her job adjustment. I am particularly interested in her work history since the birth of my patient. I want to know how much time she spent out of the home and in it. If she gave the child's care over to housekeepers or other caretakers, I want to know who they were, how long they remained in the home, and the nature of their relationships with the child. This is an extremely important area of inquiry because it tells something about emotional deprivation, a common cause of psychopathology.

The Premarital Relationship with the Father   I then ask the mother about the circumstances under which she met her husband and the qualities within him that attracted him to her. If there were previous marriages, I want to list each one and get information about them. I am particularly interested in any psychopathological trends that may have exhibited themselves in each of the previous marriages. Important questions in this area relate to who initiated the separation, what were the main problems in the marriage that resulted in the separation, and what criticisms former husbands had of the mother. Here again we see the question of criticisms other persons had of the interviewee. This can often be an important source of information about the interviewee's personality deficiencies, deficiencies that may not readily be revealed by the person him- or herself.

Projective Questions   Projective questions are routinely used in interviews with children. They are not as frequently used in interviews with adults. I myself generally use them much more in interviews with children. However, I will occasionally present them in my interviews with adults as well, when I am having difficulty getting adequate information by direct questions. In this section I will describe some of the projective questions that I have found most useful.

Five wishes The traditional question is to ask the person what wishes they would make if three could be granted. However, it is nowhere written that one must limit oneself to three. I generally prefer to ask for five wishes because I am then less likely to get stereotyped responses. The first two or three may very well be routine, everyday answers. When one must "scratch one's brain" and provide one or two more, then one is more likely to tap unconscious sources that may provide more meaningful information.

One mother gave these responses:

1. Peace of mind.
2. Fulfillment. To do something more with myself.
3. Do a better job with Michael.
4. Take care of my husband. He has high blood pressure and he's high strung. I should try to handle situations better. When he gets very upset I should try to intercede and calm the situation down.
5. Achieve a better religious and spiritual outlook. I'm compromising with my religion. I should get back to believing.

This mother left high school after three years in order to get married and at 42 felt formidable frustration over not having a gratifying career or profession. She had three children who were then in their 20s and her six-year-old son, an unplanned pregnancy, was resented from the day she learned that she was pregnant. The boy's presenting symptoms (temper tantrums, antisocial behavior, and excessive dependency) reflected, in part, a response to his mother's rejection. Although her interest in self-fulfillment outside the home was reasonable and appropriate, it was also a reflection of her desire to flee from her obligations and involvements as a mother.

The first response reflects the mother's belief that there can exist a state in which one is free of conflict, frustration, and concerns about reality. It reflects her desires to flee from the predictable frustrations of reality.

The second response provides no new information. It is a statement of her conscious wishes to enter into a fulfilling career or profession.

The third response reflects some awareness on her part that she is not doing her best for her son, and the second response has given us one of the reasons why.

The fourth response is related in part to the first. Both suggest a deep need on her part to cover over, deny, smooth over, and otherwise obliterate unpleasantries. She would want to calm her husband down when he gets upset, to prevent emotional expression and to suppress feelings. The notion that such expression could be deleterious to this man with high blood pressure, although true, serves for her as an excuse to allow vicarious gratification (through her husband) of her own need to cover up emotional expression.

Interestingly, the fifth response had direct relevance to her feelings for her son. The mother was raised a rigid Catholic and in the few years previous to the evaluation had loosened up somewhat in her religious convictions. The two main areas in which she had changed her views were that she was now using contraception and she considered abortion to be appropriate and not sinful. It is of interest that both of these digressions from strict adherence to religious belief concerned childbirth. They relate to her desire to have avoided the pregnancy with her son, my patient, and the guilt that she felt over such transgressions from her earlier religious beliefs.

Another mother made these wishes:

1. Safety and good health for all of us.
2. Equanimity for myself in daily existence.
3. An ability to see further, to be less narrow, to comprehend more the meaning of the situation *while* it is happening.
4. An ability to make and keep decisions.
5. To be less self-absorbed—to be able to give of myself.

Superficially, the first wish appears to be normal in that most people will include good health for themselves and their family. However, the word *safety* does not usually appear. It suggests unconscious hostility toward her family and then, by a process of reaction formation, she protects them from trauma. One could, however, argue that wishing one's family good health also implies an initial thought of sickness and that response could also be considered a manifestation of hostility with compensatory reaction formation. Although this may be true, I can only say that *safety* is a rare wish whereas *good health* is an extremely common one. This lends support (but certainly does not prove) my belief that they have different psychodynamics. In this case this mother did indeed harbor formidable hostility toward her husband, a domineering and overbearing individual upon whom she was quite dependent.

The second wish reveals a wish for cessation of her chronic feelings of anxiety, depression, and inner agitation that was associated with her difficult relationship with her husband.

The third wish makes more specific reference to her inability to think for and assert herself, not only in her relationship with her husband but with others as well. Her statement, "to comprehend more the meaning of the situation *while* it is happening" makes reference to her problem in considering her own thoughts and feelings when they are contradicted by others. Subsequently, she sometimes realizes how submissive she has been. Her wish here is that she be more astute and less inhibited and denying when she is allowing herself to be suppressed.

The fourth wish also makes reference to her passivity and dependency on authorities, especially her husband. She cannot make a decision because she is too beholden to the opinions of others and to keep them against resistance is extremely difficult for her.

Last, the fifth wish refers to her self-absorbed state which was the result of the above-described pathology as well as her deep-seated inhibition in giving of herself meaningfully in an affectionate way. This mother significantly deprived her child, the patient, and described how when he was very young she refused to let him come into her bed in the mornings although he stood for hours scratching at the bedroom door.

Another mother gave these wishes:

1. Traveling. I'd like to do a lot of traveling. I'd love to go to Europe, to Germany, Denmark, and Spain.
2. I'd like to live very long.
3. I'd like to have a lot of money.
4. I'd like to eat more without gaining weight.
5. I'd like my children to succeed. I'd like them to be as happily married as I am, to enjoy the world, the blue sky and the grass. I don't want them to marry money. I want them to be basic individuals. I don't want them to be impressed by prestige.

These wishes reveal the mother's basic egocentricism. The first four are all concerned with herself, and no mention is made of her husband and children. They all reveal the desire for self-indulgence. The fifth, although possibly a normal response, is not so for this mother. She was an extremely hysterical and histrionic individual. The most mundane subjects were spoken about with extreme enthusiasm and exaggeration. The mechanism of denial was frequently utilized, and no matter how unfortunate or miserable the situation was she tended to see it in the best possible light. Her references to enjoying "the world, the blue sky, and the grass" are all part of the hysterical picture and cannot be considered bona fide desires for her children to enjoy these aspects of living. In addition, her wish that her children not "marry money" and not be concerned with prestige in their choice of a mate was in her case simple reaction formation to her basic desire that they be most concerned with these considerations. This mother was quite involved with social status, but she denied this through frequent utilization of the mechanism of "undoing," and spoke of her "tolerance" of social and ethnic groups which were usually discriminated against.

Last, one mother gave these wishes:

1. I wish I could be left alone. I always feel under pressure. I'd relax. I feel under pressure from my husband to be a perfect wife. He wants gourmet cooking. He wants me to be more aggressive and I am not. He wants me to friendly to people who might be important to him for business purposes. I just can't be that way.

2. I'd like to travel a lot. I've never been to Europe. But we can't go now because my husband would rather spend money on cars. He gets everything he wants. He's very selfish. He always does what he wants and never what I want. I feel helpless because he has control over all the money.

3. To be more self-assured.

4. I wish I was more tolerant of my parents. I don't know what it is, but whenever I'm with them I cringe. I know I'm their whole life. I can't forgive them for not being more affectionate to me when I was younger. They were always working.

5. I'd like to be completely independent so I won't have to rely on my husband for everything. If I wanted to do something I wouldn't have to ask my husband for everything. I'd like to be on my own and have my own money.

These wishes need little psychoanalysis. They described, quite succinctly, this woman's main psychological and marital difficulties. It was no surprise that near the end of the first interview she stated: "Although I came here for my child, I really think I have problems of my own and I guess I want treatment for myself as well."

Verbal projective questions Although I routinely present children with verbal projective questions, I do not usually present them to adults. Again, when direct questions are not adequate to provide me with the information I desire, I may utilize verbal projective questions. Whereas with the child I generally ask questions about animals and objects, with the adult I generally ask about people. My usual question to the adult is this: "If you could not be yourself, but could live your life as any other person in history, living or dead, real or fictional, famous or not, whom would you choose?" Although this question may be immensely valuable for learning about adults, it is often of little value for children because of their limited repertoire of figures from which they can select. In addition, they will often choose superheroes or other age-appropriate figures. The stereotyped responses are not as revealing as the atypical. Accordingly, as will be seen below, the verbal projection question for people (as opposed to animals and objects) can be very useful for adults.

One mother gave these responses:

> (+)1 Rita Hayworth. I try to copy her to a T. She led a very glamorous life. She was beautiful. She was sexy-looking.
> (+)2 Maria Callas, of the Metropolitan Opera—she's not a dying thing. People adore her. People will worship her forever.
> (+)3 Happy Rockefeller. She's a dream person. She's not cheap or rowdy. She's elegant. She's wealthy.
> (−)1 a) A poor person. I'd never want to be poor.
>   b) My aunt. She was very promiscuous.
> (−)2 My mother. She was very ignorant. She had a low IQ. She wasn't neat.
> (−)3 The female murderer in the picture, *I Want to Live.* She kills other women. She was a murderer. She slept with men.

This mother was basically hysterical, exhibitionistic, deeply materialistic, and vain. Her vanity bordered on psychotic grandiosity. She looked upon those who did not profess adoration of her as being hostile. These cravings are well revealed in the verbal projective test. The (+)1, (+)2, and (+)3 responses all reveal her desire to be adored by large numbers of people, adored for beauty and wealth. The (−)1b and (−)3 responses reflect her guilt over sexual feelings, and (−)3 also reflects her guilt over hostile feelings toward other women.

Another mother gave this response:

(+)1 Jacqueline Kennedy. She has glamor. She's respected and she's elegant. She has many intellectual interests. There is more for her in the future.

(+)2 Picasso. He lives an isolated and contented life. He has inner contentment and satisfaction. He's not dependent on others. He's uninvolved with the rest of the world.

(+)3 Jay. The man I'm now dating. He's serious-minded. He has a flair for enjoying life. He captures both worlds, the real and the unreal.

(−)1 My ex-husband's brother's wife. She has no sense of morals. She has affairs with other men and she shows no reaction, no guilt. Otherwise, she's wonderful.

(−)2 My mother. She's incapable of showing warmth. She always finds the bad side of things. She thrives on misery.

(−)3 Candy, the heroine in a book. It's a sexual satire on a foolish young girl. She has sex with her father, with an uncle, with a resident doctor, with someone in a men's room, and a hunchback in the street.

This mother was an extremely infantile and self-indulgent woman. She was sexually promiscuous and neglected her children in order to go off evenings and weekends with a series of men. She was highly materialistic and extremely exhibitionistic. She was incapable of involving herself in a meaningful way with others. All these qualities are revealed in the verbal projective responses. Her choice of Jacqueline Kennedy for her "glamor" and elegance reveal her exhibitionistic and materialistic qualities. Her inability to involve herself meaningfully is suggested in the reason she gives for wishing to be Picasso, as well as the reasons she gives for not wishing to be her mother. Some guilt over her sexual promiscuity is revealed in (−)1 and (−)3 where she denigrates two other women who themselves were quite promiscuous.

Another mother stated:

(+)1 Margaret Bourke-White. She was formerly a photographer. Now she's sick. She was well traveled and she led an exciting life.

She traveled all over the world. She was married to Erskine Caldwell but they were divorced. She was very creative. She was a very aggressive woman.

(+)2 E. Nesbitt. She wrote children's books. She wrote books on poetry, English, and wild life. She supported her husband and her husband's mistress in her own home. She entertained many interesting people. She was a very strong person. She was lively and full of energy.

(+)3 My Aunt Robb. She was always held up to me as a model. She was beautiful, charming, athletic, and always enjoyed life. She always lived in an academic world, but she was not an intellectual.

(−)1 My mother. She lead a hard life. She was always mixed up. I don't like her. She has no common sense. She's done all the wrong things. She favored my brother. She was unfair to me. She gave me no preparation for life. When I had to have my tonsils out, she didn't tell me in advance. I couldn't rely on her. I've never gotten any backing from her and now I can't depend on anyone.

(−)2 My father. He's lead a very unrealistic kind of life. He never found meaningful work. Although he graduated from Harvard, he always held menial jobs. I wouldn't want to be him because he married my mother. He was never happy with her.

(−)3 A man at my office. He's a no person. He's a zombie. He has no animation. He's just a dead pan.

This mother was a very intelligent, independent, self-assertive, and a fairly accomplished woman. She had been married to a very intellectualized man who was quite dependent on her. She was somewhat inhibited in the expression of her maternal feelings. In the (−)1 response, she reveals some of the sources of her exaggerated independence and self-assertion, namely, her own mother's neglect and disinterest in her. Not being able to depend on her mother she has never felt she could depend on anyone and had thereby become extremely independent and self-assertive. In (+)1 and (+)2 she selects women who have these qualities. The (+)2 choice exhibits this to an extreme degree where she selects a woman who supports not only her husband but her husband's mistress. The (+)3 response is not in itself pathological but tends to support the kind of independent life which this mother considers to be ideal. The (−)2 response again gives information about the reasons why this mother could have little respect for men and little belief that she could depend upon them, thereby having to depend only on her own resources. The (−)3 response also makes reference to her emotional inhibition and lack of spontaneity.

Draw-a-Person and Draw-a-Family   I do not commonly ask parents to draw a person and then tell me a story about the person they have drawn. However, on occasion, I will do so. The Draw-a-Family test may not be particularly useful for children, because of the stereotyped responses they most often provide, but it can be much more useful for adults. My experience has been that adults are less prone to give me stereotyped stories. In this section I will not reproduce the pictures that the parents drew but will present verbatim the stories they provided and my analyses of them.

One mother drew a woman and told this story:

> She's a 25-year-old college girl. She lives alone is a small apartment in New York City. It's an East Side apartment. She works for a magazine as a news writer and editor. She's attractive. She has many boy friends. On her vacations she likes to go traveling. She lives frugally in order to have money to travel.
>
> She goes to England on a trip. She's in London and she meets an Indian—from India, not an American Indian. She's interested in him. They date a lot, and then he returns with her to the United States. He goes back to India, and they continue writing. They decide to marry. She goes to India for his parent's permission. His parents are very upset that he is marrying a nonHindu. He decides not to go against his parents' wishes.
>
> She then travels throughout India. She is depressed by the poverty there. She spends the rest of her life in India trying to convince people not to have children because of the population problem.

This mother was a highly intellectualized woman who married outside of her religion. I considered her clinically to be low in maternal expression, and the story reflects her deep-seated desires to be single and to proselytize nonconception as a way of life.

One mother told this story about the male figure, which was drawn first:

> It's a boy. He's warm, bright, and friendly. In school he gets into a fight with another little boy. He gets hurt and dies. His brother is not as attractive. His mother and father have always ignored the brother, who was not so attractive. He was neglected. The father is very similar to the brother who lives. But the father gives in to the domineering mother. The father tries to be kinder, but the mother browbeats and puts the father down. So the father joins the mother in saying "You should have died, and your brother should have lived. You're lazy and shiftless."

The brother then grows up and is in constant trouble. He gets into a lot of difficulty with the law. Then he married, but he can't keep a wife. He married four or five times. He never holds a job and never functions on his own. The father tries to help the boy without the mother knowing. The father sees himself in this boy. The father gets sick and he dies. As he is dying he wants the boy to be with him and not his wife.

The mother who told this story had a child with a severe school phobia. Her underlying hostility toward children is well revealed in this story. One of the mother's two children dies and the other is severely rejected. The story also reveals her feelings that it is the wife who not only controls her husband but is capable of turning him against his own child.

The same woman then drew a picture of a female and described the picture as follows:

> She's a woman of about 38. She has a square jaw. She looks determined. She is lovable but neurotic. You can't see what's going on behind that face. I'm not sure about that smile.

The statement, "You can't see what's going on behind that face" reveals this mother's tendency to maintain a façade and not reveal her real inner feelings. She was an artificial person, vain, histrionic, materialistic, exhibitionistic, and false in many of her dealings with people.

This story was told about the male figure which another mother drew:

> He has wide shoulders and a moustache. He is standing with his arms out. He's blond. He's not very happy. He has a sign. It says STOP. He's directing traffic. He's not well dressed. He's 40 years old and he's a traffic cop. He's standing on a corner. He's bored to death. He's in a rut. He doesn't know anything else. His family realizes that he's very tired, but he's good with the kids; involved with the Policemen's Benevolent Association. He dies and his wife collects PBA insurance but she's not happy either. He had a heart attack.

This story, of course, reveals this mother's hostility toward her husband whom she unconsciously wishes would die of a heart attack. He, in reality, was a psychopathic person who was constantly placing the family in great debt and she, for masochistic reasons of her own, suffered all the difficulties which this situation brought about. Her husband, depicted as a traffic cop with his hand saying STOP, reveals her view of him as an authority to be obeyed—especially when he directed her to refrain from expressing her resentment over his psychopathic behavior or her desire to flee the marital situation. Having him die appears to be one way out of this situation; but even then she would not be happy because her insurance benefits would not satisfy her needs.

Another mother told the following story about the male figure she had drawn:

> It's an astronaut who has landed on the moon, and he is surprised that the atmosphere is so suitable to man. He was able to remove his space suit. He was astounded that he could breathe. He was pleased about it and enjoyed it.

This story is most interesting in that it dovetails completely with a repetitious dream of the patient's husband (see page 142). He was the son of a rich man, and no matter how poorly he did in school, his father had always bought his way into another school. No matter how negligent he was in fulfilling his obligations, his father always assumed them. The husband had a repetitious dream in which he was drowning but, at the moment when he feared he would die, he suddenly realized that he could breathe underwater. The wife's story that she could miraculously breathe on the moon was similar to her husband's repetitious dream that he could miraculously breathe under water. These people were "made for each other" in that they were both extremely narcissistic and dependent on the husband's father, and my patient was following in his parents' footsteps in that he viewed the paternal grandfather to be the source of all support in the family, so much so that no one need do anything him- or herself to earn his or her way in the world.

Another mother told the following story about a female figure that she has drawn:

> She's all dressed up. She's ready to go on a trip. She's going to go on a holiday. She's waiting for someone to pick up her suitcases and bring her to the airport. She flies to a place where the climate is warm. She arrives at a tall, white shiny hotel. The ocean is all around. She's really been looking forward to this trip. She wants to swim. She surfs. She goes waterskiing.

While on the trip she sees a person coming down the road with bananas. She thinks this would be a good business. She goes back home and starts to import them to the United States. She starts a business in the United States importing and exporting bananas. She frequently visits the island to be sure that all is right at that end.

This mother suffered with an hysterical character disorder with much repressed sexuality and hostility. The story reveals a desire to be taken care of and indulged. The banana is most likely a phallic symbol. The importing and exporting probably reflects her ambivalence over receiving the penis or possibly whether or not she wants one herself.

The mother then told the following story about the male figure she had drawn:

He's warm, happy, and outgoing. He's the athletic type. He's a skin diver. He goes on trips that take him to all parts of the world in order to look for rare stones for museums. He's in Southern France and runs into difficulty with his scuba equipment. He has a fight with a large fish, but he comes up okay with his collection of stones.

My guess is that the stones represent the husband's testes or masculinity. She sees him as being essentially emasculated and searching the world in order to obtain his masculinity. However, when he does so they are only used for exhibitionistic purposes; that is, they are exhibited in museums. The story reflects the mother's feeling that her husband is emasculated and that if he were to achieve a greater degree of masculinity, she would use it only for exhibitionistic purposes and not take advantage of the increased sexual gratification and intimacy that such acquisition would allow.

Another mother told this story about the *family* she drew:

The mother and father are walking in Central Park with their little boy. It's a beautiful day. The birds are flying. They walk through the zoo and pass a lion in his cage. They go to a lake, get a boat, and row for a while in the sunshine. Everyone takes his turn at the oars.

Suddenly a frog jumps into the boat. The woman almost falls out of the boat because she is so frightened by the frog. She knows that it can't do her any harm, but she was shocked by its sudden arrival. She tips the boat. It overturns, but the woman can't swim. She flounders. She can't swim. The boy and the father can't swim either. In the confusion about who can save this woman she drowns.

Her obituary reads: "She drowned in confusion. Her husband and child could have helped her. She wasn't helping herself. She could have made it to the land. She slipped as the result of the mass confusion."

The mother was an extremely inhibited individual with massive repression of the extreme hostility she felt towards her only son. She had a strong need to present everything in terms of deep calmness and serenity in the service of repressing the rage within her. The caged lion reveals this tendency, especially as it appears in the setting of a pleasant walk on a lovely day. However, later in the story her unconscious reveals itself in the form of a frog which leaps out of the water into their boat, thereby upsetting the family's precarious serenity. The fact that this frog can throw this family into massive confusion, which ultimately results in the mother's drowning, reveals the great fear she has of dealing with that which is beneath the surface.

Another mother told this story about the *family* she drew:

The farmer and his wife are both 23. The children are 8 and 9. They live in the Arkansas dust bowl. They follow the crops. Then they go to Arizona. All the children are out in the field picking the crops. A reporter sees the family and details the story of their meager existence. He publishes it and it brings into national prominence their and the plight of other migrant workers. They keep working although they have trouble adjusting. They're still miserable trying to eke out a living. They do manage to save some money and their children get scholarships to college. This boy becomes a famous surgeon, but all this doesn't change their lives. The children get what the parents don't.

The mother sees herself as living in a dust bowl. She spends her life trying to squeeze nutriment out of the dry land. The work is hard and painstaking, but she manages to survive by "following the crops," that is, migrating to wherever there might be a little nutriment. Her whole life is spent in deprivation in the "dust bowl" but she manages to vicariously gratify her desires to leave it through her children's success in doing so.

Both this mother and her husband lived in an emotional vacuum. They were both severely inhibited in expressing tender and affectionate feelings and their primary mode of interaction was hostile. They bickered almost incessantly. She did indeed live in an emotional dust bowl and although she claimed gratifications of a more meaningful nature (as symbolized by food in the story), she only intermittently obtained them and was spending her life in the almost futile quest to get such satisfactions. The story was an accurate portrayal of her situation.

Dreams   I will most often ask a mother if she has had any dreams that have repeated themselves throughout the course of her life. I am in agreement with my colleagues in the field of psychoanalysis that this can be an important question. Repetitious dreams most often reflect an ongoing theme in the individual's life. If the mother has not had such experiences, then I ask her if she can recall *any* dream in her life. This, too, may be significant, especially if it is a dream that she had many years previously. The fact that she remembers it so many years later is a statement of its psychological importance. Another kind of dream that should be given serious consideration by the examiner is one that occurs before the first session. Often this may be a rich source of information about the patient's anticipations from treatment or about fundamental life problems. Unfortunately, the dream may be presented at a time when the therapist is least capable of analyzing it because of his or her unfamiliarity with the person. However, to the degree that one can analyze it, to that degree may one learn some useful information. On occasion, one files it away and may find it useful subsequently, when one is more familiar with the person.

One mother related this dream as having taken place just prior to the initial evaluation:

> I was in the waiting room of a dentist's office and there were three dogs there. They got into the garbage cans and the dentist was going to spray the dogs with MACE (that anti-riot stuff that makes you paralyzed).

The child's father was a physician who spent long hours in his office. The dream reveals the mother's feelings that the father (here depicted as a dentist) sees their three children as an unnecessary nuisance who have to be rejected and paralyzed if he is to be freed of the obligations of taking care of them. Their scrounging for food in a garbage can reveals her feeling that he has little to offer them. It is of interest, however, that she is passive to all of this and permits it to occur.

Another mother related this repetitious dream:

> I often dream that there is a fire in the house and I have to get the kids out.

The dream serves as an expression of the mother's hostility towards her children and her desire that she be free of the responsibilities and inconveniences associated with their upbringing. However, another part of her—a part which is genuinely concerned for their well being—salvages them in time. In summary then the dream reflects the mother's ambivalence toward her children.

Between her first and second evaluation sessions, a mother related this dream:

> A service man had to come to service the bidet. He didn't know what he was doing.

I understood this dream to mean that the serviceman was this examiner and it reflected the mother's feelings that I was incompetent. The mother had an hysterical character disorder with much repression of hostility and sexual feelings. I considered the bidet, as a cleanser of her genitalia, to reflect her desires that I might in some way alleviate her feelings that sexuality was dirty, or that I might in some way be involved in cleansing her sexuality. I did not attempt to analyze this dream in this case because I felt that she was not ready to deal with any of my surmised interpretations. Often a dream like this speaks poorly for the parents' commitment to the treatment process because of its implied distrust of the therapist. Fortunately, in this case, this did not turn out to be the case, and the child did well with full cooperation on the part of the parents. My guess is that the mother gradually became more confident in me, in spite of her initial hesitation.

One mother related this repetitious dream:

> I was at AB's house. She was having a birthday party for her daughter C. It really wasn't A's house but she was having a party there. She had an old-fashioned stove there, a pot bellied stove. It had a beautiful rare plant growing out of it. The plant had a beautiful

odor. I said, "Please tell me where you got this." A said, "Before you leave, I'll either tell you where I bought it or I'll give you a branch to plant yourself." It had pink and white pretty flowers. I kept asking her where she got it. Oh, yes, one other thing. The stove had originally been black, but it was painted white.

This mother had previously been in treatment for a short period, was intelligent, and was interested in analyzing this dream. As a result of her associations and my inquiries, we decided that the pot-bellied stove and plant represented the mother herself. She basically considered herself to be vulgar, inadequate (i.e., "black"), and she attempted to hide these deficiencies by presenting herself with a colorful façade. This was represented by the white paint and the beautiful flowers which everyone admired and which everyone enjoyed smelling. This may have reflected her way of dealing with her inner feeling that she "smells."

This mother was an extremely materialistic and exhibitionistic woman. She was quite wealthy and was obsessed with indulging herself with expensive clothing. She said, "I even dress up to go out for the mail." She was quite shocked after she understood what the dream meant. She subsequently went into therapy with me, and the dream served to catalyze her working on this problem.

Another mother told me she used to have this dream about once a week a few years prior to the evaluation:

A very short, ugly man came up to me. He was exactly the opposite of the kind that I like. I asked him to make love to me. He was overjoyed at the idea. He couldn't believe his luck. He then made advances to me, and I told him that I changed my mind.

The dream reveals the mother's deep-seated hostility toward men. In the dream she selects an ugly man, that is, one who is most likely to respond with gratitude and enthusiasm to her suggestion of a sexual encounter and then thwarts him in the midst of his excitation. Her hostility toward men here is obvious.

During the evaluation this mother told the following dream:

I was with a child. I was at Columbia Teacher's College. I went back and forth from making pottery to being in the apartment of a photographer. While I was making pottery, someone said that I should do it in a particular way but I insisted that I could do it better. Which was so.

This photographer was trying to take a picture of a child and he said that he was on the staff at the university. The child didn't want to let his picture be taken. I told the child that he should let the photographer take the picture. The child said that he would be nice to the photographer only until the picture was taken and then he wouldn't be nice any longer.

The child and I then went through many rooms and then we went out the back door and left.

The dream clearly reflects the mother's attitude toward the evaluation. The photographer is a common symbol for the therapist who "sees through," confronts, and accurately portrays the patient. The child is depicted in two ways: first as the pottery which the mother creates, and second in the form of a child. In the dream the mother reveals her feeling that she can do a better job in molding and forming her child's personality than I can and, therefore, insists upon doing it herself. In the dream she also has the child cooperate with me only until the picture is taken (that is, until the end of the evaluation) and then has him refuse to cooperate further.

The journey through many rooms signifies the complex inquiry of the evaluation and their leaving through the back door reveals their desire to remove themselves surreptitiously and prematurely, rather than through the front door which would reflect a desire to leave when treatment is completed.

The dream was a perfect statement of what ultimately happened and served as an accurate warning for the examiner. The child did cooperate until the end of the evaluation, and then both he and the parents decided not to pursue treatment. Although the dream was analyzed with the mother and she accepted its implications at the time, I was unable to alter the strong forces which compelled her to follow its dictates.

Another mother described having frequent fearful fantasies and an occasional nightmare that "my husband would lose both of his legs and I'll end up pushing him in a wheelchair."

This mother was extremely masochistic. Although she had a Ph.D. degree, she constantly berated herself intellectually and had always felt that she had to present herself as intellectually average or below average if she were to attract her husband. Her husband was a borderline psychotic who had little involvement with her and devoted himself to his academic pursuits (He was a professor at a university). He had her do most of the "dirty work," that is, boring research and typing, for his own doctoral thesis.

The fantasy reveals not only her unconscious hostility toward her husband, hostility which is expressed through the desire that he lose his legs, but also her feeling that the only way he could really need her was if he were to be helpless. When he was getting his doctorate degree he needed her. Following this he would no longer need her and the fantasy allowed her once again to play a meaningful role in his life. In addition, by straddling herself with a crippled man, she could gratify her masochistic desires.

The mother of an adolescent described this dream on the night before her first individual interview with me. (There had been a previous screening interview when I saw her in association with her son and husband):

> I was on one side of a sliding door. My husband was on the other side. I was trying to shut the sliding door and couldn't.

The dream, coming as it did on the night prior to her first interview with me alone, suggests that she would prefer to place a closed door between herself and her husband so that he would not see certain things which would be unpleasant for her to reveal to me. It suggested that she was not going to tell me freely very much about her real feelings about her husband. In the subsequent part of the interview this prediction turned out to be true. She described her relationship with him as a good one and had absolutely no complaints. Of him she could only say, "He's wonderful. He's good. Sometimes he talks a little too much, but that's nothing that concerns me. He talks a lot of common sense."

In reality, the husband was a person who was prone to make endless speeches over inanities. He would puff himself up and pontificate over the most simplistic issues as if he was spouting forth great wisdom. Only one of his four children was consciously irritated by these lectures. One of his sons (not my patient) identified with the father and at 21 was already filled with an air of self-importance.

The dream and the mother's subsequent comments revealed her fear of coming to terms directly with this quite alienating trait of her husband's.

I generally spend two or three interviews with the mothers, each one lasting 45 to 60 minutes. I hope the reader can appreciate that the information gained in the individual interviews provides me with a much greater knowledge of what is going on with her than is obtained in the initial two-hour consultation. In every sense of the word, the data collection in the initial interview is indeed superficial. The examiner who does not avail him- or herself of the more extensive interviews is being deprived of vital information—information that is crucial to have if one is to understand thoroughly what is going on with the patient.

Before closing the final interview with the mother, I may ask her how she views herself ten years from now. The answer provided can also be a useful source of information. The same question can be asked about her guesses about the child a decade from now. I am sure that the reader has a collection of his or her own questions that can also prove useful. In this section I have presented those that I personally have found most valuable.

THE EVALUATION OF THE FATHER

My discussion of the father's evaluation will be significantly shorter than that of the mother. This is primarily the result of the fact that many of the questions are the same and that there would be little point in my repeating the same questions in this section. However, another fact relates to my observation that fathers generally are less willing to reveal themselves than mothers and accordingly, their evaluations are often shorter. Whereas the mother's evaluation is generally two to three interviews, each of which is 45 to 60 minutes, fathers generally have nothing further to say to me after one to two interviews of the same duration. They often are much "tighter" when responding to the projective questions, as well.

The Initial Inquiry

As was true with the mother, I begin the interview with the father with an open-end question in which I ask him if there is anything special on his mind that he would like to speak with me about. He may or may not have something to discuss and, of course, I follow his lead. I then ask the father about reactions to the initial two-hour consultation. We then go on to questions in which I ask him his opinion regarding the causes of the child's difficulties. I inform him that I recognize that his main reason for consulting with me is that I should provide my opinion regarding the answers to this question. However, I advise him that his guesses and speculations can be an important source of information to me. I then proceed with the questions regarding his and his wife's dealing with the child, both assets and liabilities. I am particularly interested in whether the father involves himself in sports with the children, especially such activities as Little League, soccer, and so on. In investigating into this area, however, the examiner should find out whether the father is fanatical about it. If the father is having fist fights with the coaches at the Little League games, he is probably doing his children more harm than good. He is probably using the child for vicarious gratification to a degree beyond the normal.

Description of the Marriage

We then proceed to a discussion of the marriage. Here, especially, fathers may be particularly unreceptive to revealing difficulties in the marital relationship. A common situation is one in which a mother will claim that her husband had had an affair, and he has told her that he does not wish her to reveal this to me. In the session with me he will studiously avoid discussion of this issue, even though he knows that his wife is aware of the relationship. I ask the father the same questions about the marriage that I ask the mother, especially with regard to its strong points and weak points. If the father initially presents the marriage as "good," with no problems at all, I will state that all marriages have their areas of friction, and I encourage him to discuss those areas in which he and his wife have differences of opinion. Even with this sanction, the father may insist that there are no such difficulties in his marriage. If such a response is given by a father whom the examiner knows is having an affair (by some information provided by the wife), then there is little the examiner can do. It is hoped that she will bring the matter up during the joint session, but often she does not. As mentioned, in such situations, I often let the thing rest. To "rock the boat" may cause a disruption of the marital equilibrium, which may do the child more harm than good.

History of Psychiatric Treatment

I then ask the father whether he has ever been in treatment. Most child therapists will agree that boys are overrepresented in their patient population. In contrast, most adult therapists will agree that women are overrepresented in their patient population. I believe that this phenomenon relates to the fact that boys are generally more rambunctious, assertive, and "fighters." As every teacher and parent knows, boys are "tough customers" when compared to girls. Accordingly, they have greater difficulty complying with social constraints, especially in school. I suspect that there are probably genetic bases for these character traits in that they were probably more adaptive in evolutionary development. Hunters and fighters do better if they are more aggressive, and so men who possessed such qualities survived preferentially over men who did not. However, social and environmental factors have probably played a role as well in engendering these traits. At the adult level, however, men often feel the need to maintain their "macho image" and are less receptive to therapy—a process in which they are encouraged to reveal weaknesses and failings. If the father has been in therapy, I will ask the same questions that I have asked the mother regarding the nature of the problems for which he went into treatment and what benefits, if any, were derived from the therapy. I am especially interested in marital counseling and the marital problems that brought the parents into therapy.

Background Information

The questions to the father regarding background information are essentially the same as those posed to the mother. Specifically, I ask the father about his parents, their relationship with one another, and their relationships with him. I also inquire about his siblings, especially with regard to the presence of psychiatric difficulties. Here, I am particularly interested in the kind of parenting the father received in that his parents probably served as the model for his own parenting. I also want to know about the nature of the relationships between the paternal grandparents and my patient.

Military Service   One difference between the father's and the mother's inquiries relates to military service. If the father served in the military, one does well to find out about how he adjusted there and whether he received an honorable discharge. One should ascertain whether the father had difficulties adjusting in the service and whether he warranted disciplinary action and/or psychiatric treatment. The military generally requires a degree of integration similar to (if not more than) that which is required for adjustment in school. One must be willing to comply to a reasonable degree with authority and to exhibit self-restraint under stressful circumstances. If the father was in combat, one wants to find out whether he suffered with any psychiatric disorders commonly seen under such circumstances.

The First Memory Question   As was true for the mother, questions about the father's first memory can often provide useful information about underlying psychodynamics. I present here a few examples.

One father gave this memory:

> I was about four years old. I remember leaving my mother's and father's store. I climbed over a fence outside of the store and ripped my leg open. Then I ran back into the store.

This father, although 38 years old, was still working as an employee in his parents' store. He was extremely dependent on them and was quite passive in his relationship with them. Although he spoke on occasion of going out on his own, there was little evidence that he seriously intended to do this. Although he could not openly admit it to himself, it was clear that he was waiting for the day that they would die and then the business would become his. In his marriage, as well, he was quite dependent on his wife, who domineered him mercilessly. The memory reveals the father's basic feeling that were he to leave the domain of his parents he would be traumatized. The warning serves him well and he returns to the store where he feels comfortable and safe. This first memory epitomizes the basic theme of his life and his relationships both with his parents and with his wife.

Another father had this memory:

> I was about four years old. I was driving a little toy car and running over another kid's white shoes. He was a dandy. I was a dirty little kid. I liked to get dirty. He went crying to his mother. I don't know if after that I was chastised or what.

This father was a bright, somewhat cocky, and basically arrogant man. He was quick to anger and most of his comments about people were critical. He was in the plumbing supply business and psychologically he appeared to be "shitting" on the world. The memory reflects this life pattern. His greatest pleasure appeared to be dirtying those who were clean, that is, defecating on others. His relationship with me was in the same spirit. I felt that he saw me as a boy with white shoes and his primary mode of relating to me was hostile. He stated that in grade school his greatest pleasure came when he was head of the monitors, a position, no doubt that gave him further opportunity to be sadistic to others. After graduation from college the father was fired from his first job after six months of work. He considered his firing the result of his having been rebellious: "I didn't want to do what they wanted." He finally ended up working for his own father, with whom he described a very competitive and antagonistic relationship.

The father also stated that he feared women, stating: "I see them as aggressive birds who would want to scratch our eyes out." I considered this fantasy to be a reflection of his own hostility projected out onto women.

Another father's memory:

> I was in my crib. I must have been about two years old and I was picking the paint off the iron bars and eating it.

This father's parents were quite distant from him and he suffered definite emotional deprivation in his childhood. The recollection is symbolic of the deprivation he suffered in that he had to resort to the ingestion of inedible objects in his attempt to gain symbolic affection. The psychodynamics of his ingestion of inedible objects is similar to that of children with pica who ingest inedible objects because of neglect and a craving for oral-dependent gratifications.

Another father's first memory:

> I was two or three years old and playing in my backyard. My clothing got caught on a fence that I was climbing. A friend of mine came and had to lift me up and take me off.

This father had a schizoid character disorder and was severely dependent on his wife and parents. Although 31 and a law school graduate, he was still unable to function as an adult. He worked for his father, who was also a lawyer, and it was clear that he could not have been able to function independently in another law firm or in his own practice. The memory reveals his basic dependency problem. When he is confronted with an obstruction or some other difficulty in life, he is unable to get himself out of trouble and must depend on others to take care of him.

One father gave this response:

> I was about three years old and I remember trying to eat cement from a wall.

This man's father (that is the paternal grandfather of my patient) was a very intellectualized man who devoted himself to his scholarly interests instead of spending time with his children. The paternal grandmother had paranoid and depressive episodes for which she received ECT. At times she was suicidal. It is not hard to see how this father felt that the love and affection given to him was as digestible as concrete.

School Life I ask the father about adjustment at the elementary school level. I am particularly interested in the father's comparison of himself with my patient during this period, especially if the patient is a boy. Many fathers will say that the patient is exhibiting behavior very similar to their own during this phase of their lives. One must consider the possibility that this reflects a genetic component. However, one also wants to ascertain whether the father is sanctioning atypical behavior (antisocial) or criticizing it. Possible genetic contributions notwithstanding, sanctioning may contribute to its perpetuation.

Although things are changing, women still have less necessity to dedicate themselves as assiduously as fathers to school and career planning. I am not claiming that this is a good thing; only that it is a reality of our world, recent changes notwithstanding. Accordingly, if a mother was insufficiently motivated during the high school period, it does not necessarily reflect as much pathology as a father who was similarly unmotivated. The pressures on the father to ultimately be a breadwinner are far greater than those placed on girls during the formative years. Accordingly, a girl's lack of school and work motivation during the high school period does not necessarily reflect as much pathology as in a father who is similarly unmotivated. I am also interested in the father's social relationships throughout his school career. These lay the foundation for adult relationships, including the relationship with his wife.

Work History It is important to go into the father's work history. A long history of difficulty adjusting in jobs generally reflects psychiatric difficulties. And the father's commitment to work will generally affect the child's attitude toward school. If the child sees the father seriously involved in his work, it is likely that he will thereby serve as a good model for the child's involvement in school work. I cannot emphasize this point strongly enough. Many parents present with children who are unmotivated to do their school work. Yet the parents may provide an atmosphere in which work is viewed as odious and there is practically no intellectual curiosity. In such an environment the child is not likely to develop strong school interest unless exposed extensively to other models who demonstrate such commitments.

The Premarital Relationship with the Mother　I want to find out the circumstances under which the father first met the mother and what his initial attractions were. The examiner does well to appreciate that most people do not provide what a judicious middle-aged person would consider reasonable reasons for marriage. So common are the frivolous criteria for marriage that one has to consider them to be in the normal range. For example, a father may claim that he "fell in love." When one asks what the particular qualities were that he fell in love with, he may be hard put to give other answers other than his wife was physically attractive and that she was "sweet." One should be particularly interested here in any atypical relationships that were established during this period.

Projective Questions　Because fathers are generally more reticent to reveal themselves directly, one would think that projective questions might be useful. However, even in this area my experience has been that they are more reluctant to reveal themselves. This hesitation notwithstanding, one can sometimes still get useful information by the utilization of these questions.

Five wishes　Some fathers can only go to three wishes. When they reach the fourth and fifth wishes, they become too anxious to continue because they run out of stereotyped responses. I present here some responses of fathers to the five wishes question.

One father gave these responses:

1. That Randy be okay.
2. That I have a happy marriage.
3. That I become independent and self-sufficient.
4. I can't think of any more.

All three wishes relate to difficulties in the family. The third wish especially epitomized the father's main psychological problem, namely, that he was an extremely dependent individual. Although in his late 30s, he was very much under the thumb of his own father, whom he was working for, who was supporting him, and who controlled almost every aspect of his life.

Another father gave these responses:

1. Wisdom.
2. Patience.
3. Charity.
4. Free access to any library I wanted.
5. The writing style equivalent to George Travelli Macauley.

This father was a highly intellectualized man on the faculty of a major Eastern university. He was most fearful of intimate involvements with others and spent most of his time absorbed in his academic work. For years he had not slept in the same room as his wife and sexual contact was rare. Three of his five responses make direct reference to his intellectual and academic ambitions (#1, #4 and #5). In addition, this man flaunted his intellectual accomplishments in an attempt to bolster a very low self-esteem. This is well shown in wish #5 where he mentions the name of a person who was unknown to this examiner. When I asked him who Macauley was, he responded with condescending incredulity that I didn't know that Macauley was a famous historian. The implication of his facial expression was one of: "How stupid can you be, not ever to have heard of Macauley?"

Conspicuous by their absence is the fact that none of the responses refer to any human beings other than himself.

Another father gave these responses:

1. Good health and long life.
2. To be a contented, respected millionaire. To have enough material comfort to free me from worry.
3. To have stature and power. To be a better lawyer than anyone else and to be recognized as such. To be a member of the establishment.
4. For my children to have the same luck with their wives as I have with mine and to have as much money as I have.
5. The question I wonder about is whether it would be better for

my wife or for me to die first? It would be better for her if I went first, but you won't get me to say that I want her to die first. No, the best thing would be if there was an accident and we both died together.

This father was an extremely grandiose, self-centered, manipulative, and hostile individual. He actually considered himself to be uniformly admired, respected, and envied by all around him. In actual fact he had no real friends. His cruelty to his daughter (more verbal than physical) resulted in her being a very withdrawn and timid child.

Response #1 is within the normal range. Wishes #2, #3, and #4 reflect the already described grandiosity, materialism, and power fantasies. Wish #5 reveals his hostility toward his wife, which he then denied. Actually, this man's wife (my patient's mother) had significant personality problems, and the marriage was fraught with difficulties. However, he had to deny this in order to maintain the image of having a "perfect marriage." Under these circumstances there was formidable hostility toward his wife, reflected in his death wishes, but he could not allow these feelings entrance into conscious awareness.

Verbal projective questions Presented below are some verbal projective questions that provided important information in the fathers' evaluation.

One father gave these responses:

(+)1 Caruso or Lawrence Melchior. I can't sing very well, and I'd love to be a great singer, to be able to entertain people that way.

(+)2 Jacques Cousteau. He leads an active, interesting life. He's adventurous; he's in the outdoors; he does a lot of skin diving.

(+)3 "Dr. H. He's a very good surgeon. He does a lot of good for the people. His hours probably aren't too bad.

(−)1 Frank Sinatra or the Beatles, or others in the public eye. They have no private life. They're mobbed wherever they go.

(−)2 A politician. Most of them are phony phonies. They lie all the time. I couldn't keep track of all the lies.

(−)3 Just plain Joe. I want to get some recognition in life.

My full clinical evaluation of this man revealed him to be relatively stable and free from significant psychopathology. Although one might find evidences of psychopathology in the above responses, I considered them to be within the normal range. The (+)1 and (+)3 responses suggest that this father might have inordinate desires to be famous. However, his life situation was one in which he appeared to be very secure and adjusted in a fairly respectable but certainly not famous position. He was an engineer who was owner of a small manufacturing company. The (−)2 reply suggests the possiblity that the father himself engages in duplicity or would like to do so. However, this was not substantiated by the rest of my clinical evaluation. It is important for the reader to appreciate that repression of unacceptable material exists in all people, and projective tests reveal what is being repressed. In our culture there is probably a tendency in most people to lie at times and to crave fame. Lying and inordinate ambition are not acceptable traits and may very well be repressed. This does not mean that the person harboring such desires is suffering with psychopathology. It is only when there is acting out, obsessive preoccupation, or when these trends interfere significantly with one's life pattern that the term psychopathology can justifiably be applied.

Another father gave these responses:

(+)1 Elvis Presley. He's rich and famous. He's honest; he doesn't gamble. He's a good family man. I've always been a great fan of his.

(+)2 Mickey Mantle. I like to play ball. He's my idol. I adore his strength and skill as a ball player. He's also an upright family man. He doesn't have much of an education, just like me.

(+)3 John Kennedy. He had a close relationship with the common man, in spite of all his money. But he wasn't a big shot. He had compassion for the common man.

(−)1 Fidel Castro. He deceived people. He manhandled people. He caused a lot of pain and heartache.

(−)2 Hitler. He mistreated the Jewish people terribly. He rose to power by stepping over everybody.

(−)3 Jimmy Hoffa. He engaged in many underground activities. He's a vicious leader who robbed the union membership.

This 28-year-old father worked at the dairy counter at a supermarket. He graduated high school with mediocre grades and married at the age of 20. The paternal grandfather showed the father little warmth, and abandoned the home when the father was 18 years old.

The persons that this patient selected in both positive and negative categories could very well be within the normal range. However, the reasons he gives for choosing these people reflect certain manifestations of his personal psychopathology. In the (+)1 and (+)2 responses he introduces the "family man" theme, which are clearly personal associations to these figures, and certainly not typical. They suggest preoccupation with and cravings for a close-knit family in compensation for the deprivations he suffered as a child in this area. In the (+)3 response he chooses John Kennedy, in part because of his "compassion for the common man." His (−)1, (−)2, and (−)3 responses are all people who in one way or another have taken advantage of, deceived, and even killed the common man. These responses reveal this father's basic feelings of impotency in a world which he sees as malevolent and overpowering. He craves the protection of a benevolent authority symbolized by John Kennedy.

Another father gave this response:

(+)1 Paul Getty, for his business shrewdness. He got the oil reserve depreciation bill passed by Congress. He had no family life, so I wouldn't want to be like him for that.

(+)2 My old hometown doctor, Dr. O. He's someone who has done a lot for many people. He could talk to you about anything. He was a good family man.

(+)3 Supreme Court Justice White. He's an athlete. He's smart. He leads a well-rounded life.

(−)1 Adolph Hitler. He was a killer. His super-race idea was all wrong.

(−)2 Walter Reuther. He's a legalized crook. He warps our economy with the strength of his union.

(−)3 Malcolm X. He was trying to get a job done and wasn't doing it the right way. He was using violence rather than discussion.

This father had little interest in the patient, his adopted stepson, and spent 16 to 20 hours a day, six to seven days a week at work. He had strong psychopathic tendencies as well.

The (+)1 response reveals both his psychopathic tendencies as well as denial of his disinterest in family life. In the (+)2 reply we again see the denial of his disinterest in his family via his admiration for Dr. O, the "good family man." I considered the (+)3 and (−)1 responses to be within the normal range. The (−)2 response again relates to the father's psychopathy because I considered the father himself to be a "legalized crook." The (−)3 response as it stands cannot provide too much information. Had time been available to discuss the Malcolm X associations further, more revealing information might have been obtained.

One father gave these responses:

(+)1 Nathaniel Bowdich. He was a 19th century New Englander. He was a self-taught navigator and ship owner. He established many of the principles of navigation for whaling ships. Mariners still use Bowdich's book on navigation. He was very sharp and skilled. He taught mathematics at Harvard as well.

(+)2 Thomas Jefferson. He was a happy man. He had many interests. He enjoyed life.

(+)3 Jerry G., a colleague of mine. He's articulate, outgoing, and gets a bang out of life.

(−)1 Nat Turner. Although he was free, he was really still a slave. He had obsessions that he could not let go of. He was a double-dealing shackled madman.

(−)2 Nixon. He doesn't know what he wants. He doesn't know where he's going. He's not up to the responsibility. He has no convictions of his own.

(−)3 A psychiatrist. There's too much intimacy. They're bowed down with the inner world, which is a horrible one.

This father, although a successful professional man, was a borderline psychotic whose main symptoms were withdrawal and obsessive ruminations. He had little genuine interest in his family and only out of a sense of duty did he make attempts to involve himself with them. Consistent with this lack of involvement is the fact that in none of these responses is any mention made of family involvement. The (+)1 person, although admirable in many ways, appears to epitomize 19th century new England independence and self-assertion. He is the kind of a person who rises above hostile forces in nature and the hardships of life in a determined and single-minded manner. The choice of the navigator probably relates to the father's feelings that he himself needs some navigation and direction if he is to weather the storms of his life, especially those associated with the welling up of feelings (as represented by the ocean waves) which are so threatening to him. In the (+)2 and (+)3 responses the father reveals his desire to get some pleasure out of life, something he was not getting because of his psychiatric disturbances.

The (−)1 response reveals the father's basic feelings about

himself. He, like Nat Turner, is enslaved by his obsessions and his duplicity (which was associated with his contrived and artificial involvement in his family) and cause him to think of himself as "a double-dealing shackeled madman." In the (−)2 response reference is made to the father's indecisiveness related to his obsessive doubting and massive ambivalence. The (−)3 response again makes reference to the father's psychic conflicts and fears of relevation of his primitive eruptions from the unconscious.

One father was asked the animal questions in addition to the person questions. These are the responses he gave:

(+)1 A poodle dog. It gets good treatment.

(+)2 A black panther. It's shrewd and it's cunning. It's fast.

(+)3 A turtle. It goes on slowly but looks back to see if it's right or wrong.

(−)1 A cat. It's too self-reliant. It doesn't give. It just takes.

(−)2 A pig. It's only here to be eaten.

(−)3 A reptile or snake. It's misunderstood. People kill them and don't realize that they're just doing their own thing.

This father was an extremely psychopathic person. He had little interest in the patient, his adopted stepson, and spent most of his time away from the home at his job. He was a very conniving and materialistic individual who used people ruthlessly in order to obtain his own ends. His primary attaction to his wife, who was 10 years his senior, was that she was a good cook.

The (+)1 response reveals his strong impulses to passively lead a life of luxury. The (+)2 response reflects his admiration for psychopathic qualities. The (−)3 response suggests unconscious respect for the psychopathic personality type who is most circumspect, calculating, and reflective of his behavior.

In the (−)1 response the father's criticism of the cat who "doesn't give, just takes" is a clear statement of his denial of these qualities within himself, because he was a most taking person. The (−)2 response relates to the same attitude in that the father, seeing the world as a place where one is "eaten," chooses to be the "eater." The (−)3 response is a clear-cut rationalization for psychopathic behavior. The reptile and the snake are highly symbolic of the devious, the unacceptable, the cunning, and the surreptitious. The father cannot provide a logical justification for accepting such behavior but merely requests that these animals be accepted because they are "doing their own thing," and that in itself should be enough for people to accept them.

The verbal projective questions can also be used with adults to describe other family members. Just as the child is asked to select animals and objects that will suit his or her mother and father, the parent can be asked to present people, animals, and objects that will suit other family members, especially spouse and children. This father gave the following responses when asked to select animals that suited his wife's personality:

(+)1 A mynah bird. It's like a parrot. It's always jabbering.

(+)2 A rhinoceros. It goes where it wants. It doesn't have much of a brain. It tromps over everything in order to get what it wants.

(+)3 A Pekingese house dog. It has no worries. It's fed, then taken out to shit, and then put to bed.

(−)1 A mallard. It's graceful; she's not.

(−)2 A leopard. It's quiet and stealthy. She's loud. She has no tact. She's noisy.

(−)3 An alligator. He lives in the water and she's afraid of the water.

This father had very little respect for or involvement with his wife and the verbal projective associations clearly reflect this. The responses clearly reflect the massive feelings of disdain and disgust he had for her, and each response reveals a different type of deprecation. Here we see how all of these derogatory attitudes are on the conscious level.

Another father gave these responses when asked to select animals that suited his wife's personality:

(+)1 A lion. It's majestic. It's a leader. It's quiet and unassuming. It has perseverance. It likes to get things done in a quiet way. She's respected like the lion by the rest of the animal kingdom.

(+)2 A Mastiff dog. It protects the house. It's a strong animal yet it's gentle. It's respected by everyone.

(+)3 A deer because of its beauty and gracefulness. It's shy except when protecting its young and then it becomes very forceful. It's clear. It leads a quiet life. It's a choice food of carnivorous animals.

(−)1 A cat. They're nice until you go against them. Then they will turn against you. She won't do that.

(−)2 A snake. She's not repulsive. She doesn't instill fear in anyone.

(−)3 A bat because it's a spreader of disease. It's repulsive. It's a scavenger. It hides away from view.

This father was extremely passive and submissive in his relationship to a remarkably domineering masochistic-martyristic wife. She was extremely controlling and coercive to all members of the family, but her manipulations were rarely overt. She played on their guilt through her martyristic self-sacrificing tendencies. Both the father and the children were very much in fear of her.

These qualities are reflected throughout the verbal projective responses. She, like the lion, is the "leader" and gets things done in a "quiet" and "unassuming" way. The "respect" that the lion enjoys from the "rest of the animal kingdom" is clearly the fearful subservience she has extracted from the members of her family.

The Mastiff dog, of course, exhibits qualities similar to the lion. The mother, like the Mastiff, is the "protector of the house" and is "respected" (= feared) by everyone. In the (+)3 response the statement that the deer is "the choice food for carnivorous animals" reflects the father's primitive and repressed hostility which he harbors toward the mother. By identifying himself with a carnivorous animal for whom the deer is "choice food," he can vent the rage he feels toward her. In addition, the fantasy probably represents a desire to acquire her strength through primitive incorporative, cannibalistic maneuvers.

The (−)1 response is denial pure and simple. The mother is a person who will turn against the father if he turns against her, and he lives in fear of her retribution. The (−)2 response reveals his true feelings towards the mother, namely, that she is repulsive and he lives in fear of her. The (−)3 response is again a clear statement of the real feelings the father feels about the mother. He sees her as "repulsive" and "a scavenger." The subtle and somewhat surreptitious coercive maneuvers that the mother utilizes are reflected in the comment that the bat "hides away from view."

Another father gave these responses:

(+)1 A tiger. She's ferocious at times. She yells and screams a lot.

(+)2 A horse. She likes horse races. She watches many on TV. She loves all sorts of gambling, but not to excess. She's a $2.00 better.

(+)3 Dogs, any kind of dog. She loves them and I despise them. She'd want to be a dog. (What kind?) A brown Scotch Terrier. I can just associate her with dogs. I don't know why.

(−)1 A cow. It's fat, cumbersome, and odd. She's not like that.

(−)2 A giraffe. It has a high neck and long strides. She doesn't have a high neck and she takes short strides.

(−)3 A snake. It's slimy. She's not.

The 12-year-old daughter of this man was constantly bickering with her mother, whereas he tended to indulge his wife. The mother was not a very strongly maternal person, and the patient turned to her father where she felt she could get greater affection. An hereditary loss of hair was a source of serious concern to the mother, although the father denied that it in any way lessened his attraction for her. When first seen, the family was going through what I would consider an "oedipal crisis," with the father and daughter strongly attracted to one another and denying their attraction with intermittent bickering. The mother was quite jealous over the relationship between the father and daughter and directed much of her jealous rage toward the daughter.

The (+)1 response refers not only to the father's awareness of the mother's overt hostility expressed toward the daughter but, in addition, probably reveals his sensitivity to some of the mother's additional hostilities as well. The (+)3 response reveals the father's inability to overtly express his anger and his lack of physical attraction to his wife. He could only go as far as saying that he "despises" dogs and he somehow associates his wife with a dog. Denial and reaction formation were strong defense mechanisms in this man. In the (−)1 response he reveals his basic feelings about her lack of attractiveness, and there is also suggested his awareness that she is not a very maternal person in that the cow lends itself well to being viewed as a powerful maternal symbol. Although the (−)2 and (−)3 responses could also reveal his lack of attraction to her, they also could be considered to be within the normal range of responses.

Draw-a-Person and Draw-a-Family One father presented this story about the person he drew:

> He is a man who is awakened in the middle of the night to find that his house has burned down, killing his wife and children. His feeling was one of bluntness and unfeeling. Sadness and loss and overwhelming numbness. There is nothing to do.
>
> He always sat after that. He goes back to his work as a blue-collar worker, as a machine operator. He works in a factory where they make furniture legs.

He doesn't think he's ever going to get back on his feet, but he is young and he eventually recovers.

The story reveals clearly the father's wish to remove himself completely from his wife and children, and to start life anew with others. In addition, the father, a successful professional man, depicts himself basically as a person much lower on the social scale.

It took another father ten minutes before he could begin drawing a picture. Each time he placed the pencil on the page he removed it anxiously with the excuse that he did not know what to draw, that he was sure it would not come out right, that he had never drawn pictures before, et cetera. The picture he finally did draw was very lightly and hesitatingly drawn. Although a head was present, facial features were completely absent. The picture reflected the father's basic lack of a sense of identity. The hands and feet had no definite shape and appeared to be evaporating into space. This reflected the father's lack of feeling that he had any capacity to handle his environment and his profound sense of instability. A large crotch defect was present, revealing his basic feelings of masculine inadequacy. The picture, in short, was one drawn by a man with severe feelings of impotency.

It was extremely difficult for this father to tell a story about the figure he had drawn. He stated, "He's just standing there. He's a farmer. He's just finished working. He's surveying everything that he has just accomplished, the work in the fields, he has harvested and reaped everything. He has sown the field and he has reaped the harvest."

This father was indeed a most impotent man, not only in the narrow sexual sense but in life in general. He worked for his own father and was completely under the latter's domination. His picture revealed his sense of impotency and the story he told was a feeble attempt at compensation.

One father drew a picture of a family and told this story:

> The family is on a hike. They pack their lunch. They are at Bear Mountain. Their son, Johnny, hears a yell and a crash. The father has lost his footing and slipped off the edge of the trail. He's lying fifty feet below the trail, holding onto a small tree, with several hundred feet of drop below him. The mother is hysterical.
>
> Little Johnny is very bright and has learned lessons in the Boy Scouts. He lets himself down to his father. He knows he doesn't have the strength to pull his father up. He ties the rope around the father.

He climbs up to the trail, takes the rope with him and ties it around a tree on the trail and then the father is able to climb back onto the trail. The family is overjoyed at the rescue. The parents are very proud of the boy.

The story reveals the father's feelings that his son will be his savior. This father did indeed place great pressures on his son to excel both in sports and in the academic area. He himself was poorly educated, although he did excel in sports. The family was constantly boasting about the child's unusually good performance in both of these areas. The story reveals the father's feelings that his well-being and possibly his very existence depends on the boy's performance.

This father of three boys drew a picture of a man, a woman, and a daughter. He told the following story:

> They are going for a walk in the park. The daughter is attached to the father. The father doesn't see her much, and so he wants her to be near him. The mother is resting because she has too much of the daughter every day so she wants some relief. They are a happy family and this is their time for relaxation. The man looks ugly, but the other two look cute.

The usual response is to draw one's own family. This drawing revealed clearly the father's desire to have a single daughter instead of three sons. This related to conscious feelings that the presence of his sons took away his wife's time from him. Somehow he saw a daughter as less of a threat. But the story also reveals that even if he were to have a daughter he would be neglectful of her, and he sees a wife as being neglectful of her as well. All this is denied at the end when he states that the family is happy. In addition, his basic feelings about himself is that he is ugly, as manifested in his final comment about the male figure.

Another father drew a picture of himself and his wife with one boy standing next to his wife and another boy standing next to him. He told the following story:

> The wife's hand is interlaced with her husband's. The children are side-by-side with the parents. They are happy children. The two people grew up together in life. The man achieved success with his wife growing up with him. They learned the importance of sharing. They learned to live with each other's idiosyncrasies. They learned to live with one another.

After the husband graduated from graduate school, he met his wife and wanted to get married. The wife went to work. They struggled and worked together. Their children are happy.

This man's wife decided upon a divorce just prior to my first session with my patient, the older of their two sons. During our first interview he tried to get me to convince his wife not to go through with her divorce plans. The story is replete with references to a cohesiveness and sharing that never existed in the family. This is well confirmed by the fact that the father makes reference in the first sentence of his story to the interlacing of the hands of the two parents. In fact, in the picture he drew this was not the case. The parents were drawn entirely separate, without any hand contact. The mother had decided upon divorce because of the inability and disinclination to tolerate the father's idiosyncrasies. The story reflects the father's desire that his wife be more tolerant of them. The happiness of their children is also in the service of denial, because their two sons were indeed most unhappy young boys.

This father drew a picture of a man, a woman, and a little girl. In actuality the family consisted of the parents, a 12-year-old boy (the patient), and two younger daughters. He then told the following story:

> A sociologist took a trip to England. He met a woman there who was a domestic. Although from totally different societies and social levels, and although mentally and emotionally they were far apart, they enjoyed one another.
> He knocked her up and rather than get an abortion, she decided to have the baby. Later they realized it was a mistake. They were delighted that they didn't get married. He earned enough money to care for the child. He left and returned to the United States, and she and the child managed quite well. She married a milkman, had two more kids, and they lived happily ever after.

The drawing itself reveals the father's wishes to remove himself and even abandon his wife and children. He was a cold and isolated man and could only involve himself to a minimal degree with his wife and three children.

This man left graduate school just prior to receiving his Ph.D. in engineering and married when his wife threatened to discontinue the relationship if he did not marry her. He never involved himself significantly in the marriage, and there were long periods during the patient's childhood when he worked seven days a week and came home late at night, resulting in his hardly ever seeing the patient.

This story reveals his basic feelings that he can only attract a woman far below him socially and intellectually. It also reveals his desire to involve himself in a most minimal and distant way. He does not marry the mother of his child, puts the Atlantic Ocean between himself and her, and abandons his child as well. He ends the story by assuaging some of his guilt over such rejection of his child and woman friend by having someone else assume the responsibilities.

Dreams   The husband of the woman whose fantasy was described on page 115 reported this repetitious dream:

> I dream that I am submerged under water. I think that I can't breathe and that I'm trying to get to the surface. I then discover that I can breathe under water and I feel much better.

The father was completely dependent upon his own father who owned a large business. As he grew up he always knew that no matter how poorly he did in school he would ultimately end up owning the business. He never applied himself and each time he failed out of prep school or college, his father managed to buy him into another. He had many psychopathic qualities and felt no obligation to spend time with his children, be faithful to his wife, or commit himself in any way to anyone.

The dream reveals his basic life pattern—that he will be magically saved from catastrophe. Actually others would have suffered the consequences of such a life of self-indulgence, but he seems to feel that he has come away unscathed. Others get drowned; he can breathe under water. The dream epitomized his life pattern, especially his relationship to his overprotective father.

This father described the following repetitious dream:

> I was taking a test and I never had time to finish it. I felt pressured and pushed. I kept feeling that I wasn't going to finish.

This is a common repetitious dream of people from homes where the academic pressures have been great. In analyzing this dream with both parents and patients, I have most often found it to reflect a feeling that the people will not be able to live up to the standards of their parents, both in the academic as well as in the nonacademic areas of life. Because so much emotional investment has been directed to the academic realm, it serves as a general symbol for success in life. I have also found the dream to reflect ambivalence on the person's part toward successful achievements in life. Failing the test is not simply the academic test, but the test of life's success as well. Often the parents of such a patient have been ambivalent themselves with regard to their children's successful performance.

This father was a borderline psychotic who was a highly educated and moderately successful professional man. However, his extreme psychopathology prevented him from getting anything but the slightest gratification from his professional and nonprofessional life.

Another father related this dream:

> I was reading one of my competitor's private reports. He walked in and I was ashamed. I put the papers down.

Although this father did not exhibit specific psychopathic trends in the clinical interview, he was a fiercely competitive, materialistic, grandiose, and coercive individual. Although ostensibly ethical in his business dealings, the dream reflects an aspect of his personality that was not apparent in the clinical evaluation, but would certainly be consistent with his character structure. This dream demonstrates how a parent's dream may provide the examiner with added information about character structure—information that may be useful in understanding the child's psychopathology. In this case, some of the child's antisocial behavior could be considered the result of identification with his father's psychopathic traits and the desire to fulfill the unconscious wishes of the parent.

Throughout his life, one father had this repetitious dream:

> I had a gym all to myself. I spent a lot of time there with kids, teaching them to play basketball. I have no problems there when I am in the gym.

The father, although 38 years old, was still very much a child. He was still employed by his parents in their small store, and he was very much under the domination of his wife. He spent much time out of the house coaching young boys in various sports. This activity not only served as a way of removing himself from the domination of his wife, but also provided him with a feeling of authority and competence—which he lacked in his relationship with both his parents and his spouse. Furthermore, sports enabled him to express vicariously much of his pent-up hostility. Last, the dream enables him to engage in childish activities beyond the extent to which he involved himself in reality. It is a dream of an adolescent dreamed by a man who psychologically was still an adolescent.

Concluding Comments

My goal here is to show that the individual, whether mother or father, who is reluctant to give information directly may provide meaningful data with projective tests. However, analyzing such material can be risky. I am certain that many examiners may have come to different conclusions regarding the interpretations I have given to the material presented. In my defense, I might say my interpretations are made on the basis of my direct clinical experiences with the families. Analyzing this material in isolation from such clinical data is extremely risky and is generally a poor idea. But even when one does have clinical information, there is no question that there is still a certain amount of speculation. These drawbacks notwithstanding, I find such projective material useful, especially for the parent who is not comfortable revealing him- or herself in the direct clinical interview.

12 EVALUATION OF THE CHILD

Introduction

Pediatricians sometimes compare themselves to veterinarians in that both cannot rely on their patient's verbalizations to assist them in making their diagnoses. Carrying this analogy further, the child psychiatrist could be compared to the "veterinary psychiatrist," because neither can learn much by asking his or her patient: "Tell me about your problems." Both must rely on more indirect and nonverbal modalities of communication. This drawback of gaining information from children notwithstanding, there is still much that the therapist can learn.

When psychogenic problems are present, I generally devote

three sessions to the intensive evaluation of the child. And this is the kind of evaluation I will be describing here. If, on the basis of the information I obtain in the initial two-hour evaluation, I conclude that neurologically based difficulties are present, then a longer, extended evaluation is often warranted. I not only have to assess for the presence of the neurologically based problems, but for psychogenic problems as well. And the latter may fall into two categories. The first are those psychogenic problems that are secondary to the neurological impairment. They are derivatives of such impairment and would presumably not be present if the child did not have a basic organic disorder. The second are those that are independent of the neurological disturbance and often result from family problems and/or improper child-rearing practices. Of course, the two categories may overlap and each contribute to the intensification of the other. Obviously, the evaluation for these difficulties is much more complex and generally takes five to six meetings with the child.

It is important for the examiner not to pressure the child to participate in any particular part of the evaluation. The child's defenses *must* be respected. A severely disturbed child may become so upset by projective tests that he or she may close off any further revelations by this route for many months. The child who says that he or she cannot think of a story may be mildly encouraged, but certainly not shamed, cajoled, or otherwise forced into telling one. Children of low intellectual capacity, who mask their feelings of inadequacy, may become quite embarrassed over not being able to answer certain questions. The examiner does well to sense such reactions and not push the child further. It is generally preferable not to gain the information than to do so under duress, because data elicited under stress is not only of questionable validity, but worse, extracting information coercively interferes with the formation of a good therapist-patient relationship. The authors of the Group for the Advancement of Psychiatry report No. 38 aptly state (1957): "A test is never so important that a child should have to undergo severe anxiety or panic because of it."

On occasion, a child may be more comfortable with a mother or father present during the course of the interview. Many examiners object strongly to the parental presence and do everything possible to see the child alone. I, personally, do not have such strong feelings on this subject. If the parents' presence, especially at the beginning, makes a difference between the child's being cooperative and significantly uncooperative, I will generally allow the parent to be present. I cannot deny that I may be entrenching immaturity and dependency here, but I am willing to pay that price for the advantages of having a calmer and more cooperative child. Of course, as the child becomes more comfortable with me, it is generally possible to have the parent leave the room.

The presence of the parent has advantages in its own right. One may observe interactions between the child and the parent that would not otherwise have occurred. In addition, when the parent observes exactly what I am doing, the discussions during the final presentation become more meaningful. Having seen the instruments being administered and having observed the child's responses, the parent is more likely to have conviction for the examiner's conclusions. I am fully aware, however, that the parental presence may have a squelching effect, in that the child may not be as free to reveal certain material (both consciously and unconsciously) when the parent is there.

All these considerations result in my taking the flexible approach to the question of parental observation. In practice, most often children are comfortable enough to proceed without the parents being present. The reader who may be wondering at this point about how the child's confidentiality affects my decision as to whether or not the parents should be in the room, should appreciate that I have less respect for the role of confidentiality in child therapy than do most therapists.

It is important for the examiner to appreciate that the purpose of the extended evaluation is more than simply data collection. An equally important, if not more important, goal is to lay the foundation for a good therapeutic relationship. This is not likely to be accomplished in one or two pressured interviews. The more relaxed the circumstances, the greater the likelihood the therapist will be able to engage the child meaningfully.

Direct Verbal Inquiry with the Child

When engaging children in direct verbal discussion, it is important for the examiner to appreciate certain basic facts about interviewing techniques with children. As mentioned already, children most often do not have insight into the fact that they have "problems" and the examiner is well advised not to attempt to get them to develop such insight. In fact, most children (especially younger ones) are not cognitively capable of making the kinds of linkages and associations that are necessary for an analytic type of inquiry (whether it be diagnostic or therapeutic). Accordingly, the examiner should not be looking for any kind of testimonial in this area. Furthermore, what we call "problems" are not generally viewed as such by children. To them the problem is often the people who are "on their backs" trying to get them to do things they don't want to. But even those children who clearly have differentiated the behavioral patterns which their parents consider pathological from those which their parents deem acceptable and desirable, are not likely to be motivated to direct themselves to alleviating the "unhealthy traits."

I will often start the interview with the traditional open-ended question: "So what's doing with you?" or "So what would you like to talk about?" On occasion (I would say about 5% of the time) the child will have something on his or her mind to discuss. But most often (whether it be in this evaluative session or in the therapeutic session), the child has nothing particular to tell me about. Examiners who feel frustrated about this might consider going into another field. This is the way our patients are, and it behooves us to work around this rather than to forcibly extract a conversation on the child's problems.

Abstractions and conceptualizations are of far less therapeutic value than concrete examples. This principle is especially important in the interview with the child. Questions beginning with "why" are far less valuable than questions beginning with "when, where, what, or how." Of course, as therapists we are interested in knowing *why*, but we are less likely to learn the reasons *why* from *why* questions than we are from questions utilizing other interrogatory words. For example, to ask a child why he or she misbehaves in school is waste of time and words. To ask the same child a series of questions about when, where, with whom, and under what circumstances there is trouble in school is more likely to provide useful data. Even here, because of the child's defensiveness, one may not get reasonable answers because the questions are related to the child's "problems"—a touchy subject if there ever was one. A preferable way to lead into a revelation about academic problems, for example, is to ask very specific concrete questions such as "What grade are you in?"

"What's your teacher's name?" "How many children in your class?" "How many boys, how many girls?" "Who is the smartest kid in the class?" "What do you like about him(her)?" "What don't you like about him(her)?" "Who is the dumbest student?" "Do you like him(her)?" These questions may then ultimately result in the child's talking about his or her own attitude toward academics, and this may be one of the presenting problems. Other questions that might lead into a discussion of the child's academic problems are: "What subject do you like most in school?" "What subject do you hate the most?" "What subjects are you best at?" "What subjects are you worst at?"

In order to discuss behavioral problems one might lead into the issue with questions such as: "Who are the kids in your class who get into trouble?" "What kinds of things do they do?" "What does the teacher do when they get into trouble?" The reader will note that I am talking here about *other* parties, not the patient. "Does the teacher yell at them?" "What does the teacher say to them when they get into trouble?" "What do the other kids feel about those troublemakers?" "What kinds of punishment do they get?" "Who's the best person in the class in conduct?" "Do you like him(her)?" From this point one might say, "*All* kids get into trouble once in a while in class, what kinds of things do *you* do that get *you* into trouble?" By stating first that "all" children get into trouble, at times, it becomes easier for the child to describe the situations when he or she has behavioral difficulties. The reader will note also that I do not ask yes-no questions. These are most often of little value because, after one has received an answer, one does not know if it is really valid. Questions requiring specific answers are much more likely to be useful.

In order to learn more about peer difficulties, one again might start off with specific, nonthreatening questions, for example: "Tell me the names of some of the kids who live in your neighborhood?" "Who are the ones you spend the most time with?" "Who is your best friend?" "What is it about that person that makes you like him(her) so much?" "What kinds of things do you like doing most with him(her)?" "What kinds of things do you *not* like doing with him(her)?" "Of all the kids in the neighborhood which one do you dislike or hate the most?" "What is there about that person that makes you dislike or hate him(her) so much?" "What do you think are the things that a child can do that will turn off other kids?" For the child who is teased and/or scapegoated, one might ask what are the specific things other children say to him or her when taunting is occurring. These children might also be asked what things their parents and siblings tell them they do that get them into trouble. One might also talk here about the various activities the child involves him- or herself in and, if there are difficulties, the details regarding why.

With regard to pathological behavior in the home, again, the examiner does well to follow the aforementioned principles. Some good lead-in questions: "What do you like doing most with your mother(father)?" "Of all things you like doing in the house, what things are the most fun?" "What are the things you don't like doing with your mother(father), the things that are no fun at all?" "All kids get scolded sometimes. What kinds of things do your parents scold you over?" "All kids get punished sometimes. What kinds of things are you punished for?" "Who punishes you?" "What kinds of punishments does your mother(father) give you?" "How long do they last?" "Are these fair punishments?" "I want you to tell me the best things you can about your mother?" "Now tell me the worst things about your mother?" "Now I want you to tell me the best things you can about your father?" "Now tell me the worst things about your father?" "What's the best thing that ever happened to you in your whole life?" "What's the worst thing that ever happened to you in your whole life?"

In my discussion of the interview with the mother, I mentioned "grandma's criteria" for assessing maternal and paternal capacity. One can question the child, as well, to get information about parental capacity. This can be done by going through the events of the day, from the time the child gets up in the morning until the time he or she goes to sleep at night. In association with each event, one tries to find about which parent is involved and the nature of the involvement. For example, one might ask which parent gets the child up in the morning and whether there are difficulties, and continue with such questioning about the whole course of the day. Particular emphasis should be given to those times when both parents are available. Most often, this is during the evening. In the discussion one could ask about homework—who helps with the homework, who has the most patience, and whether there is any conflict and fighting over it. The bedtime scene, also, can provide useful informaton about parenting capacity. One should find out about who reads the child bedtime stories and how much patience each parent has regarding reading to the children. Also, one can learn about cuddling. Rather than saying, "Does your mother(father) like to cuddle?" one does better to ask, "Is your mother(father) the kind of person who likes to cuddle?" By using the latter form, there is the implication that there are two kinds of mothers(fathers): cuddlers and noncuddlers, that neither is better than the other, and that the examiner is just trying to find out in which category the child's mother(father) is. When questions are posed in a way that there is minimal disparagement implied of any of the involved parties, the examiner is more likely to get an honest answer.

The examiner must be aware that children generally have weak egos and will utilize a variety of maneuvers to avoid direct confrontation with their deficits. They commonly utilize such phrases as "I don't know." Accordingly, the examiner should pose questions that circumvent embarrassing confrontations. To say to a child, "Tell me about the things you're scared of?" or "What are the things that frighten you?" is an injudicious way of finding out about a child's fears. A preferable way of getting information in this area is to say: "Most children have some things that scare them once in a while. What things scare *you*?" By presenting fears as a normal response, the child is more likely to divulge what his(hers) are. Also, by starting off with the positive, easily admitted aspects of an issue, it is often easier to get into the embarrassing opposite. For example, one might ask, "What are the things about yourself that you are most proud of?" I will then go into a detailed inquiry of the sources of the child's pride. With ego enhancement, then, as a buffer one is in a better position to ask the question: "Everybody has times when they do, say, or think things they're ashamed of. I'd like to hear one thing that you're ashamed of." Again, the question is so posed that shame is presented as a normal phenomenon and all I'm asking of the child is to mention one thing that has caused him or her shame.

Some children in treatment are particularly fearful of expressing their feelings. On occasion, feelings are relegated to the unconscious, and questions about them prove futile. However, there are some children who can verbalize their feelings but are uncomfortable doing so. The worst way to elicit his or her feelings from a repressed child is to ask the question: "How do you feel about that?" or "How does that make you feel?" One could ask the question, but should not be surprised if the repressed child does not answer. In such cases, the examiner might say, "You must have felt really sad when your parents told you they were going to split up." "You must have *really* felt lonely when the children didn't want to play with you." Even then one might get the answer: "It doesn't bother me!" One might respond then with, "Well, I find that hard to believe. I believe that you *do* have feelings about it but that you're not comfortable talking about it now. I hope the time will come soon when you'll feel more comfortable talking about these things."

There are occasions, however, when the aforementioned kinds of catalytic questions do serve well to precipitate an emotional response on the part of the child. They serve to fan and enlarge sparks of feelings that were only dimly appreciated by the child. Another way of facilitating the expression of such feelings is to precede them with comments that make them socially acceptable: "Most kids get very upset when they learn that their parents are going to get a divorce. What were the kinds of feelings you had?"

A discussion of the child's interests and hobbies can be very useful. Sometimes, the examiner does best to start the interview with this topic, because it is the least threatening. At other times, it may be useful as a way of decompressing a situation and diverting a child from a particularly difficult area of inquiry. One might ask very simply: "What are your hobbies?" or "What are your favorite games?" or "What do you like doing after school?" "What's your favorite sport?" These can serve as a point of departure for a discussion in which the therapist discusses his or her own knowledge of this area. Such discussion can serve to entrench the therapist-patient relationship. Sometimes the discussion may reveal pathological trends. One boy may say that his hobby is dinosaurs. However, the discussion of dinosaurs reveals that he has such a massive preoccupation with the subject that he spends little time on anything else. When asked about his favorite TV program, one child responded, "Divorce Court." A psychotic child's favorite hobby may be watching the phonograph player's turntable revolve.

I have already mentioned that I routinely give every child at the time of the first session, whether it be for a consultation or treatment, a copy of my *Stories About the Real World*, Volume I (1972). As mentioned, the issues raised in this book are likely to be pertinent to most children's therapy. Sometime during the first evaluative session I will ask the child if he or she has read the book. If the answer is affirmative (the case for most children), I will inquire about which stories the child liked the most and which the least. I attempt to use the book as a point of departure for further inquiry. If the child is vague or nonrevealing, I may ask about a particular story that I suspect is likely to be most relevant to the child. For example, I might ask the child to tell me what he or she remembers of *Jerry and the Bullies,* a story that deals with self-assertion, the use of profanity, and fighting back. I might ask a shy child about *Helen, The Girl Who Wouldn't Try,* or the child who lies might be asked about the story, *The Hundred-Dollar Lie.*

Three Wishes

Whereas I generally ask adults for five wishes, I usually ask children for only three. My main reason for this is that I have found this question to be less useful for children than for adults. More often, children provide somewhat stereotyped responses that are age appropriate and not particularly valuable sources of information. The unusual or idiosyncratic response may, however, provide useful information. A common response a child gives is "a million dollars" or "all the money in the world." Generally, a list of toys and other material objects is provided, a response that I consider to be in the normal range. Another normal response, that also serves the purposes of resistance, is "all the wishes I wanted." In response I will generally advise the child that this answer is not acceptable and that the child must select specific things that he or she would want to happen or have.

Fred, an eight-year-old boy, gave as his first wish, "Love from everybody." The response implies that the patient felt deprived of affection and wished that everyone in the world would give him love in order to compensate for the deprivations that he suffered at home. His second response was, "Peace all over the world." I considered this response to reflect Fred's desire that there be no anger, either within himself or within everybody else. The response served to squelch or repress all the resentment that existed both within Fred and his parents. His third response: "Respect to everybody." This was clearly a unique response. It again related to his desire to suppress the hostility he felt toward his parents.

Sally, a nine-year-old girl, presented with symptoms of immaturity and dependency. Her mother worked full-time and left her to the care of a succession of maids. The patient was very involved with her pets with which she spent significant time when she was alone. Her first wish: "Pets, all the different kinds of pets in the world, except insects." Her second wish: "Money to buy things for the pets, birdfeed, peanuts for the elephants, bananas for the monkeys." I considered the first and second responses to represent the patient's strong identification with lower animals. By gratifying their needs, she was vicariously gratifying her own. By projecting herself into the animals she fed, she could gratify vicariously her own dependency needs. She was also demonstrating at the same time how inferiors and underlings should be treated. Her third response: "A bird, because it can fly anywhere it wants." I considered this response to reflect her desire to remove herself from her home environment because it was not particularly gratifying.

A ten-year-old girl presented with symptoms of depression, stuttering, poor relationships with peers and generalized tension. Her mother was extremely punitive and her father passively permitted the mother's sadistic behavior. Her first wish: "To have magical powers to make someone exactly like me. We'd then go and live in a big mansion in Florida." I considered the first wish to reveal her desire to have a "clone," someone just like herself. She would then have a playmate to compensate for the deprivation she suffered in her household. The playmate, of course, would be kind to her, unlike her mother. She would also remove herself from the home and go to Florida which represented, I believe, a climate of emotional warmth, ease, and relaxation. Her second wish: "I'd have a farm of horses." Although this might be a normal response, in this girl's situation I suspected that it related to her desire to be in the company of animals because her experiences with human beings had been so difficult. Her third wish: "To grow up fast and get married to a man who would love me a lot and take good care of me." Considering this child's background, the meaning of the wish is obvious. It is another reflection of the patient's general unhappiness in her home situation. Although ten, she was preoccupied with sexual fantasies involving teenage dating, seductivity, and kissing. This was partially derived from her mother who, in addition to her hostility, was a seductive woman, preoccupied with sex, but was basically a sexually inhibited person.

The mother of a nine-year-old boy had a schizoid personality and was not able to give him very much affection and attention. His father, a businessman, was extremely materialistic and was constantly boasting about the monetary values of his cars, boat, homes, et cetera. The patient's presenting symptoms were antisocial acting out in the classroom and temper tantrums at home. His first wish: "Never break anything like I do when I have a temper tantrum." I considered this wish to reveal some guilt and remorse over the anger he was exhibiting. In a sense, it was a good therapeutic sign in that the child wanted to do something to reduce this symptom. His second wish: "Every year I'd buy all the cars I like and I'd have enough money to do it." This wish, although it might be age appropriate in our society, had heavy loading from the family because of his father's exhibitionistic consumption of material things. He was clearly modeling himself after his father. His third wish: "Be a teacher at the Abraham Lincoln School because they give good lunches there." I considered this response to reflect this boy's emotional deprivation. Although the family was quite wealthy, he was significantly deprived of affection. Although I did not ask him for a fourth wish, the patient spontaneously gave me one: "Have a gigantic garage for thousands and thousands of cars." Although his second wish revealed some cravings for consumption and exhibition of material goods, the fourth wish carries this to an absurd extreme—not surprising for a child with such a father. (And his mother had no complaints about the father's materialism. In fact, she enjoyed the same indulgences.)

First Memory

A child's first memory is generally a less valuable source of information than that of adults. One might argue that the child's first memory is more likely to be a useful source of information because the time gap between the event and the time the question is posed is much shorter than the time lag for the adults. When adults are asked this question, they are reaching back into the distant past and are selecting the event from a much larger storehouse of recollections, and thus it usually has a much greater psychological significance. One cannot label a child immature or regressed if he or she remembers being in a crib, being fed a meal, or being taken care of in bed when sick. As is true in all projective information, one must take care to differentiate the age-appropriate from the idiosyncratic and atypical.

A very bright 11-year-old boy had great difficulties in his relationships with his parents. His mother was an extremely cold, critical, coercive, and controlling individual. His father did not protect the boy adequately from his mother's maltreatment of him. When asked for his first memory, the patient responded: "I was being put into a crib a few minutes after I was born." I believe that the patient was being honest with me; however, I also believe that the fantasy had a reality for him because it was so deeply entrenched in his psychic structure and so well lent itself to symbolizing his life situation with his mother. It reflected well his feelings of having been separated from his mother a few minutes after he was born and placed where he could not enjoy any contact with her.

A ten-year-old girl's mother was self-centered, materialistic, and exhibitionistic. Her father was quite rich and prided himself in how much he could indulge his wife. This child was essentially raised by a series of caretakers. The parents traveled extensively, to various parts of the world, and on occasion, brought the patient with them. At such times, her care was entrusted to nursemaids and other caretakers. This was the response she gave to the first memory question: "I was 14 months old. It was London. I didn't want to take naps. I stayed in my crib. I screamed. The maid said, 'Let her cry.' I tried to climb out of the crib, but I didn't make it. Somebody came and took me out. I was mad at my mother for making me take a nap. I ran and I jumped up and down on her bed. She wasn't there." The response reveals the patient's feelings of having been abandoned by her mother. Her cries for contact with her remain unanswered. Even the maid, under whose care the rejecting mother left her, does not respond to her cries for warmth and affection. "Someone" (not her mother) does finally remove her from her imprisonment. She then runs to her mother's empty bed. The implication of this is that she hopes to gain some affection from her mother there. However, her mother is not there and she responds angrily by jumping up and down on her mother's bed. Not being able to express her hostility to her mother directly, she vents it on her mother's bed.

A nine-year-old girl was brought to treatment because of poor motivation in school and difficulty in her relationships with friends. Her mother was rejecting of the patient and left her care to a housekeeper, Anna. The mother also treated Anna somewhat shabbily. This was the response she gave to the first memory question: "I was three years old. We had a Portuguese maid. Her name was Anna. She's still with us. I hate hot dogs and I've always hated hot dogs. Anna made them when my mother didn't want them. My mother didn't speak up to Anna and tell her not to make them. So Anna gave me the hot dogs and I didn't like eating them." First, the realities were that Anna would not have defied the mother, so hostile and strong was the mother and so weak and passive was

Anna. The memory, probably a distortion, served to split the patient's mother into a "good mother" and a "bad mother." Anna, here, is made the "bad mother." She forcefeeds the patient hot dogs (a food the patient doesn't like) in spite of the mother's objections. Implied in the mother's objections is the notion that her mother did not want to give her the undesirable food. The patient thereby suppresses hostility felt toward the mother for her rejection and coercion of her and puts the blame on Anna. It is safer to blame Anna because Anna is not as likely to retaliate.

An eight-year-old boy suffered with a neurologically based learning disability, associated with gross and fine motor coordination problems. He was a disappointment to his mother who had high academic aspirations for him. And he was a disappointment to his father who had hoped that his only son would be more outgoing and athletic. One of the ways he handled the home difficulties was to regress. This is the response he gave to the first memory question: "I was a little boy. I was in the bathtub. I was taking a bath. Someone was cleaning me with soap." Although one might argue that the memory has regressive, "return-to-the-womb" fantasies, as symbolized by emerging in water (possibly symbolic of amniotic fluid), I am dubious about this explanation. More important, I believe is the emphasis on the cleansing process. I believe that the fantasy revealed the patient's view of himself as dirty and as being cleaned symbolized his desire to cleanse himself of the dirty feelings about himself derived from his parents' frequent criticism of him.

This 12-year-old boy's parents both had minimal involvement with him. His father was a hard-driving businessman, a workaholic, who was often absent from the home because of long business trips. His mother was a frustrated, angry, embittered woman who ranged from tolerance of the patient to utilization of him as a scapegoat. This was the first memory he provided: "I was in kindergarten. The school nun was there. The milk she gave me was frozen and I was scared to tell her that the milk was no good. The other kids told her for me. I was afraid that if I bothered her, she would yell at me." The fantasy needs little analysis. The frozen milk is a clear statement of the patient's view of his mother as unmaternal. In addition, he fears complaining about her lack of affection because he might then be traumatized in retaliation and thereby add to the difficulties he was already suffering in association with his emotional deprivation.

A 14-year-old girl was referred because of severe outbursts of rage. She described this event occurring when she was five:

> My mother went down a one-way street in a car. She went the wrong way. A policeman stopped her. I didn't like police at that time. I thought they were mean. I was scared of them. I cried a lot and said, "Don't hurt my mother." I was screaming and crying and yelling. It got him so frustrated that he said, "The heck with it," and he got rid of us. And he didn't give us a ticket.

The patient's mother was a woman who felt overwhelmed by the world and was often confused about where she was heading and what her future would be. One manifestation of this was her poor sense of direction, which prevented her from adequately driving distances more than a few miles from her home. The patient's recalling of her mother going down a one-way street is a statement of her view of her mother as a woman who doesn't know which way she is going in life. The patient's recollection of avoiding the consequences of her behavior by having a violent outburst of rage epitomizes her life pattern. The patient's temper outbursts did indeed enable her to avoid the consequences of her unacceptable behavior. Early in life she had learned that if she were to rant and rave long enough, she would get her way. In this case the policeman, the symbol of the punitive authority, is dissuaded by her tantrums from administering appropriate punishment.

Free Picture

As mentioned in the initial two-hour evaluation, I generally provide the patient with a blank piece of drawing paper and crayons and request that he or she draw a picture and then tell me a story about it. In the intensive evaluation, as well, I will often utilize this technique once or twice more. It is one of the standards in child therapy that deserves its good reputation. Drawing is something that most children enjoy and telling a story about a picture is a common childhood activity. Again, one must differentiate between age-appropriate, stereotyped pictures and stories and those that are atypical. As mentioned, I do not accept designs, which often are used as a way of resisting revelation of unconscious fantasies. In addition, if a boy draws a picture of rockets, airplanes, spaceships, and tanks in battle, one learns very little. It is difficult, if not impossible, to differentiate between the normal utilization of such fantasies for socially acceptable release of hostility and the pathological use of these vehicles for such release. I do not "reject" such stories but merely recognize that they are of little psychological significance in most cases and then go on to other instruments. I present here some examples of the way in which these pictures and their attendant stories provide valuable information about a child's underlying psychodynamics.

This ten-year-old boy's parents were involved in vicious custody litigation. He was continually being used as a weapon and spy by each of his parents, especially his father. Furthermore, he recognized that his mother was being seriously traumatized by his father. The boy drew a bird whom he described as "a blue and red-footed flying dragonbird." This is the story he told about the bird he drew:

> He became famous because he saved tons of birds from being shot by arrows and being eaten at the king's banquet. He flew where the bow and arrows were being made and the trees were chopped down for firewood for roasting the birds. He grabbed the trees and logs with his claws and went into a dive and dropped them (the trees) on the men and their tools. He dropped the logs in a circle and set fire to them. He broke the arrows with his claws and burned the bows and arrows up. He then became king of the birds.

I considered the king in the story to represent the boy's father and the flock of birds his mother. Birds are a common symbol for females because of their beauty and grace. The hero of the story, the "blue and red-footed flying dragonbird," represents the patient himself. He prevents the king's men from making weapons to kill the "tons of birds." By destroying the arrows and bows and burning up the king's men, he puts a cessation to all hostilities, especially the ability of his father to traumatize his mother. In addition, he protects himself from the traumatization that he himself suffered as a bystander and intermediary in the parental warfare.

This eight-year-old girl was the oldest of three children. The parents were highly intellectualized professional people whose involvement in their academic pursuits was so extensive that the children were significantly neglected. The father, especially, was away from the home for long periods in association with his professional lectures and academic pursuits. The mother, although more involved with the children, was quite ambivalent in her relationship with them. At times she would reach out and at other times she would withdraw. The patient dealt with this situation by passive-aggressive maneuvers. She was obstructionistic and at times tantalizing. When her mother would reach out to her, she would gain sadistic gratification from rejecting her.

The patient drew a picture of a boat in the ocean. Above the boat is a bright yellow sun and beneath the boat are three fishes. A clown is in the boat, reaching toward the fishes below the surface. When asked to tell a story about the picture, she related the following: "The clown is trying to catch the fishes with his hands. But he can't. The sun is shining." When I asked her to relate more, she stated that that was the whole story.

I considered the three fish to symbolize the patient and her siblings. I considered the boat to represent her mother. The boat, like the womb, holds within it human life and lends itself well, therefore, to symbolizing the mother. She views her mother as enjoying the sunshine, warmth, and affection. However, she views herself and her siblings as being below the surface of the water, under the boat, where the sunshine does not reach. Because fishes cannot generally get into boats, the picture further reflects her feelings of separation from her mother. The story about the clown reaching out for the fish, but their eluding him, is a reenactment of what actually went on in her relationship with her mother (the clown being depicted as a male notwithstanding). She did make a fool out of her mother by her elusive behavior, thus the symbolization of her mother as a clown. This game with the mother provided the patient with an outlet for the hostility she felt toward her because of the mother's ambivalence and frequent rejection.

A six-year-old boy was referred because of disruptive behavior in the classroom and hostile acting out. He stole, lied, and did dangerous things to his classmates such as throwing scissors and knives at them. His mother was an extremely petulant, irritable, fault-finding individual. Both he, his sister, and his father could do no right. She was basically a miserable, bitter, unhappy woman, who made the lives of those around her equally unhappy. The boy drew a picture of a whale and then told the following story about it:

> The whale is swimming under the water. He's trying to catch a school of fish. He eats all of them. There was a boat above him, and it was connected to the bottom of the ocean to a plug on a long chain. He electrocuted himself because of the plug under the water. He put his mouth on it, and he got electrocuted, and he got pulled into the

fishing boat. They cut him up, cleaned him out, put him in a package, and sent the pieces to the market. Then people bought him and ate him.

I considered the whale to represent the patient himself and his swimming under water, his feelings of being submerged and over-whelmed by the environment. As was true of the previous example, the boat symbolizes the patient's mother and the long chain, her umbilical cord. Because of his significant deprivation of affection, he has an inordinate appetite and eats up a whole school of fish. Then he attempts to form contact with his mother by eating the end of her umbilical cord (the plug at the bottom of the ocean). When he bites it, in order to form a bond between himself and his mother, he is electrocuted. This is a dramatic statement of his feel-ings that attempts to gain dependent gratification from his mother can be lethal. He is not only electrocuted when he tries to reestab-lish a bond between his mother and himself but is also cut up into little pieces and eaten by others. This represents his view of his mother as being murderous and may also be a statement of his feel-ings that he might ultimately prove of some value to someone, that is, others might gain nourishment from his dead body.

Another patient's father had an inordinate need to be loved by the world and devoted just about every waking minute to that end. He was a lawyer by profession but spent practically every evening furthering his political career. On weekends, as well, he was most often away from the home. And even when at home, he was ever available to friends and neighbors to help them do repairs on their houses, take their children to emergency rooms, listen for hours to their problems, and so on. He failed to appreciate, however, that his family was paying a heavy price for his ostensibly benevolent ego trips. The patient's mother was extremely angry over these dif-ficulties in her marital relationship. Rather than express resent-ment to her husband, she directed her hostility to her daughter, whom she used as a scapegoat. When the patient was asked to draw a picture, she drew a house. On the window sill was a flower box in which there were yellow flowers. Overhead was a bright blue sky with the sun and clouds. The grass was green and the house quite pretty, with colored curtains. This is the story she told.

They're flowers on a lady's window sill. They're all yellow. They're fake. They couldn't stay yellow that long because the woman forgot to water them. They say goodbye and they jump out of the window and they crack their heads. The lady says goodbye to the house and she jumps out of the window and lands on the flowers and smells like flowers. The lady gets married because someone liked the smell of her flowers.

If one were to look at the picture, it would appear to be a normal, healthy one for a seven-and-a-half-year-old girl. The sun is shining, the grass is growing, the sky is blue, the house is pretty, and all appears right with the world. However, the story reveals something quite different. I considered the flowers to represent the patient. Their being fake reveals her basic feelings of lifelessness and her need to present a façade of happiness. The flowers are deprived of life-giving qualities by the woman who does not water them, that is, her mother is not providing her with enough affection, and therefore she feels somewhat dead. She then abandons this rejecting home (the flowers say good-bye and jump out of the window), but sees herself as being traumatized upon leaving her house (they crack their heads). However, her mother joins her and the fragrance that the mother thereby derives from the flowers serves to attract a suitable husband.

Although the story involves a girl and her mother, no mention is made of the father which, of course, is an accurate reflection of the fatherless home she was basically growing up in. The story reflects her desire that her mother attract another man and the patient plays an active role in the luring process. The picture itself (as is often the case) does not enable one to come to specific conclusions about the child's psychodynamics. It is only when one hears the related story that one is able to appreciate the picture's true significance. When one looks at the picture then, one is likely to conclude that it is a statement of reaction formation and denial by this depressed, unhappy girl.

This ten-year-old boy entered treatment because of academic underachievement, poor peer relationships, and behavior problems in school. He was taunted by other children because of his oddball behavior: silliness, inappropriate laughter, and "saying the wrong thing at the wrong time." His father, a car salesman, was very involved in his business and gave little time to the boy. He therefore had little, if any, paternal model. His mother was a self-centered woman whose primary sources of gratification were shopping, playing golf, and spending time at her hairdresser. The free picture he drew was one of a fairly ugly looking creature standing in the middle of a blank page. This is the story he told:

> It's Frankenstein. He's lonely and he hardly does anything but just stands there. He has no friends. He just stays at home. Everything he tries to do would just scare people, so he never had any friends. He looked like he was going to hurt people, but he really didn't want to. He didn't care and so he stayed at home.

The description reflects clearly the patient's feelings about himself. He considered himself ugly. He was teased by friends and handled their taunts by withdrawal. The patient tended to deny his own participation in his alienation, especially his hostility toward others. The statement, "He looked like he was going to hurt people, but he really didn't want to" reflects the basic anger he felt and his inability to express it directly. And the statement: "He didn't care" is a reflection of the denial mechanisms which the patient utilized extensively.

Draw-a-Person and Draw-a-Family

I generally confine the Draw-a-Person and Draw-a-Family tests to the initial two-hour evaluation. On occasion, I will administer the instruments again during the course of the extended evaluation. The examples presented here were derived from that phase.

This seven-year-old boy's mother was extremely rejecting. She openly admitted that she harbored hostility toward all men, including her husband and two sons. She related this to the maltreatment she had received from her father during her childhood. Her son entered treatment because of hostility toward her and acting out in school. The boy drew a picture of a little girl picking flowers. When asked to tell a story, he stated, "She's picking flowers. She's smiling. She wants to find a butterfly." The butterfly, like the bird, lends itself well to symbolizing a female. It is pretty and graceful. In the picture there is no butterfly. The little girl wants to find a butterfly. There is nothing more to say about this picture and the story. The patient's few words say it all.

This nine-year-old girl came to treatment because of low academic curiosity and motivation in spite of high intelligence. She was the youngest of three children, having two teenage brothers. The older siblings were excellent students whom the mother referred to as "superstars." The patient felt that she could never live up to her parents' expectations of her and psychologically had "dropped out" of the academic race. This is the story she told about the person she drew:

> This little girl lived with her mother and father. She had two brothers and two sisters. One day she went out for a walk. She saw a hurt baby rabbit. She bought it to a vet. It had a broken leg and he fixed it, and she brought it back home, and she let it go where she had found it.

On occasion the story in the Draw-a-Person test provides information about the patient's relationship with the therapist and his or her expectations from treatment. In this story the patient revealed her basic feeling of being traumatized and she looks upon the therapist (the vet) to cure her. However, he does so in such a way that her only participation is that of passive compliance. She does not actively participate in her own cure. In addition, the story reveals her basic feeling that she is not a member of the household and that even after therapy she would still be an outsider.

On occasion, during the course of the evaluation, I will provide the patient with a responding story if I am clear about the meaning of the patient's story and if I believe that a responding story might be useful at that point. I am especially likely to do this if the story reveals the patient's unrealistic expectations from treatment, as was the case here. This is one of the ways in which I introduce children to the mutual storytelling technique. In this case I told a story about a sick rabbit who was required to do various exercises and take a variety of medicines in order to assist the vet in the healing of his broken leg. When he was lax in his following through the doctor's recommendations, the leg did not heal well; when he was assiduous in his application of the treatment, the leg healed more rapidly.

This eight-and-a-half-year-old boy entered treatment because of timidity, exaggerated response to the teasing of his classmates, excessive weight, and frequent utilization of psychosomatic complaints to avoid stressful situations. This is the story he told about the person he had drawn:

> He's a 12-year-old boy. He's working with his chemistry set. He wants to make a smoke bomb with his friend. He's going to throw

the smoke bomb up in the air in front of somebody and then run away. He's going to blindfold the person he threw the smoke bomb at. He's a man and he's 20 years old. Then he's going to take the man to his own house and hypnotize him and make him tell him what the secrets are that he knows. He then is going to let the man go away. (Therapist: "What secrets is he going to learn from the man?") That the man is going to go to the 12-year-old boy's house and try to find out information from the boy—information about his club and what he's going to do the next day. And if the 12-year-old boy is going to do something to the man.

The story reveals clearly the patient's marked fear of the therapeutic inquiry. The 20-year-old boy represents the therapist and, of course, the 12-year-old boy, the patient himself. In order to avoid the therapeutic inquiry, he is going to throw smoke screens around the therapist, blindfold him, then hypnotize him, and do to the therapist what he anticipates the therapist is going to do to him, namely, force him to reveal his inner secrets. The patient's response to the therapist's question regarding what secrets the boy will learn lends confirmation to this explanation: he anticipates that the therapist will come into the boy's house, that is, enter into his psyche and find out information about his clubs, his movements, and his whereabouts. The patient was indeed a timid and inhibited boy who was extremely fearful of revealing himself. The story confirmed well the clinical situation.

An 11-and-a-half-year-old girl came to treatment because of antisocial behavior both at home and at school. She was very resistant to the idea of coming for treatment, told this to her family, but not to the therapist. This is the story that she told about the family she drew:

This family was very happy. They had one dog, but he didn't get his picture taken. He wanted to be in the picture, but the family wouldn't let him be in it.

The next-door neighbors, they were snooping around trying to find out why the family wouldn't let the dog have his picture taken. They found out that the dog kept jumping on the cameraman all the time. They had to shut the dog up in a closet so that he couldn't get on the cameraman.

The reason the dog was always jumping on the cameraman is because the dog thinks that every time the cameraman would take a picture, a gun would come out of the camera and kill the family.

Finally one day the neighbors told the family why the dog was doing that—because he thought the cameraman had a gun. The family laughed and said, "There's nothing. There is no gun."

But then the cameraman did shoot the family. He was a robber and he wanted jewelry. Then the neighbors called the police and the police put him in jail and gave the dog a medal for capturing the cameraman.

The dog, of course, represents the patient. In the beginning of the story the dog's failure to get his picture taken reflects early treatment anxieties in which the patient does not want to be seen by the eye of the camera, that is, by the therapist. Depicting herself as a dog also reflects her feelings of low self-esteem. She sees herself as being rejected by the family and "locked in a closet." The cameraman's murder of the family represents her own hostility toward her family members and the cameraman is used as the perpetrator of the crime, thereby assuaging her own guilt over the act. The dog has little remorse over their demise. By having the camerman jailed she further assuages the guilt she feels over her hostility. Providing the dog with a prize serves further to reinforce suppression of hostilities.

This seven-year-old boy's mother was an extremely harsh and critical individual. She utilized biting sarcasm as a primary mode of interacting, expecially with men. She was a highly intelligent woman, but was clearly envious of male prerogatives in society. The patient's younger brother reacted to the mother's anger by withdrawal and inhibition in the expression of his anger. My patient reacted with antisocial behavior, directed both at his mother, father, and teachers. The picture he drew consisted of a father and two sons. This is the story he told:

The mother lived and died. The stepmother loved the children dearly and very well. And they lived happily ever after. The end.

The meaning of the story is clear. The mother is removed as a statement of the patient's desire to obliterate her from his life. The story reflects his wish that she be replaced by a loving and more benevolent stepmother.

This nine-year-old boy's mother was an extremely angry, rigid, condescending, and arrogant individual. She was mercilessly critical of the patient who, although very bright, entered treatment because of academic underachievement. He was an only child. The family of three that he drew was clearly grotesque. All of the heads seemed to be off-center and the eyes were odd-shaped, as were many of the other bodily features. This is the story the patient told:

> The kid has a funny neck. It's off-center (laughter). They all look funny and messy. All of their necks are in the wrong place. Their necks come off their shoulders.
>
> This is the Kook family. The little boy is Johnny Kook. The mother is Lady Kook. The father is Chris Kook; no, him name is Bill Kook. (The patient's father's name was Chris.)
>
> Lady Kook is making breakfast for her son. He trampled down the stairs. He broke his skull and had a concussion. That puts him out of the story. Lady Kook fainted and went to the hospital 'till the end of the story. Bill Kook worried. He went to the hospital and stayed with them 'till they both came out of the hospital.

The story reveals the patient's concept of his family as "kooky" or atypical and disturbed. The off-center heads and necks also reveal this. He sees himself as damaged in the head and his mother as one who psychologically removes herself by the loss of conscious awareness of her environment. He sees his father as the only stable person in the family, who comes to the rescue of both himself and his mother.

Verbal Projective Questions

The verbal projective questions described in the initial two-hour evaluation can be elaborated upon to their full degree in the extended evaluation. Generally, time does not permit the presentation of all questions in the initial evaluation. The basic questions that I have found most useful are, for younger children, the animals and objects that they would like to be if they had to be so transformed (positive and negative, first, second, and third choices) and the animals and objects that would suit each of their parents (first, second, and third choices, positive and negative). As mentioned, the person transformation question is not generally useful for younger children because of their limited repertoire.

This 11-year-old boy came to treatment because of severe conflicts with his father. His father was a shrewd businessman who prided himself on his business acumen. However, he was insensitive to others, to the point of being psychopathic. The mother was passively submissive in her relationship with her husband, thereby abandoning the boy to her husband's maltreatment of him. These are the responses he gave to the question regarding which persons he would choose to be changed into had he to be so transformed:

(+)1 The actor who played "Oliver." He was an orphan boy. He lived in an orphanage. He had very little food. He unknowingly meets his grandfather, and then he lives happily ever after with his grandfather.

(+)2 Mr. Robinson. He's the father in the TV program "Lost in Space." It's a space family and they go around exploring space. In one program the father was drifting from the ship into space, and they catch him just in time. They catch him just in time to get away from monsters. He's the pilot. He's the leader of the family.

(+)3 President Johnson. He signs civil rights bills, making sure that all races have equal rights.

(−)1 Mary Martin. I saw her in that play, *The Sound of Music*. She makes this mean father into a nice man. He was very strict to his kids and she changes him so he isn't strict. I would not want to be there in the beginning of the picture when she was married to the mean father.

(−)2 My sister Ruth (age 14). She's a real kook. She thinks of love all the time. If the house was on fire and she was talking to her boyfriends, she wouldn't make an attempt to get out.

(−)3 My sister Jane (age 16). She's a big shot. She thinks she's real great. She bosses everybody around all the time. She snitches on me to my parents.

Response (+)1 reveals the patient's feelings of having been abandoned and rejected by his father and his desire to be protected by him. The (+)2 response reflects the patient's ambivalence toward his father. On the one hand, he would want him separated and removed (drifting into space) and exposed to the dangers of monsters. On the other hand, he would want him retrieved. In the (+)3 response, his desire to be President Johnson stems here from the wish to be assured equal rights, that is, to be given humane treatment from his parents.

The (−)1 response reflects the patient's desire that someone come into his home and transform his father into a benevolent and loving person. The (−)2 and (−)3 responses are, in part, normal responses for a 12-year-old boy and reflect usual sibling rivalry problems. However, in (−)2 the introduction of the house burning down theme reflects the patient's hostility toward his family. There is possibly a sexual element here as well: the fire representing his sexual desires which he harbors toward his sister and the devastating results should he express such.

Both of this 14-year-old girl's parents were extremely rejecting and angry people. The patient herself harbored deep-seated retaliative hostility toward her parents which she was unable to express. I considered such feelings to be playing a role in the anxiety attacks which she presented for treatment.

> (+)1 A bird, a small one, a bluejay. It's sweet. It can sing and fly. They care for their children even though they are animals.
>
> (+)2 A deer. It's gentle, sweet and pretty. Deers care for their children.
>
> (+)3 An otter. It's playful. Their main objective is not to kill.
>
> (−)1 A lion. All animals are scared of you. Lions kill, and I wouldn't want to do that.
>
> (−)2 A snake. They're mean and ugly and horrible.
>
> (−)3 A bug or spider. They're horrible. They're so horrible and creepy, but I couldn't kill it. I can't kill any insect.

In (+)1 and (+)2, the patient admires birds and deer because they "care for their children," a quality which she does not enjoy from her parents. The (+)3 choice, the otter, whose main objective is "not to kill," reveals the patient's desire to repress her own murderous rage.

The same holds true regarding her desire not to be a lion (−)1 because a lion kills, that is, she wishes to disown her own hostility. The (−)3 response clearly reveals her basic feelings that she is like a bug or spider, prone to be obliterated by overwhelming forces. In addition, her inability to kill small insects reveals her great conflict about the expression of hostility.

This seven-year-old boy came to treatment because of social difficulties associated with his neurologically based learning disability. I considered his parents, especially his mother, to have dedicated themselves in an unusually healthy way to his education and treatment. These are the responses he gave to the animal questions:

> (+)1 A horse. It's fun to go on a horse. Cowboys go on horses.
>
> (+)2 A cow because I like to pet a cow and get milk.
>
> (+)3 A skunk. It smells. It's fun to make smells to people.
>
> (+)4 A pig. They can go oink-oink.

(−)1 A lamb. I can't say the sound of a lamb.
(−)2 A llama. It has a bad smell.
(−)3 I don't know no other animals.

The (+)1 response is normal. The (+)2 response relates to the patient's affection for his mother and his dependence on her. It speaks well for their relationship which, clinically, was an excellent one in that she was warm and tender and was unusually patient with him. The (+)3 answer reveals the so-called "sweet-lemon" way of dealing with a defect. In this process, which is the opposite of "sour grapes," the person lessens the psychic pain he or she would experience regarding a deficiency by turning it into an asset. The patient basically considers himself to smell like a skunk, and this attitude toward himself is related to his awareness of his deficits. This self-loathing contributed to an actual symptom in which he considered himself to smell. By using the odor in the service of expressing hostility—and rationalizing then its usefulness—he thereby reduces his feeling of self-deprecation. In (+)4 he again reveals his low self-esteem and again claims to enjoy those qualities within himself which he inwardly despises.

The (−)1 response suggests something about feelings of performance impairment but little else can be said about this answer. In (−)2 the bad smell theme appears again, but this time he more overtly wishes to reject those qualities within himself which have become epitomized in the "bad smell symptom."

This 11-year-old boy entered treatment because of a difficult relationship with a very competitive father, who not only competed with colleagues but with his own children. This sequence is presented because it demonstrates how, on occasion, the three questions can bring about responses that go progressively deeper into the unconscious. In this case, the boy's third response made reference to a symptom of his mother's (compulsive laughing) that he denied being consciously aware of.

(+)1 A beautiful butterfly. When she's dressed up in formal clothes, she's really beautiful.
(+)2 A colorful bird. She's nice. She's so busy she needs a natural way of transportation, like flying.
(+)3 A mocking bird. She talks a lot.

The (+)1 response is a socially acceptable comment reflecting the patient's conscious admiration of his mother's appearance, and could be considered a normal response. However, response (+)2, although initially complimentary, introduces critical elements: "She's so busy. . . ." In (+)3 he expresses overtly a critical response: "She talks a lot." However, the response is most interesting for another reason. As mentioned, this patient's mother suffered with a compulsive laughing problem. She could not control herself from laughing loudly in situations where the appropriate response was sadness, depression, contrition, etc. For example, when told of the death of people she considered herself close with, she would compulsively laugh, much to her own and her husband's embarrassment. The patient denied any awareness of this problem, and yet the response "mocking bird" clearly reveals that at some level he appreciated its presence. The use of the mocking bird also reveals his appreciation of the hostile element in his mother's symptom.

The next series of responses to the animal question is presented because it basically provides normal responses. The patient entered treatment because of excessive sibling rivalry with an older brother who was doing far better than he academically. In addition, he would often use somatic complaints in order to avoid going to school. His relationship with his mother was essentially a good one and his responses to the questions related to animals that would suit his mother's personality did not reveal significant difficulties in his relationship with her.

> (+)1 A soft kitten. She's playful, helpful, happy, fun to be with.
> (+)2 A butterfly. They go places. They're fast. They never touch the ground. My mother's always doing something.
> (+)3 A deer. She likes to investigate and find new things.
> (−)1 A bear. She's not grouchy.
> (−)2 A beaver. She doesn't like to destroy things. A beaver will cut down a tree.
> (−)3 An ant. My mother wouldn't like to be small. She wants important things. She works for the PTA and in the community.

These are examples of normal responses. There is nothing here that is significantly pathological. In (+)2 the mother's going fast from place to place is not a reflection of actual rejection on her part or such active interest in other things that the patient is neglected. Knowing the clinical situation here helps in making the decision as to whether the response is normal or pathological. In (−)2 we see some evidence of ambivalence in that the child is sensitive to certain hostile elements in the mother but the degree here is not pathological. One expects ambivalence and a certain amount of repression of unacceptable ideas about a parent. These are considered pathological when they deal with morbid themes or are excessive.

This eight-year-old girl was brought for psychiatric consultation because of power struggles with her parents, especially her mother. She thwarted her mother in practically every household activity and chore. From the moment she got up in the morning she balked at dressing, eating breakfast, and going to school. On the weekends she refused to cooperate in family activities and household chores. Even getting her to go to sleep resulted in frequent power struggles with her mother. In school she was not concentrating and showed little inclination to complete her school work. Rather, she enjoyed talking with the other children and defied the teacher's reprimands and disciplinary actions.

The patient's maternal grandmother was a woman with very little interest in her daughter, the patient's mother. The mother, too, exhibited little maternal involvement in her own daughter, the patient. She much preferred to spend time with her friends or in her small, part-time business. Although well meaning, the mother could not devote herself with conviction to child rearing for a significant period.

During her second session of consultation the patient gave these responses to the question regarding which animal would most suit her mother's personality if she had to be transformed:

> (+)1 Wild horses. She'd like to be one. She could run free and do what she wants and wouldn't have to do things for children. If a child says, "Take me out for candy," the child has to keep begging her and she won't do it.
> (+)2 A puppy. They're cute and she is.
> (+)3 A lion. She lays around a lot. When I come home from school at 3:15 she's still in her nightgown and sleeping.
> (−)1 A pig. She doesn't eat like one.
> (−)2 A German Shepherd. When someone comes in she doesn't just jump up and bite them.
> (−)3 A kangaroo. She doesn't have a pocket to carry her baby in. She doesn't jump up and down like one.

The (+)1, (+)3, and (−)3 responses all reveal well the patient's view that her mother is deficient in her maternal capacities. Like a wild horse, she would prefer to run free and remove herself completely from all maternal obligations. And like the lion (as the patient views it) she would prefer to remain lying around than getting up and fulfilling her maternal obligations. Of course, the most poignant symbol of her mother's impairment in maternal involvement is the comparison between her mother and the kangaroo. Whereas the kangaroo lends itself well as a powerful maternal symbol with its womb in a sense being external, the patient's mother is just the opposite. She doesn't have a pouch to carry her baby in, that is, she doesn't have the capacity to hold a child.

This 11-year-old boy came to treatment because of severe passive-aggressivity in the home and at school. His obstructionism was a constant source of irritation to his teachers and school personnel. The patient's father was an extremely insecure and inadequate man who compensated with a pathetic pseudo-intellectuality. He fancied himself an arm-chair philosopher and as a man who was exquisitely sensitive to the deeper processes and workings of the human mind. His seemingly erudite pontifications were most often fatuous. When frustrated, he exhibited severe rage outbursts. These are the responses the patient provided to the question regarding which animals would most suit his father if his father had to be so transformed:

(+)1 Half-gorilla and half-lamb, because sometimes he yells and sometimes he's nice.

(+)2 Half-cat and half-lion, because sometimes he yells and sometimes he's nice.

(+)3 Half-tiger and half-playful dog, for the same reason. Sometimes he screams a lot and other times he's nice.

(−)1 A gorilla. He doesn't always yell.

(−)2 A tiger, because he doesn't always yell.

(−)3 A lion, because he doesn't always yell.

When providing answers to these questions, it was clear that the patient was not going to exert himself or in any way inconvenience himself to think of elaborate answers. The easiest thing for him to do was to perseverate the same reasons for his choices. However, his resistance notwithstanding, he provided meaningful material. The perfunctory way in which he gave his responses, as well as their repetitious similarity, revealed his basic passive-aggressivity. His (+)1, (+)2, and (+)3 responses all indicate that the patient appreciated his father's dual personality. On the one hand, the father is "half-gorilla," a reflection of the patient's appreciation of his father's rage outburst problem. On the other hand, his father is "half-lamb," a reflection of the patient's appreciation that his father is basically a weak person. The gorilla is also a façade and serves to compensate for the basic feelings that his father is a lamb. The (−)1, (−)2, and (−)3 answers are basically repetitions of the gorilla, tiger, and lion themes, given without much thought and deliberation. Nevertheless, they reveal his appreciation of the compensatory personality traits of his father.

At this point, I present in detail (with many verbatim vignettes) a child's responses to the verbal projective questions. I will demonstrate here not only the use of the child's responses as a source of information about underlying psychodynamics, but as a point of departure for the acquisition of additional information and therapeutic interchange. Charles was brought to treatment at age 13 because of destructive behavior in the classroom, poor academic performance in spite of high intelligence, defiance of his parents at home (especially his mother), and alienating behavior toward peers. He was fiercely rivalrous with his nine-year-old brother who was more successful in the classroom, in the neighborhood, and in his relationship with their parents.

During the initial consultative session I was not able to determine the sources of Charles' difficulty in the family. Charles' mother was a housewife and, to the best of my knowledge, was dedicated to his upbringing and showed no manifestations of significant psychopathology. His father, however, was a somewhat "uptight" individual who was inhibited in expressing his feelings. In spite of this he did devote significant time to both boys, especially on weekends, and involved himself extensively in their recreational activities where he served as a coach for a variety of sports.

Charles' problems are said to have started when he was three-and-a-half years old, following the birth of his younger brother. By the end of my two-hour consultation I concluded that fierce sibling rivalry was probably playing an important role in Charles' difficulties, and I could not ascertain any other significant family problems that might have contributed to his antisocial behavior. In addition, Charles had a weight problem from excessive eating—a problem for which he was frequently criticized by his parents (especially his father).

In the second session, the first of my extended evaluation, I asked Charles the first animal question. His response: "A tiger because I would be able to defend myself from other animals. Also, they're very fast."

Charles' second choice: "A bird." Consistent with the principle that one does well to ask for species in that there are a wide variety of birds that can symbolize many different things, I asked Charles what bird he would like to be. He responded, "A robin because they can fly wherever they want." I then asked Charles where he would fly to if he were a robin. He responded, "To Florida. I've never been there. I want to go there with my family."

Charles' third choice: "A seal because everyone likes them. They can swim wherever they want."

Before we had the opportunity to go on to the animals Charles would *not* want to be, he asked me if it was all right to change his first choice from a tiger to a chimpanzee. I told him there would be no problem there, but asked him why he wanted to be a chimpanzee. He responded, "Because they're smart and intelligent. They're active and people love them because they're cute." He then told me he would like to leave the tiger answer as his fourth choice. Again, I told him there would be no problem with that.

We then went on to the animals he would not want to be. His first choice: "A rhinoceros because everyone hates them because they're strong and they kill other animals. People are afraid of them because of the way they look with their big horns."

His second choice: "A hippopotamus because they're big and ugly. People are scared of them because of their looks."

His third choice: "A shark because everyone is scared of them. No one wants to be near them. They're killers."

I believe that Charles' request to substitute the chimpanzee for the tiger was a reflection of his strong desire for the chimpanzee response to take priority over the other three. His reasons for selecting the chimpanzee related to the problems for which he entered treatment. He described the chimpanzee as smart, intelligent, active, and "people love them because they're cute." Doing poorly in school, Charles did not consider himself smart or intelligent. Both he and the chimpanzee are "active." Charles' "activity" was associated with antisocial behavior and resulted in his being alienated from others. The chimpanzee's activity, however, does not result in such alienation; rather, "people love them because they're cute." The response reveals Charles' desire to be loved in spite of his alienating behavior. The robin and the seal responses share in common the desire to be free from constraints. At times this is a normal response, given by many children who view school and home restrictions to be constraints from which they wish to free themselves. Last, Charles' original first choice, the tiger, was chosen because of its capacity to defend itself from other animals. The response suggests that Charles sees himself as vulnerable to attacks by outsiders and would like to be strong enough to defend himself.

The three animals that Charles chose not to be share in common the hostility element. The rhinoceros "kills animals." People are "scared of" the hippopotamus. And sharks are "killers." In addition to the hostility there is the appearance element that is described in the rhinoceros and hippopotamus responses. Of the rhinoceros Charles stated: "People are afraid of them because of the way they look with their big horns." And with regard to the hippopotamus: "People are scared of them because of their looks." The hostile elements in the undesired animals may very well be in the normal range. However, they may also reflect inordinate hostility which Charles wished to disown. One cannot justifiably come to this conclusion from these three responses taken in isolation from other data, especially because they were given in response to the question regarding what animals he would *not* want to be. Not wanting to be an animal that is ferocious is within the normal range. Bringing in the element of appearance, however, is definitely idiosyncratic and suggests that Charles has special feelings about how he looks. This may have related to his mild obesity problem in that Charles was frequently criticized by both of this parents (especially his father) for being overweight.

Charles was then asked what objects he would want to be changed into, if he had to be so transformed. His first response: "I'd want to be a computer. It knows a lot of stuff. It knows more than a man. It's smart and intelligent. People like to use them." We begin to see here a theme emerging on the issue of intelligence. The responses suggest that Charles has feelings of intellectual inadequacy associated with his academic underachievement. His revised first choice on the animal question was the "smart and intelligent" chimpanzee and now his first choice on the object question again relates to intelligence.

Charles' second choice of object: "A pen because people would use me a lot and I'd have a lot of people around me." Charles was then asked what was the particular value of that and he replied, "People need them. People need them to write and writing is important." The response here not only reflects Charles' need for others to respect him for his abilities, but the particular quality for which he wants respect is that of writing. And writing, of course, is best done by those who are "smart and intelligent."

Charles' third object: "A stereo. People love to listen to music. I'd be used a lot." The response reflects Charles' desire that he be liked and be needed by other people, probably a reaction to the alienation he suffered from parents and peers because of his psychological problems.

The first object Charles would not want to be: "A box for corn flakes because once people are through with it they throw you away." Again we see the theme of being needed and the fear of being viewed as useless.

His second choice: "A baseball bat. You're always getting hit with a ball and someone can break you. People don't treat you well. You're just a piece of wood to them. They just throw you around." The response again reveals Charles' feelings of being rejected by others and being viewed as subhuman, as someone whose feelings are not considered. In addition, there is the element here of maltreatment from others, and this response is similar to one of the reasons why he did not wish to be a tiger, namely, because it is unable to defend itself from other animals.

The last object he would not want to be: "A gun because I wouldn't want to be used to hurt anyone else." Although one might ascribe hostility here, it is also possible that the response reflects a humane attitude toward others. Of course, both needs would be gratified by this response.

Charles was then asked what animals would suit his mother if she had to be so transformed. His first response: "A chimpanzee. They're nice, but when you get on their bad side they won't be nice to you." I then asked Charles how he gets on his mother's bad side. He replied, "If I don't listen to her she gets mad." I then asked him what he could do about this and he responded, "By stopping myself from being on her bad side." I next asked him why he was still continuing to be on her bad side and why he couldn't stop doing so. His reply: "I know I shouldn't. If I get into my moods I just think 'Who does she think she is bossing me around like that?' " I finally tried to elicit from Charles information about what factors contributed to his getting into one of his "moods." He was unable to provide me with any meaningful response and so we proceeded.

Charles' second choice of animal that would suit his mother: "A bird." Again, I generally do not accept readily such a response and asked him what specific *kind* of bird would most suit his mother's personality. He replied, "A bluejay because she is a nice person. Bluejays keep on coming back if you are nice to them and give them food. If you are nice to them, they'll be nice to you, and it's like that with my mother. I've got to stop being on her bad side." I asked Charles if he thought he could do so and he replied, "Yeah, I've got to try harder. If I put my mind to it. The problem is, I've got to put my mind to it." When asked why he had not done so in the past, he replied, "I don't know. I just get into one of my moods." Again, Charles was asked what situations get him into one of his moods. He replied that when he has trouble with other children, he gets moody. Although I was able to get him to see that his difficulties with peers related to provocative behavior on his own part, I did not feel at that point that my message was sinking in. And so we proceeded.

The third animal that Charles considered to suit his mother's personality: "An owl because they're smart. She's smart. She knows a lot of things I don't know. She knows a lot of math and she can help me with my math." Again, the issue of intelligence emerges and Charles is stating here that he views his mother to be a smart woman, as someone who could help him with his studies. Children generally view their parents as smarter because that is the reality of the situation. Parents do help children with homework and generally have a much vaster fund of knowledge. I suspect, however, that Charles' response here is not simply related to this reality. Rather, it probably relates to feelings of intellectual inadequacy resulting from his academic underachievement.

Charles was then asked what animals would not suit his mother's personality. His first response: "A shark because she isn't a mean person. A shark is." His second animal: "A pig, she's a neat person and she's smart. A pig isn't." His third animal: "A gorilla, because she's not like a savage." The first and third responses could very well be considered to be within the normal range. The pig, however, again reveals the theme of intelligence, lending weight to the conclusion that this issue is very much on Charles' mind.

I then proceeded to ask Charles what animal would suit his

father if he had to be so transformed. His first response: "An owl, just like my mother. I have the same answers for my father as I do for my mother." At this point I urged Charles to come up with different responses for his father in that his father and mother were two different people and I was sure that he could think of animals that indicated these differences. Giving the same answers is a common avoidance maneuver, and the examiner should encourage children to ponder the question a little longer before taking the easy route of giving identical responses for both parents. In response Charles replied, "Okay then, a cheetah. He's fast and he can defend himself."

At that point, Charles interrupted and asked me if he could give me another animal that would suit his mother because one had just come to mind. Of course, I agreed and he responded: "A dog and a cat." I suggested that we start with the dog and that he name a specific kind of dog. I cannot emphasize this point strongly enough to the reader. There are a wide variety of dogs, each species of which lends itself well to symbolizing a different personality characteristic. And, as the reader will see in just a few seconds, my asking Charles to select a specific kind of dog provided useful information. His response: "A Saint Bernard, because you can depend on them. If you have a problem, you can tell them and they'll help you. They're famous for rescuing people in the snow." The response reveals Charles' view of his mother as nurturing and protective. However, it also suggests that he feels himself in a situation of emotional deprivation (lost in the snow). Perhaps this relates to his father's problems in expressing feelings and his mother's capacity to provide him with the affection that his father cannot.

Because Charles had stated that his mother resembles a "dog and a cat," I asked him then why he had chosen a cat. He responded: "You can also depend upon them. If you need a friend it's always there, and they're always by your side." The response again is a statement of Charles' view of his mother as warm, nurturing, and reliable. It is important to appreciate that this response, coming as it did as an interruption, must be given extra attention and credibility when assessing a child's responses. Just as the chimpanzee interruption provided useful information earlier in the inquiry, this interruption did so as well. The examiner does well to view these interruptions as reflecting significant pressure by unconscious processes to express important issues. The comments about Charles' mother's warmth, protectiveness, and affection came in the midst of descriptions of his father. They suggest that his descriptions of his father's coldness was anxiety provoking and that he needed his mother's warmth and protection as an antidote.

We then continued and Charles gave as the second choice of animal that would suit his father: "A dog, a Saint Bernard." Again, I asked Charles if he could give me a different animal because I considered the Saint Bernard response to be a manifestation of resistance in that he had just given that animal as one that would suit his mother. Without much delay he stated, "A Dalmatian, because you can depend on them for help." It is difficult to assess his answer, coming as it did immediately after one that described Charles' mother as being someone on whom he could depend. I believe that Charles' father *was* dependable in certain areas such as involvement with Charles in sports. What he could *not* depend upon from his father was open displays of emotion, intimacy, and warm tender feelings. His father could, however, *do* those things that were necessary for adequate child rearing.

The third animal that would suit Charles' father: "A beaver because it works hard." Charles' father's work occupied him for long hours during weekdays; however, he was available to a significant degree on weekends to devote himself to his sons. From the ensuing discussion I could not be certain whether or not Charles felt any deprivation in association with his father's midweek work obligations. He denied such feelings. I suspect that the reality was that Charles did not consciously experience his father as depriving because he was there to a significant degree on weekends. The deprivation that he was not consciously aware of was the emotional deprivation which is more subtle—but deprivation nevertheless.

In answer to the question which animals are not similar to his father, Charles replied: "A lion because he is not mean or savage." The second animal unlike his father: "A fox because he is not a con artist." And the third animal: "A snake because he is not a slippery snake that goes around biting people." I considered the first and third responses (the lion and the snake) to be within the normal range, not only with regard to the animals chosen but the reasons why. However, the second response is, in my experience, atypical. And atypicality is one of the criteria for ascertaining psychopathology. It certainly is an unusual response and suggests that the patient, at some level, may consider his father to be duplicitous. It may be of interest to the reader to learn that on the day following this interview I did have an individual interview with the father.

There was no question that he was not candid with me. He described the marriage as always having been a good one and denied that there were any problems. Charles' mother, however, during the interview prior to the one with Charles in which the verbal projective test was administered, described a number of serious marital problems, among which were infidelity on her husband's part. Although Charles' response here created only a mild suspicion that his father was duplicitous, and although such a view was not supported by subsequent responses on the test, there was indeed "fire beneath the smoke," and the initial suspicions engendered in me by this response proved to be verified in the next interview with his father.

Charles was then asked questions regarding the objects that would suit his mother's personality. His first response: "A bandaid because she helps me heal." His second response: "A chair because she is comfortable." And his third response: "A computer because she is smart and so intelligent." The first two responses, of course, make direct reference to his mother's nurturing and protecting roles. The third again is another example of the theme related to intellectual functioning which, as we know, was an area of difficulty for Charles.

When asked what objects would not suit his mother's personality, his first response was, "A knife because she's not a dangerous person." His second response: "A machine gun because she doesn't go around hurting people." And his third response: "A camera because she doesn't spy on people." As is usually the case, it is more difficult to make firm statements about the meaning of the negative responses than the positive. Negative responses do not necessarily indicate unconscious material that the patient is guilty and/or anxious about and must thereby relegate impulses to unconscious awareness. They can also be explained simply as age-appropriate negative attitudes that the child has derived from the environment. Here again, one looks for atypicality for leads to psychopathology. The knife and machine gun are, in my experience, normal responses, although the machine gun may be a little strong in that a simple gun is more often chosen. The camera serving as a vehicle for spying, however, is a more atypical response and suggested feelings that the patient has that his mother spies on him. However, most children have these feelings, and so I cannot consider this response to be significantly representative of psychopathology, especially because there was no repetition or pattern of such imagery throughout the assessment.

Charles was then asked what objects would suit his father's personality. His first response: "A computer because they're smart." Once again, we see the concern with intellectual capacity, clearly a problem for Charles.

His second response: "A thermostat because it keeps you warm and cool." This was an unusual and somewhat confusing response and so I questioned Charles for further details. Accordingly, Charles was then asked to elaborate on the point that his father, like the thermostat, keeps one "warm." In response he stated, "If I have a problem, he'll say don't worry about it and that makes me feel better." When asked to elaborate on the association between his father and the thermostat helping someone become "cool," he replied, "He's comforting and he helps you." When I tried to understand better what Charles was referring to here, the best I could determine was that he was using the word *cool* in the sense that many adolescents use it, that is, to refer to one's being unemotional and not taking upsetting experiences seriously. To the degree that this response implies improper suppression and repression of feelings, to that degree it is pathological. In my subsequent interview with Charles' father, I found him to be quite inhibited in expressing his feelings and suspected that Charles' response here related to this aspect of his father's personality.

Charles' third response: "A car." Again, just as I asked Charles to tell me the specific *kind* of dog and bird he had selected, I asked him to tell me the specific *kind* of car that would suit his father's personality. There are many different kinds of cars and they lend themselves to different kinds of symbolization. In response, he stated, "A Ferrari, because he has one and he's interested in cars." The response suggests that Charles' father may be swept up in the common materialism of our society. This is not to say that every person who buys a Ferrari is necessarily exhibitionistic; only that there are many purchasers of this car who certainly are so, and the response should alert the therapist to look into this issue.

Charles was then asked to name those objects that would not suit his father's personality. His first response: "A hand grenade because he doesn't kill people." His second response: "A knife because he doesn't stab people." His third response: "A match because he doesn't burn people." Although the level at which normality ends and pathology begins may be difficult to ascertain with the negative questions of the verbal projective test, I believe that the responses here go beyond the normal frequency of dangerous implements that one gets in response to these questions. They suggest Charles' view of his father as inordinately hostile—hostility that Charles is trying to suppress and repress. Considering the fact that Charles had an acting-out problem, the responses here suggest that a contributing factor to this symptom related to Charles' relationship with his father, especially with regard to hostile elements that often contribute to such difficulties.

As mentioned, the interchanges derived from my administration of the verbal projective test with Charles are presented in detail in order to familiarize the reader with the administration of the test and its utilization not only for learning about psychodynamics but for providing material that may serve as a point of departure for further inquiry, both diagnostic and therapeutic.

Dreams

Children are less capable of analyzing their dreams than adults, but the dream may nevertheless be a rich source of information about a child's underlying psychodynamics. The ability to utilize the dream metaphor probably exists at about the age of two or three in most children. However, the ability to appreciate the process, that is to separate cognitively the symbol from the entity that it denotes, is a later phenomenon and for the average child does not take place until the age of 10 or 11, the age at which the child reaches what Piaget refers to as the stage of *formal operations*. Accordingly, I will often be interested in a child's dreams, especially during the extended evaluation. However, I do not generally spend much time attempting to help the child gain insight into the dream's meaning. Rather, I use the information in the course of the treatment. Later, I will discuss dream analysis for the rare child who can be involved meaningfully in this procedure.

I ask the child to tell me any dreams he or she can remember, and that I am particularly interested in repetitious dreams. As mentioned, these often provide valuable information about basic themes that pervade the patient's personality structure. Here I will describe and analyze some dreams that children presented me during the intensive evaluation. I will present my understanding of the dream's meaning. I will not go into detail about any discussions I may have had about the dream's meaning. My primary purpose here is to demonstrate how a child's dream can often be a rich source of information about underlying psychodynamics. Even when the child is not capable of analyzing the dream, the examiner's hunches and speculations about the dream's meaning can often be useful in the child's treatment.

This ten-year-old boy presented with complaints of severe difficulties in his relationships with peers, both in the classroom and in his neighborhood. He was extremely bright and did well academically. However, he would flaunt his academic successes to his peers and this, of course, was alienating. He would not share and had a low frustration tolerance in play with other children. When he won a game, he would also flaunt his success to his opponent. He was an only child and had severe power struggles at home with his mother who was an extremely cold, aloof, and condescending woman. Throughout my total experiences with her, she was continually critical. I most often work closely with parents—to the point where they actively work with me in the session. This mother was so condescending and hostile, that I considered it best for the boy's treatment that she sit in the waiting room throughout most of the session. She was not the kind of person whom I could confront with these difficulties and who would be receptive to my suggestion that she give some thought to her attitude. I viewed her as a fixed negative constant in the family and the child's treatment. The patient's father was totally blind to his wife's alienating personality traits. He too was an unemotional individual who, like his wife, had little capacity to extend warm, tender feelings to the child. The patient told me this dream during the extended evaluation:

> I was in clockland. Everyone there turned into a clock and I turned into a clock. I had a hard time getting out of there and turning human. I was an alarm clock and I rang my bell in the guard clock's ear. He was guarding the gate and so he popped and broke and so I was able to get out of the gate and turn human again.

I considered the clock, as the central figure in the dream, to represent the patient. The guard clock probably represented his mother. Depicting himself and his mother as clocks is a statement of his view of himself and her as mechanical devices, that is, not human. In addition, his viewing himself as an alarm clock may represent some desire to communicate to the world (especially this examiner) the terrible conditions under which he was living. It may also represent the threatened eruption into conscious awareness of profound hostility that had to be repressed and suppressed if he were to protect himself from even further rejection from his parents (especially his mother). His ringing his bell in the guard clock's ear is therefore a hostile manifestation as well as a plea for help. The only way he can escape is to destroy the guard clock. However, it is not he himself who destroys the guard clock; rather, the guard clock spontaneously "popped and broke," and so he was able to escape (without guilt over having killed the guard) and "turn human again." The dream is a clear statement of this boy's view of his family as one in which he is living amongst mechanical devices, is a mechanical device himself, and the only way he can become a human being is to escape.

This ten-year-old boy came to treatment because of impaired motivation in the classroom. He had little academic curiosity or motivation and did not seem to be bothered by the fact that he was getting low grades and was on the verge of being asked to repeat the fifth grade. The patient's paternal grandfather was a self-made multimillionaire who owned factories in various parts of the world. The patient's father (see page 142) was basically a ne'er-do-well. He too had little interest in schooling and had flunked out of a series of private schools over the course of his education. Each time, however, the paternal grandfather used his money and influence to gain his son admission to another preparatory school. In high school the patient's father began drinking heavily and his four years in college were basically spent womanizing and imbibing alcohol. Then, he went into the paternal grandfather's business where he automatically rose up the ladder, without any particular competence or skill. He was basically disrespected by the people with whom he worked, but he had to be tolerated because of the fact that he was the owner's son. The patient's mother (see page 115) had been a model and had little interest in being a homemaker or mother. Both she and the father had had affairs during the marriage. With regard to his school problems the patient openly stated that there was no point in his studying very hard because he would ultimately go into his grandfather's business. During the initial two-hour consultation and during the extended evaluation, the patient reported this dream, which was essentially the same on both occasions:

I was looking out the tower window at my grandfather's farm. My grandfather's car was coming down the road. He parks the car in a parking lot and he opens the tailgate door. My sister and I come out of the house to meet him. He takes out everything with a white sheet over it. He puts it on the ground. He takes out some other stuff and lifts off the white sheet. Then I saw an electric minibike. I asked whose it was and he said it was for me. I say, "Can I ride it now? How can I start it?" And then I awoke.

The dream reveals the patient's view of his paternal grandfather as the provider of material things. He provides the patient with a minibike, that is the vehicle for moving along life's course. The paternal grandfather, not surprisingly, was the one who provided the patient's father with a new automobile every year. The minibike, like the automobile, lends itself well to symbolizing an individual's view of him- or herself with regard to the capacity to move independently along life's path. Here, it is the paternal grandfather who provides the minibike, that is, who provides the vehicle which the patient will use to move along life's course. And this, of course, was the case with the patient's father as well. But the patient does not know how to ride the minibike and asks the grandfather to teach him. This fantasy is a reflection of the patient's insecurities about his own capacity to move along life's course and his viewing his grandfather as the person who can teach him how. The complete absence of the father, and the view of the grandfather as the provider and teacher, was certainly a reflection of the reality of this boy's situation.

This eight-year-old boy was referred for treatment because of timidity, depression, somatic complaints, impaired motivation in school, and passivity in his relationships with friends. His mother was a homemaker and his father a businessman. However, his father had a moderately severe drinking problem and, when inebriated, would on occasion beat the patient's mother. She passively accepted this situation as a necessary concomitant of the marriage. During the extended evaluation, the patient described this repetitious dream:

I saw this old-fashioned train. It was very dirty. It needed to be washed. Some people were trying to clean it, but it was very dirty.

I considered the train to represent the patient's father. From a child's point of view, a parent can readily be considered "old-fashioned." The train needs to be washed. This I believe represents the patient's view of his father as "dirty" and in need of cleansing. Certainly, when the father was inebriated, he presented a most unsavory appearance and his personality qualities, especially those associated with his beating the patient's mother, were characteristics that the patient justifiably considered to warrant cleansing.

This eight-year-old boy entered treatment because of depression, excessive worrying, and poor school performance in spite of high intelligence. He was the proverbial "worrywart." He had little capacity to enjoy himself and took the weight of the world on his shoulders. He would see the worst in most situations, and his pessimism compromised his capacity for enjoyment. The patient's father was an extremely successful lawyer who spent little time at home, so involved was he in his practice. Even on weekends, he spent little time with his family. His mother was also a pessimistic, depressed, worrysome individual whose capacity for pleasure was compromised significantly. During the first session of the extended evaluation, the patient told me about the dream he had had the previous night: "My parents are run over and I become an orphan." I considered the dream to provide a vehicle for the expression of the considerable hostility this boy felt toward his parents because of the deprivations he suffered in his relationships with them. However, he recognizes that if these hostile wishes were to be fulfilled, he would be left an orphan.

During the second evaluative session, the patient brought in another dream: "My brother and I were sitting alone in the back seat of our car. No one was in the front seat. The car was rolling. I was scared." The dream is a poignant statement of the patient's feelings that neither of his parents are in the driver's seat, that is, available to provide him with guidance, support, and direction in life. He and his brother feel alone, abandoned, and fearful of the consequences of being so rejected.

This 11-year-old girl presented with psychosomatic complaints, especially headaches, nausea, vomiting, and occasional diarrhea. She had a variety of allergies as well. Her mother, who was an extremely tense and angry woman, had little meaningful capacity for child rearing. The mother openly stated that she should have never become a parent. Her relationship with her husband was a difficult one because he too felt frustrated over his wife's tension and rejection of him. When either he or the children (the patient had a 14-year-old sister) would express any anger toward the mother, she would have violent rages which were extremely frightening to both the children and their father. The patient related this dream during the extended evaluation:

> I was at the beach with my friend at Atlantic City. I was in the water. A giant wave came. I had to duck under. Another big wave came and it drowned me.

This is a common dream. I consider the most likely explanation for a dream in which a patient is being drowned or submerged by waves to reflect the feeling that suppressed or repressed emotions are going to break out of the unconscious into conscious awareness. The emotions, however, are viewed as dangerous and even lethal. Often patients will wake up from the dream relieved that they have not been drowned. And I believe that this explanation was applicable to this girl. The feelings here represent the massive hostility she felt toward her mother—hostility that could not be expressed overtly lest she suffer even further rejection and retaliation. Her feelings overwhelm her and she will drown in them. I considered many of her symptoms to be manifestations of the tension she felt in association with her attempts, both conscious and unconscious, to suppress and repress her anger toward her mother. Her dream confirmed my clinical speculations.

This 14-year-old boy asked his parents to bring him to therapy because of strong homosexual fantasies. His father was an extremely domineering, controlling individual who always presented with a façade of reasonableness. However, in any discussion in which differences of opinion were expressed, he maintained a rock-like rigidity. The patient's mother was passive and submissive in her relationship with the father. Neither parent had much capacity to involve themselves emotionally with the patient and his older sister, then 17. During the extended evaluation, he described this repetitious dream:

> My family and I were in a car going up the driveway to my school. It was a school day. There was a little shack next to the school. I went into the shack. There was a hand there in a white glove. It was a mechanical hand. I had to be very quiet. It was very dangerous, so I couldn't make any noise. Once I sneezed and the hand went over my mouth.

I considered the little shack, next to the school, to symbolize the patient's view of himself as isolated from the mainstream of his peers and possibly his family as well. I considered the mechanical hand, covered by a white glove, to represent his father who did not allow the patient to express his genuine thoughts and feelings. Even the sneeze, which the patient could not control, is suppressed by the white-gloved hand. It is a statement of his great pressure for expression of the patient's repressed thoughts and feelings. Viewing his father as a mechanical hand in a white glove is a statement of his belief that his father is machine-like rather than human. The white glove implies sterility and cover-up of "blackness" and other undesirable personality qualities. It also symbolizes the father's veneer of reasonableness to disguise inhumane (mechanical) qualities.

Concluding Comments

The kinds of inquiries and assessment instruments described above are the primary ones that I utilize in the extended evaluation of the child. They generally provide me with a wealth of information. However, on occasion, I will utilize other instruments. Younger children (ages four to six, the youngest I treat directly) may engage in doll play. The fantasies that I elicit in association with such play are sometimes useful. I say *sometimes* because they are often merely normal age-appropriate and stereotyped fantasies. One less often elicits the kind of idiosyncratic material that is the richest source of information. Also, during the extended evaluation, I will spend some time (generally 15 or 20 minutes in each of two sessions) playing *The Talking, Feeling, and Doing Game*. My purpose here is not simply to gain some data. Rather, I am interested in ascertaining how successful I will be in engaging the child. Of course, I am assessing this with other modalities such as straight discussion, mutual storytelling, and the ability to gain insight (as mentioned, not a promising area). But *The Talking, Feeling, and Doing Game* involvement will enable me to learn about just how formidable resistances are in that only the most severely resistant children will not play the game. Last, I will sometimes refer children for psychological tests. I feel comfortable doing the WISC-R and the WIPPSI but I do not consider myself trained to do the Rorschach Test and I will occasionally refer a child for this assessment.

3 JOINT INTERVIEW WITH THE PARENTS

Following the individual interviews with each of the parents alone, I will conduct a joint interview with both parents together. It is extremely important that the examiner conduct this interview as part of the extended evaluation. At times, parents may object to this because they will claim that each parent has already provided information. Sometimes, they will even claim that the information has already been given twice, in that mother has related it during her individual interview and the father during his. When I explain to them that I often get different renditions of what is happening in the home, they will become more receptive to the joint interview because they recognize that it is important that any distortions which have been introduced into the evaluation should be corrected. Besides utilizing this interview to gain the most accurate data, the interview enables the examiner to observe interactions between the parents. This is truly a situation in which the whole is greater than the sum of the parts. It is a rare situation in which I do not learn new things from the joint interview. This relates both to the acquisition of new information as well as the things I learn from the interactions. During the initial two-hour consultation, only a limited time is spent in the joint interview so that the opportunity for observation of interactions is small.

The Correction of Distortions and Other Kinds of False Data

It is extremely important for the reader to appreciate that all human beings distort their perceptions in situations of stress. At the Columbia University School of Law, it is not uncommon for a professor to stage a totally unanticipated interruption in the class. Specifically, a group of young men and women may suddenly charge into the classroom. There is screaming, a scuffle, shouts, shrieks, and angry words. Feigned gun shots, knife stabbings, and other forms of violence are likely to ensue. Then, as quickly as it began, the group suddenly leaves the room. The professor then asks each member of the class to write exactly what he or she observed. He advises them that they have been witness to a crime and that they will be asked to testify under oath regarding what they have seen and heard. The class is generally around 300 young people, just about all of whom have been extremely high in their college classes and have performed extraordinarily well on the Law School Aptitude Test. Presumably, then, we are dealing here with a very bright group of young men and women. The professor generally receives 300 different renditions of what occurred. And each of these young people is being honest. Such is the nature of the human mind. So great is the capacity to distort under situations of stress.

Another example of this phenomenon. As the reader may know, I lecture extensively throughout the United States and occasionally abroad. Most often, I give a full-day of presentations, generally three or four lectures. The most common format is four one-and-a-half hour presentations, two in the morning and two in the afternoon. Frequently, a person will ask me a question in which there is a misquotation and/or a misunderstanding of what I had previously said. When I inform the person that I have been completely misunderstood and that I said exactly the opposite of what he or she is attributing to me, the individual often responds with incredulity. I have often had the thought that a wonderful experiment would be to make a videotape of the first presentation. Then, I would hand out an objective test (such as one with multiple-choice questions) that would be based *entirely* on the material just presented during the previous hour and a half. I am convinced that most people in the audience would give some incorrect answers and would, in addition, swear that their recollection of what I said was accurate. Then, we would get the videotape's opinion regarding what I said. These individuals would react with amazement that they could have so misunderstood me.

Our memories play tricks on us, especially if the topic is one that is emotionally charged. And when one lectures in the field of psychiatry, one is likely to touch on emotionally charged situations. If I am lecturing on the subject of divorce, there are likely to be many individuals in the audience who have been or are going through the process of divorce, and this is likely to be a charged subject for them. Under such circumstances, distortion is almost inevitable. I am not being critical of these individuals who distort or misinterpret what I say. I myself would be likely to make such errors occasionally were I in their situation. And when one is interviewing parents about their marriage and the ways in which they deal with their children, especially in a psychiatric interview, it is inevitable that distortions will arise. The joint interview can serve to correct these for both the parents and the examiner.

It is extremely important for the examiner to appreciate that one's interpretation of any situation is determined by two factors. One is the actual facts, the actual reality, and the other is what one brings to it, what one interprets it to mean, what one *wants* to understand about the significance of the events. As mentioned earlier, I often say that life is like a Rorschach test. In fact, one could view this as a fundamental dictum of human experience. All phenomena can be divided into two factors: the reality and what the human being brings to the reality. The viewer's hopes, anticipations, denial mechanisms, et cetera, are all going to play a role in determining what the individual sees and how he or she reacts. Both the external entity and the viewer's thoughts and feelings about it are realities in their own right, and both play an important part in determining how one will react in a particular situation. There is a glass with water in it. One person sees it as half full, another sees it as half empty. And when parents are talking about their marriage and their children, the likelihood of these superimposed attitudes playing an important role in their discussions is very high. In fact, it is so great that I consider it to be universal. Accordingly, distortions, misrepresentations, and exaggerations are inevitably going to be present, and it is in the joint interview, especially, that the examiner is in the best position to determine what these are.

In the split-screen sequence from Woody Allen's move *Annie Hall*, both Woody Allen and Diane Keaton complain bitterly about the other with regard to sexual interests. Woody, lying on the couch, complains to his psychiatrist about Diane's unreceptivity and frigidity; Diane complains to her therapist about Woody's voracious sexual appetite. Woody's psychiatrist asks him how often he has sexual relations. He answers in complaining tones, "Only two or three times a week." Diane's therapist asks her how often she has sexual relations. She answers in angry tones, "Two or three times *every* week!" Both agree on the two-to-three times a week frequency, but they have very different attitudes about this frequency and both experience pain and discomfort; Woody because he feels he has too little sex, and Diane because she feels she has too much sex.

Accordingly, the examiner must recognize that the information gathering process in this interview occurs at two levels. One must attempt to ascertain, to the degree that one can, exactly what is happening. Sometimes this is possible if the two individuals come to some kind of a compromise or when one's credibility is clearly greater than the other's. At other times it may not be possible and the examiner does well to go on to the next issue. In such cases, I might say, "Well, you say one thing and your husband(wife) says just the opposite. We've gone back and forth a few times and you each stick to your own positions. I suggest we go on to another issue. Perhaps in the future, I'll learn what's really going on."

The other level, and possibly the more important, is the attitudinal. It relates to the thoughts and feelings of the individual about the particular event. Shakespeare's Hamlet said it well: "There's nothing either good or bad, but thinking makes it so." A father, for example, may put his three-year-old son on his lap while driving the car, and while both of their hands are on the steering wheel, the father gives the child the impression that he is helping drive the car. Early in the marriage, when there was a loving relationship between the parents, the mother may have considered the father's act to be a benevolent one, one designed to help the child feel like "a big man." In contrast, at a time when the marriage has deteriorated, she may complain vehemently to the examiner about the kinds of dangerous things her husband used to do with the boy, and she may give this as an example.

In the individual interviews, one may get diametrically opposed stories resulting in a complete inability to find out what has really gone on. In the joint interview, one can sometimes "smoke out the truth." For example, in the individual interviews, each parent might describe attendance at all school functions to which parents are invited, both curricular and extracurricular. However, during the joint interview the mother may say, with regard to the father, "Yeah, he came, but I always had to pull him. It was a big struggle. And when he finally got there, he used to fall asleep during the plays and recitals." The father may then sheepishly admit that he "sometimes" did fall asleep for short periods but that his wife is exaggerating the frequency and the duration of the time spent sleeping. In the subsequent discussion, the father may admit reluctance and occasional sleeping. Although the two may differ regarding the degree of reluctance and the frequency and duration of sleeping episodes, the examiner has still learned about the father's lack of enthusiasm for these events. And this I would consider to be a parental deficiency.

"The Whole May Be Greater Than the Sum of Its Parts"

The joint interview with the parents is one of those situations in which the whole may be greater than the sum of its parts. In fact, in most of the interviews, I find that the whole proves to be greater than the sum of its parts, because information is derived which was not or could not have been obtained in the individual interviews. This phenomenon is the result of the interaction between the parents. Because of the shortness of the joint interview during the initial two-hour evaluative session, time often does not allow for the emergence of this additional information. It is only under more relaxed circumstances, during the extended evaluation, that there is a greater likelihood that this additional data will become available.

Let us take the example of a passive and somewhat quiet man who is married to an assertive and more talkative woman. In the short joint interview, during the two-hour screening evalation, one may sense that this is the nature of the relationship, but questions are still being directed toward both parties. In the individual interview(s) with the father, the examiner is spending most of the time posing questions (as described in detail in the above section on the interview with the father). More than 95% of the time is spent with the father's talking. He is a "captive audience." The individual interview should not be conducted like a classical psychoanalytic session in which the examiner sits back silently and waits for the patient to talk. (This does not preclude, however, an occasional open-ended question.) Rather, the examiner is generally concerned with obtaining answers to a whole series of questions. In the joint interview, however, one may observe directly how the mother may actually consume 99% of the time, while the father sits silently, allowing her to "roll." Now that he is no longer captive audience, now that the examiner is not posing one question after the other, now that he is being permitted to either talk or remain silent as he chooses, his severe problem in verbal inhibition becomes apparent. In addition, his passivity problem also manifests itself, especially when he remains silent on issues of disagreement with his wife. The father may say, "I was never one who had much to say in social situations. I never had the 'gift of gab.' I guess one of the reasons why I was attracted to my wife was because she always had something to say at all times." And, with this lead, the examiner may also learn about the father's passivity in his relationship with the mother and his fears of asserting himself. A derivative of this would be a discussion of the patient's identifications in these areas, with the father and/or the mother.

A father may claim in the individual interview(s) that the marriage is a good one, that there were never any difficulties, and that there was never any talk of separation. In her individual interview(s), however, the mother may claim that on two occasions during the course of the marriage, she found love letters from other women. She suspects that there were probably other infidelities that she cannot be certain of. She claims also that when her husband was confronted with these letters he admitted to her that he had been unfaithful and that he would discontinue the affairs. In some circumstances I will recommend that the mother bring up the issue of infidelity in the joint meetings with her husband, and on other occasions I will not. On the one hand, I may consider it important for the child's treatment to do so, especially if the mother has good reason to believe that there is an ongoing affair taking place during the time of the evaluation. On the other hand, I may consider it antitherapeutic to do so in that it might cause additional marital discord which I suspect both parents would rather avoid. One just doesn't go after the truth, no matter what the consequences. One goes after the truth in the service of doing what is best for the child's treatment. In order to determine whether or not this issue should be brought up, I will ask the mother her opinion on the subject, and her input here will be very important. Of course, I too will have input into the decision. All marriages involve a certain amount of acceptance and resignation of qualities in the other party that one would prefer did not exist. The examiner must respect such equilibria and not attempt to change every single source of marital difficulty. If one is going to "rock the boat," then one should be sure that one is in a position to deal completely with the repercussions of such a disruption of the marital equilibrium.

Let us say that both the mother and I decide that it would serve the best interests of the marriage and the patient for her to bring up the affair in the joint session. In the joint meeting, the mother confronts the father with her suspicions about ongoing infidelity. She expresses incredulity that his "business meetings" so frequently go on until two in the morning. She also expresses her disbelief that they always take place at places where he cannot be reached and cannot call her either and tell her that he has been detained. She expresses her conclusion that she believes that he is with another woman (or with other women) and that he is either at their homes or in hotels. In response the father somewhat sheepishly and unconvincingly gives various explanations. At this point the mother may say, "Doctor, I've been living with this man for 15 years. I know him inside out. Right now he's lying. Look at that shit-eating grin on his face. That's how he looks when he's lying." The father might still hold to his original story and claim that his wife has a vivid imagination and that she has delusions of jealousy. On occasion, under such circumstances, the mother may turn to me and ask my opinion on the subject. My response, under these circumstances, has been along these lines: "Well, I can't be 100% certain. Your wife, however, is certainly giving some very convincing reasons why she suspects infidelity, and your responses don't seem to have much credibility to me. Although I'm not sure at this point—pending more convincing information from you— I'm inclined to believe that your wife has good reasons to be very suspicious."

However, I do not stop there. I will then say something along these lines: "Regardless of whose version is valid here, there is no question that you and your wife have some serious marital difficulties. However, you are not candidates for marital counseling at this point, at least on this issue. Either she is delusional and believes her delusions or you are lying. In either case, people like yourselves, with this kind of a conflict, are not candidates for marital counseling." I then proceed with other issues. My point here is that the joint interview enables the examiner to learn better about a parent's personality characteristics. In the example cited above, I learned about the father's probable duplicity. On other occasions, under the same circumstances, I have learned something about the mother's delusional system. In both situations, the confrontation by the spouse provided important input in my determining what was most likely the situation.

Many other forms of interaction can be observed in the joint interview. For example, sado-masochistic tendencies that may not have been apparent in the initial screening interview may manifest themselves. As the joint interview progresses, a father may become increasingly hostile toward the mother, speak in a condescending way to her, and denigrate her. Rather than asserting herself and expressing her resentment that her husband is treating her so shabbily, she may passively sit and accept his deprecations. These personality traits of the parents are likely to be playing a role in the child's difficulties. Or, a mother may continually interrupt her husband with nitpicking and hairsplitting corrections. Rather than tell her how offended he is by her behavior, he passively explains himself repeatedly, continually trying to justify himself. Again, these patterns are not likely to have manifested themselves in the individual interviews.

The Marriage

It is in the joint interview, with both parents together, that one is likely to learn much more about the marriage than in the individual interviews. Confrontations between the parents not only enable the examiner to correct distortions but to make observations in which the interactions often provide more information than actual statements. Because marital difficulties are such an important factor in bringing about psychogenic pathology in children, I will often devote a significant portion of the joint interview to the details of the marital relationship. Although some parents who bring children to treatment will not have any difficulties in this area, my experience has been that this is uncommon. Accordingly, I most often have little trouble getting parents to discuss the marital problems; often, each has discussed them at some length during the individual interviews.

On occasion, a parent who has discussed the marital problems in individual interview will show hesitancy in discussing them in the joint interview. Most often, I consider such discussion warranted. Therefore, in order to catalyze the discussion I may make a comment such as: "Each of you has told me at length what you consider to be both the assets and the liabilities, the strengths and weaknesses, of your marriage. I would now like to discuss them here with the two of you together. Why don't we start off with the strong points." At this point, I do not specify which parent I would like to start; rather, I leave it open because I would like to ascertain which parent is going to be the more assertive and forthright with regard to the marriage, both its assets and liabilities. Suggesting that they talk about the assets first generally "breaks the ice" and makes it easier to discuss the liabilities thereafter.

On occasion, one or both parents will be reluctant to discuss the marriage and say that they don't understand how their marital difficulties have anything to do with their child's problems. Others will go further and state that my delving into the marriage is improper and that if they wanted marital counseling, they would have asked for it. I try to explain to such parents that their view of child therapy as a process which is focused on the child primarily, if not exclusively, is improper and injudicious. I explain to them that I cannot separate their child's difficulties from their own, that there are therapists who would be willing to treat their child without any contact with them, but I am not that kind of therapist. I try to explain to them that children exposed to and/or embroiled in marital problems are likely to develop psychological difficulties themselves. The parents may respond that they have been completely successful in protecting their children from any knowledge of their marital difficulties. In such cases I try to explain to the parents that this is practically impossible. I try to get across the point that if the parents are unhappy this is going to compromise their parenting, even if the children don't know exactly what the parents are unhappy about.

I also advise them that my view of therapy involves my counseling parents on how to take care of the children and deal with their problems, and I hope that they will be receptive to this part of the therapeutic program. It is the rare parent who is unreceptive to this; in fact, I cannot recall a parent saying that he or she did not want my advice regarding how to handle the children's problems. I also advise them that treatment for their own problems is an overlapping but separate issue. If they *wanted* treatment for their problems, I would be happy to discuss with them the question of whether I should do such counseling or someone else should. In such discussions I point out the advantages of my doing it, but try to avoid giving the impression that "I am looking for extra business." Rather, I impress upon them the fact that by having one therapist treat the whole family, I will be more in touch with those issues that are affecting the child than I would be if another therapist were to do the marital counseling.

On occasion, it will become apparent that the child's problems are a small and incidental spinoff of the parents' difficulties and that the main thrust of the therapeutic approach will have to be with the parents if there is to be any hope of alleviation of the child's problems. (I will discuss this issue in the section devoted to the final presentation of my findings.) On occasion, it has become apparent that one of the parents is basically using the child's symptoms as an "admission ticket" for marital treatment. At some level the parent recognizes that the major problems lie within the marriage, and the hope was that by bringing the child, the parental difficulties would surface and perhaps a reluctant parent would be more motivated for therapy. My experience has been that this is a common situation and that the mother, much more than the father, is likely to have been the initiator in such a process.

On a number of occasions, it has become more apparent during this joint interview that the marital problem must be considered a fixed constant in the child's treatment. Sometimes one of the parents is adamantly against any kind of counseling. My experience has been that the person who is most often resistant to the counseling is the father. On other occasions, a parent may recognize that there are serious problems in the marriage but may be afraid to "rock the boat." My experience here has been that it is the mother, more than the father, who is often in this position. One has to respect defenses in a marriage. One has to respect the equilibria and the benefits of maintaining the status quo, the drawbacks of such silence notwithstanding. All marriages involve a delicate balance between healthy and pathological forces, and the examiner must respect these balances and not bulldoze the parent into "putting everything out on the table." The likelihood of people gaining anything from such tactics is small, and the therapist, under such circumstances, may do the family much more harm than good.

Dealing with the Children

The second important area that I generally focus on in the joint interviews is the parental dealings with the children. Generally, I have asked each of the parents in the individual interviews to describe him- or herself and the other parent with regard to this area. Here I want to get feedback that each parent has about the other. I generally encounter far less reluctance and resistance in the discussion of child-rearing practices than I do in the discussion of the marriage. I usually start with a general question such as: "Now let's talk about the children and how each of you handled the various problems that have arisen." This is generally enough to get things moving. Sometimes I will have to be more specific with questions such as: "Although we've covered child-rearing practices to some degree in the individual sessions, I'd like to go into further detail here, especially with regard to how you see each other in this area. So why don't we talk first about what you see as your own strong points and the other party's strong points with regard to dealing with the children." Again, I do not ask a particular parent to start speaking. Rather, I want to see who initiates the discussion.

Following a discussion of the strong points and assets, I then shift to the more difficult subject of liabilities. Again, I want a statement by each person regarding how he or she sees his or her own weaknesses and how the other party sees them. Sometimes I will divide the liabilities issue into specific areas of inquiry. For example, I may ask a mother what she suspects her husband's criticisms of her have been with regard to punishment techniques and/or what she recalls him to have said in this area. Then, I will turn to the husband and ask him directly what his criticisms are. I will then repeat the procedure with the father's stating first what his recollections are of the mother's criticisms of his disciplinary techniques and then ask the mother directly to state them.

In the course of the discussion on child-rearing practices, I may give advice. Although my primary goal in the extended evaluation is to collect as much data as possible, this does not preclude my spending time providing recommendations. I am not referring here to the kinds of recommendations that can only emerge from extended experience; rather, I am referring to those that are simple, short, and do not detract significantly from the time spent in the data-collection process. But such *en passant* recommendations can also serve the purpose of data collection in that parents' reactions to my suggestions often provide additional information that may be useful. I am particularly interested in the parents' degree of receptivity to my advice. And there is a whole range here from the parent who passively and gullibly accepts every bit of advice to those who are completely resistant and antagonistic to it. The ideal is that they be at some point close to the receptive end of the continuum, but not to the point of blind acceptance of everything I say. I would like them to have conviction for my recommendations because when they do, it is far more likely that they will implement them effectively. In addition, parents who are too passive in their relationship with me serve as poor models for their children. The children should not view me as their parent's "boss"; rather, they should view their parents as receptive to my advice but retaining the final decision-making power.

Concluding Comments

The joint interview with the parents not only serves the goal of data collection but, if successful, can help entrench the parents' relationship with the therapist. The establishment of a good relationship with parents is one of the cornerstones of effective therapy with the child. It is here, more than in the other interviews, that one may learn about criticisms each has about the therapist, criticisms that may not have been revealed in the individual interviews. Here, one parent may bring these criticisms up in the presence of the other. And it is crucial that they be discussed. Otherwise, the parents may harbor their resentments silently, and this can compromise the treatment and even bring about its cessation—without the therapist's knowing exactly what has gone on to compromise the treatment.

Before closing the joint interview with the parents, I discuss the family interview. Generally, I want teenagers present and those younger children who can be relied upon to contribute significantly. My experience has been that a good cutoff age is five or six. Although one may learn from the observations of interactions between the parents and the preschool nonpatient sibling, the disruptions of their presence throughout the course of the interview may outweigh the advantages of such observations. Furthermore, even children of five to eight may not be valuable contributors and may just sit there quite bored during the course of the family interview. After eight or nine, the older the youngster, the greater the likelihood of meaningful input. (The reader should not view these ages as fixed guidelines; rather, they are approximate.)

Once the decision has been made regarding which children shall participate, we discuss the issue of what to tell the siblings regarding the purpose of the family meeting. I generally advise the parents to tell the siblings that it will be helpful to me in my work with their brother or sister to get information from them about what is happening in the family. I advise the parents to reassure the siblings that they want them to be open and honest and that there will be no repercussions for their divulgences. On occasion, parents are reluctant to tell the siblings about the patient's treatment because they fear that the siblings might taunt the patient, tell others, or involve themselves in other inappropriate reactions to the disclosure. Most often, I advise the parents to tell the siblings about the treatment and to deal with any inappropriate reactions if and when they arise. I impress upon them the fact that keeping the patient's treatment a secret is likely to contribute to and even intensify the patient's feelings of low self-worth, because such withholding implies that the patient is suffering with a disorder that he or she should be ashamed about. There are occasions when a sibling is so sadistic and disturbed that the divulgence might indeed work against the patient, but this has been a rare situation in my experience.

14 THE FAMILY INTERVIEW

Here I discuss only some basic principles of the family interview in the extended evaluation. It is important for the examiner to appreciate that both the patient and the siblings may be quite tense at the beginning of the family interview. The patient is likely to be uncomfortable over the fact that his or her siblings are now going to discuss embarrassing issues. And the siblings may be fearful of criticizing their parents or may be appreciative of the fact that what they say may be upsetting to the patient. Accordingly, I generally do not sit silently at the outset of this session and wait for someone to open up. Rather, I myself begin with some reassuring statement to the various parties. I will turn to the siblings and say something along these lines: "I appreciate your coming here today. I want you to know that my experience has been that brothers and sisters can often provide me with very valuable information that helps me in the treatment of their brother or sister. I now that this is probably uncomfortable for you. But I know that I speak for your parents when I say to you that they want you to be open and honest with me and you shouldn't be afraid that there'll be any terrible consequences afterwards if you say critical things about them." At this point, I may actually ask the parents to make some statements along these lines. I will also say to the siblings: "I want you to know, also, that I appreciate that I am placing you in a difficult position with regard to the things that you're going to say about your brother or sister. However, I hope you'll appreciate that it's important for me to have this information and that you, probably more than anybody else, can provide it to me."

I will then turn to the patient: "I know that this is difficult for you, as well. I appreciate that I'm asking your brother and/or sister (or whatever the number and sexes are) to say things about you that may be upsetting and embarrassing. I hope, however, the you're big and strong enough to appreciate that it's important for me to get this information if I'm to help you." When I make this statement, I generally do not expect the child to agree with me that such divulgences are likely to be in his or her best interests; I make the statement, however, in the hope that some of it does get through, and the child does appreciate my sensitivity to his or her situation.

I will then ask the siblings why they think their brother(sister) is coming to see me. This is an important base from which to operate. The derivative questions make more sense if this issue is brought out first. On occasion, the siblings do not know of the basic problems, but most often they do. In addition, their opinions regarding the problems may be at variance with the parents and this can also be useful as clarifying data. Furthermore, their confrontations may help the patient gain some insight into the fact that he or she has problems although, as mentioned so many times previously, I don't push for this.

At this point I may ask the siblings to talk about the parents. I may ask them to say good things about their parents and things about their parents that they do not like. I start with the parents here because I want to take the focus off the patient and discuss criticisms of the parties who have "thicker skins," namely, the parents. Often, the information about the parents that the children provide me at this point proves quite useful. They may come up with parental characteristics that were not previously brought to my attention. I may then go on to the subject of exactly how they see their parent's personality problems and difficulties to have contributed to the patient's. Sometimes siblings will give me very insightful information about this relationship. For example, a teenage sister might say, "I think Billy's main problem is my mother. She spoils him sick. He's the big baby of the family. She doesn't know how to say no to him like she used to say to me and my brother." Although I may recognize that an element in such criticism may be jealousy, there also may be significant truth to the allegations. I will then use this as a point of departure for family discussion. For such a criticism, I may turn my attention to the mother and ask her for her response. I may ask Billy himself what he thinks about this criticism. The likelihood is that Billy (age eight) does not consider himself to be too indulged; in fact, he may believe that his mother is too withholding from him and indulging of his sister.

The general principle I follow when conducting family interviews is that I use each issue as a point of departure for further back and forth confrontations and discussion. Usually I ask each party what he or she thinks about what the other party has just said. Sometimes I will ask an individual what he or she thinks about what has been said previously by a few members on a particular point. I try not to let things become chaotic; rather I try to come to some tentative conclusions on each issue raised. Getting input from the other family members serves to clarify as well as generate family discussion, interaction, and information about their various relationships. Last, the family interview may have direct therapeutic benefits in that it may open up, sometimes for the first time, the kind of discussion that has never taken place previously—and this cannot but be therapeutic for the patient. I cannot emphasize this point strongly enough. The data collection interviews are often stressful to the patient and other family members. To the degree that one can help the family derive therapeutic benefits during the course of these interviews, to that degree will the therapist be compensating the family for these negative elements in the extended evaluation.

I generally do not set aside a standard 45-minute interview for the family. Rather, I will set aside an hour to an hour and a half, depending upon how much information I suspect will be emerging. It is not my intention during this time to follow up every issue to its limit. Rather, I want to focus on major problems and collect some information about each of them. I am not conducting family therapy here; rather, I am collecting data about the family, my patient, and the various interactions of the family members. On occasion, a second family interview may be warranted. Also, on occasion, the initial family interview may have served as a breakthrough for the family, and ongoing family therapy may be agreed upon. What was originated, then, as a diagnostic data-gathering procedure, ends up being an important therapeutic experience.

15 PREPARATION OF THE PRESENTATION

I recognize that the extended evaluation that I conduct is probably more time-consuming and involved than that conducted by most examiners. In fact, I myself do not *routinely* conduct such extended evaluations. On occasion, on the basis of the two-hour initial consultation, I sense that all the aforementioned interviews may not be necessary. For the purposes of this book, however, I have described in detail the full evaluation and recognize that the reader (like myself) will find situations in which it is not warranted. Similarly, the preparation of the final presentation may not necessarily be as intensive as that which I describe here. Again, for the sake of this book, I present the full preparation procedure.

The ideal way of organizing the formidable data that the examiner may have accumulated is with the use of a word processor. The examiner who has one available will save much time. Those who do not have one available must utilize the more primitive procedure that I used prior to my acquisition of this valuable instrument. Accordingly, I will first describe the method I use with the word processor and then describe the more painstaking method that I utilized previously. In addition, if the examiner enjoys the indulgence of a secretary, this can obviously save time. If not, then the examiner must perform these procedures him- or herself. Fortunately, I have both a word processor and a secretary and can indulge myself these shorter and more efficient procedures.

I begin the dictation by instructing my secretary to set up on the word processor a series of basic topics. Then, I will go through my material—from beginning to end—and dictate comments and quotations within each of these categories. The secretary scrolls up and down the screen inserting the material within each of the topics. The topics are: Basic Data, Presenting Problems, Mother's Assets, Mother's Liabilities, Father's Assets, Father's Liabilities, Patient's Psychodynamics Derived from Patient Interviews, Patient's Psychodynamics Derived from Parents and Family Interviews, Conclusions and Recommendations. When dictating the material, I do not concern myself with organization of the material *within* each of the categories. Rather, it serves the purpose of the final presentation to the parents to have just the aforementioned degree of organization. If I want to use this material in the preparation of a written report, then I will reorganize (again by word processor) the material *within* each category, but utilize the aforementioned outline as my starting point. On occasion, when the question of the child's having a neurologically based learning disability has also been raised, I will include a section in which the results of special tests in this area are also presented. I include this immediately after the section on the child's presenting complaints. I generally entitle it: Evaluation for the Presence of the *Group of Minimal Brain Dysfunction Syndromes* (GMBDS).

The basic data material is often taken directly from the face sheet of the parents' questionnaire. It generally includes the patient's name, age, date of birth, grade, and whether in a regular or special class. It also includes the names and ages of the parents and their occupations. In addition, I include the names and ages of the siblings and what grades they are in. Stepparents, also, are included.

With regard to the chief complaints, I generally start with those that have been presented by the parents (and sometimes the child) at the beginning of the two-hour consultation. I select here only those problems I consider to be psychological difficulties and not those mentioned by the parents which I have decided are not. I include here, as well, those problems described on page 2 of the questionnaire where I request the parents provide me with a three line summary of the main difficulties. I will then scan pages 9 through 12 of the questionnaire and select those symptoms that I consider worthy of therapeutic focus. I do not generally include here every single item checked off by the parents because some parents will list as a symptom atypical behavior of normal frequency, my warning to this effect in the introduction on page 9 notwithstanding.

In the section on parental assets and liabilities, one does well to include quotations. The quotations here enhance the accuracy of the presentation and may also prevent inappropriate antagonism toward the therapist. If one takes care to quote criticisms from the opposite parent, one is likely to prevent such occurrences. Such quotations are especially important if a written report is to be prepared. In these days of burgeoning malpractice, one wants to be certain that one's written report is not used to one's disadvantage in any possible subsequent litigation. And accurate recording of quotations can serve this end in that it is not the therapist who is making the critical allegation but one of the family members. (It is a sad commentary on our times that his must be mentioned here, but not to do so would be a disservice to the reader.)

When dictating the section on the child's psychodynamics, I not only describe each observation, but the meaning that I ascribe to it. This might include a behavioral manifestation and then an interpretation, or it might refer to some verbal projection and my interpretation. For example, I might quote certain key statements from the story that the child told in association with a human figure that was drawn, and then I will dictate my understanding of the meaning of the child's story. The same is done with the verbal projective animal and object questions. With regard to the verbal projective questions about those animals and objects that would suit the parents, I make sure to state that this is how I interpret how *the child* sees the parent(s) and emphasize to the parents that this may not necessarily be the way they are, but the way the child sees them. This is not only a more accurate way of stating things, but also can assuage the pains and discomforts of more defensive and/or insecure parents.

In the conclusions and recommendations section I will summarize the major themes in the family that are contributing to the child's difficulties. This generally ranges from two or three to about ten or twelve elements. It may include genetic predisposing factors and psychodynamic issues, both interpersonal and intrapsychic. This summary statement can also be useful in the course of therapy in that I may refer to it from time to time to refresh my memory about the variety of problems for which the child has presented as well as to assess progress. I then state the recommended treatment program with regard to the number of sessions per week (generally one or two) as well as who shall be involved in the treatment. If the reader does not have a secretary and word processor, then the aforementioned must be done by hand. One generally writes the titles on separate sheets of paper and then skips back and forth from page to page inserting the proper information under each category.

6 PRESENTATION OF THE FINDINGS TO THE PARENTS

I generally set aside an open-ended session for this presentation. It generally takes about two hours, sometimes longer. I make it open-ended in order to insure that we are not rushed. Sometimes I invite the child to join us and sometimes not. The older the child the greater the likelihood he or she will be invited. The primary criterion that I utilize, however, is not the child's age but how much therapeutic benefit I think the child will derive from attendance. Younger children are more likely to squirm during the course of the presentation and not attend for long on the information that I present. In addition, younger children are not likely to appreciate my discussion of underlying psychodynamics as well as family factors that may be contributing to their difficulties. Generally, I will invite children from ages nine or ten and upward, although the reader should not view this age level as a sharp cut-off point.

I usually begin the interview by telling the parents how I prepared the presentation. I directly show them the computer printouts and enumerate the various categories within which I have placed the information as it has been dictated. I then go step by step, from one section to the next, reading and commenting on what has been written therein. I advise the parents to interrupt me at any point if they have any questions or wish further discussion. I prefer that the issues raised serve as points of departure for limited discussion, but not the kind of extended discussion that might be more appropriate during therapeutic interviews. Sometimes, I may have been in error with regard to a particular point or quotation and I invite the parents' correction. I inform the parents that my goal here is not to be "right" but to be "accurate." Unless there are a formidable number of such errors, the parents will generally appreciate my receptivity to corrections. If the child is present, I will invite his or her participation as well.

On occasion, I will have ordered psychological tests. I generally make a photostatic copy of the psychological report, give the parents one copy, and we read them over together in detail. This report is their property and they take it with them at the end of the meeting (regardless of whether or not they have chosen to have a full written report prepared by me). Examiners who do not give the parents a copy of this psychological report are asking for trouble. The parents are entitled to it and not to give it to them exposes one to justifiable criticism. They are also entitled to discuss the report in detail with the examiner, especially because such reports are often confusing and anxiety provoking to parents. Obviously, when such a report is discussed in the final presentation, it is going to add to the meeting's length.

The discussion of the final treatment program is quite important. Because it comes last, I want to be sure that we have the time to discuss this in depth. And this is one of the main reasons why my final presentation is open-ended. Parents will often ask how long the treatment will take. I generally advise them that I cannot know in advance and that the most important determinants relate to how successful I will be in engaging their child and how receptive they will be to involvement in the therapy. Of course, by this time I have definite information in this area and will make comments on it. It is a serious error for the therapist to even proffer a guess with regard to the number of weeks, months, or years treatment will take. No matter how many qualifications he or she may give, the parents are still likely to put a circle on their mental calendar (if not their real calendar). Only the number becomes branded in the parent's brains; the qualifications never seem to have reached their ears. Even if accused of being vague, obstructionistic, or hostile, the therapist should not speculate about how long the treatment will take. It would be a rare situation in which he or she would not regret having made such a speculation.

I also discuss with the parents the nature and degree of their participation. Most often the parent who brings the child will be invited in at the beginning of the session and then remain to varying degrees depending upon the situation. Often this involves the parent's remaining throughout the course of the whole session. I will generally invite the parent who will not be bringing the child most often to feel comfortable to join us without necessarily providing advance notice. If greater family involvement is warranted, I will discuss this issue.

I will also talk about the difference between counseling the parents on dealing with the child vs. treating the parents for marital difficulties which they may have. It is important that the examiner not coerce the parents into treatment regardless of how formidable the marital problems are. Rather, the examiner does well to ask questions like: "Do you consider yourself to have marital problems?" "Have you ever given thought to having therapy for such problems?" and "What do you think about obtaining therapy for these problems?" It is crucial that the examiner take a passive attitude here and merely sound the parents out on their receptivity. To use coercive or guilt-evoking tactics is contraindicated, for example: "If you want to salvage your marriage, you're going to have to go into treatment. I can't imagine the marriage surviving without it" or "For the sake of your child, it's important that you people have treatment for your marriage. If you don't, it's going to be extremely difficult, if not impossible, for me to help your child."

People who enter treatment in response to such threats are not likely to be helped. If the parents decide that they want therapy for the marital problems, then the therapist does well to make a statement along these lines: "Well, as I see it, you have two choices here. One is to work with me and the other to work with someone else. As you know, I do treat parents of my child patients and have often found the combination useful, but recognize that some parents feel more comfortable working with someone else on their marital problems, while being counseled by me regarding how to deal with their child. I am interested in your thoughts and feelings on this; however, it's important that you be direct and honest with me and not hold back your true feelings from fear that I might be offended. Many parents have chosen to see others and I respect that choice." This approach, I believe, protects the therapist from the parental reaction that "he(she) is looking for business." It does, however, provide the parents with an option that they may not have appreciated they had and helps them clarify both the pros and cons of each alternative—information they are entitled to have.

If medication is warranted, I will discuss this with the parents at this point. Here again, one must leave ample time for such discussion in order to assuage unnecessary or irrational fears that the parents may have. It is likely that they have some unrealistic ideas about what medication can do and cannot do, and the therapist must give them the opportunity to express their ideas if he or she is to correct distortions (very likely). For parents who are very reluctant to have their child on medication, I will emphasize that I am only suggesting a *trial* on medication and that they not commit themselves to a full course of treatment before knowing about the drug and ascertaining empirically whether or not it will prove helpful to their child. Often, by reassuring them that a few pills are not likely to produce lifelong damage to the child's body, they will be more receptive to the trial.

Before closing this meeting, the therapist should invite the parents to ask any further questions. Often they may have heard of quicky-type treatments that promise results in a shorter period of time. I will generally ask them about the particular form of treatment and present them my views on it. When contrasting psychotherapy with these other forms of therapy, the examiner should be cautious with regard to making any claims about the efficacy of psychotherapy. The examiner does well to emphasize to the parents that there is no "proof" that psychotherapy works but that the examiner has definite convictions that it can be useful for certain children and their families, especially those who involve themselves with commitment to the process.

Finally, before closing the session, I ask the parents if they would like a full written report prepared. Examiners who charge for the extra work involved in the preparation of such a report should have told the parents about this much earlier. I make mention of it in the face sheet to my questionnaire so that the parents know about it even prior to the first meeting. Examiners who do not use such a document do well to mention this charge during the initial consultation. Otherwise, I believe parents have a justifiable complaint when they are advised of this new extra expense at such a late point. Even here many parents have "forgotten" about this charge and will express surprise (and even resentment) that it will cost them more money for me to prepare this report. If the parents choose to have a written report, I prepare a copy for them, give it to them directly, and let *them* decide whom they wish to give it to. This is an important point; in fact, it may be the most important point I make in this book. In these days of burgeoning malpractice litigation, the safest course is to give the parents the report themselves and let them decide whom they wish to give copies to, whether it is the school, the child's pediatrician, or anyone else. In this way, the examiner cannot be accused of having sent out critical and/or personal information to parties to whom the parents did not wish to have this information available.

Sometimes parents will ask me to prepare a modified report for certain parties, such as a school. I generally refuse to do this. I say to them, however, that if they wish to delete certain parts of the report before turning it over to the school, that is their privilege. However, I strongly urge them to make a copy of the report, cut out the deleted paragraphs, and advise the school of such deletions. Some may do this, some may not. I tell them about the injudiciousness of not telling the school that the report has been altered. But, if they do not follow my advice, I cannot be considered to have been at fault. The therapist does well to appreciate that we are living in a time when there is approximately one lawyer for every 850 individuals in the population. With such a ratio, there are many hungry lawyers who view malpractice litigation to be a very promising livelihood. (Remember the bumper sticker: "Become a Doctor, Support a Lawyer.") Giving parents the report and letting them make copies for distribution to others is an excellent way of protecting oneself in this unfortunate atmosphere.

References

Alexander, F., and French, T. (1946). The principle of corrective emotional experience. In *Psychoanalytic Therapy: Principles and Application*, pp. 66–70. New York: Ronald.

Beery, K. E., and Buktenica, N. A. (1982). *Developmental Test of Visual-Motor Integration*. Chicago: Follett.

Gardner, R. A. (1969). The guilt reaction of parents of children with severe physical diseases. *American Journal of Psychiatry* 126:636–644.

_____ (1970). The use of guilt as a defense against anxiety. *The Psychoanalytic Review* 57:124–136.

_____ (1972). *Dr. Gardner's Stories About the Real World*. Vol. 1. Cresskill, NJ: Creative Therapeutics.

_____ (1973a). *The Talking, Feeling, and Doing Game*. Cresskill, NJ: Creative Therapeutics.

_____ (1973b). *Understanding Children—A Parents Guide to Child Rearing*. Cresskill, NJ: Creative Therapeutics.

_____ (1976). *Psychotherapy with Children of Divorce*. New York: Jason Aronson.

_____ (1977). *The Parents Book About Divorce*. New York: Doubleday.

_____ (1978). *The Reversals Frequency Test*. Cresskill, NJ: Creative Therapeutics.

_____ (1979a). *The Parents Book About Divorce* (Paperback edition). New York: Bantam.

_____ (1979b). *The Objective Diagnosis of Minimal Brain Dysfunction*. Cresskill, NJ: Creative Therapeutics.

_____ (1982). *Family Evaluation in Child Custody Litigation*. Cresskill, NJ: Creative Therapeutics.

_____ (1986). *Child Custody Litigation: A Guide for Parents and Mental Health Professionals*. Cresskill, NJ: Creative Therapeutics.

Gardner, R. A., and Broman, M. (1979). Letter reversal frequency in normal and learning-disabled children. *Journal of Clinical Child Psychology* 8:146–152.

Gardner, R. A., and Gardner, A. K. (1978). *A Steadiness Tester for Objectively Diagnosing Hyperactivity and/or Attention Sustaining Impairment*. Lafayette, IN: Lafayette Instruments.

Gardner, R. A., Gardner, A. K., Caemmerer, A., and Broman, M. (1979). An instrument for measuring hyperactivity and other signs of minimal brain dysfunction. *Journal of Clinical Psychology* 8:146–152.

Kritzberg, N. I. (1966). A new verbal projective test for the expansion of the projective aspects of the clinical interview. *Acta Paedopsychiatrica* 33:48–62.

Machover, K. (1949). *Personality Projection in the Drawing of the Human Figure*. Springfield, IL: Charles C Thomas.

_____ (1951). Drawing of the human figure: a method of personality investigation. In *An Introduction to Projective Techniques*, ed. H. H. Anderson, and G. L. Anderson, pp. 341–370. Englewood Cliffs, NJ: Prentice-Hall.

_____ (1960). Sex differences in the developmental pattern of children as seen in human figure drawings. In *Projective Techniques in Children*, ed. A. I. Rabin and M. R. Haworth, pp. 230–257. New York: Grune & Stratton.

Murray, H. (1936). *The Thematic Apperception Test*. New York: The Psychological Corporation.

Schneidman, E. J. (1947). *The Make-A-Picture Story Test*. New York: The Psychological Corporation.

Wechsler, D. (1974). *Wechsler Intelligence Scale for Children-Revised (WISC-R)*. New York: The Psychological Corporation.

Index